Engendering Human Security

Feminist Perspectives

Engendering Human Security

Feminist Perspectives

Edited by

THANH-DAM TRUONG

SASKIA WIERINGA

AMRITA CHHACHHI

Zed Books Ltd.
London & New York

Engendering Human Security
was first published in India in 2006
by
Women Unlimited
(an associate of Kali for Women)
K-36, Hauz Khas Enclave, Ground Floor
New Delhi - 110016

Printed in the rest of the world by
Zed Books, 7 Cynthia St, London N1 9JF, UK and
Room 400, 175 Fifth Avenue, New York, NY 10010, USA, in 2006
www.zedbooks.co.uk

Distributed in the USA exclusively by Palgrave Macmillan
a division of St Martin's Press, LLC
175 Fifth Avenue, New York 10010

A catalogue record for this book is available from the British Library
US CIP data is available from the Library of Congress

ISBN: 1 84277 779 3 pb
978 1 84277 779 4 pb 13-digit ISBN

Cover design: Shruti Sanganeria

Typeset at Tulika, 35A/1, Shahpur Jat, New Delhi - 110049
and printed at Raj Press, R-3 Inderpuri, New Delhi - 110012

Contents

Preface   vii

Introduction:
Gender Questions in the Human Security Framework
THANH-DAM TRUONG, SASKIA WIERINGA,
AMRITA CHHACHHI   ix

Part I: Human Security, Gender and the Body   1

1 Gendering Transitional Justice:
   Experiences of Women in Sri Lanka and Timor
   Leste in Seeking Affirmation and Rights
   SUNILA ABEYSEKERA   3

2 Reproductive Rights and Gender Justice in the
   Neo-conservative Shadow
   GITA SEN   36

3 Gender Power Dynamics in Jamaica's Ghetto Trap:
   Southside
   IMANI M. TAFARI-AMA   56

4 The New Regulation of Prostitution in the
   Netherlands
   JOYCE OUTSHOORN   80

v

Contents

Part II: Human Security, Work and Care   99

5   Combating Trafficking in Women and Children:
A Gender and Human Rights Framework
NOELEEN HEYZER   101

6   The Politics and Culture of Care:
Some Issues in the Netherlands
CARLA RISSEEUW   124

7   The Globalisation of Domestic Care Services
RACHEL KURIAN   147

8   From State Duty to Women's Virtue:
Care under Liberalisation in Vietnam
THANH-DAM TRUONG   169

**Part III: Human Security:
Prospects for Feminist Engagements**   189

9   Globalisation, Social Movements and Feminism:
Coming Together at the World Social Forum
VIRGINIA VARGAS   191

10   Measuring Women's Empowerment:
Developing a Global Tool
SASKIA WIERINGA   211

11   Eroding Citizenship:
Gender, Labour and Liberalisation in India
AMRITA CHHACHHI   234

12   The Plasticity of Gender in Social Policy Formation
PATRICIA MOHAMMED   277

13   Engendering Science and Interdisciplinary
Environmental Research for Environmental Security:
The Case of the Nariva Swamp
RHODA REDDOCK   297

Contributors   327

Preface

This book has emerged out of the networks established through the Women, Gender and Development Programme at the Institute of Social Studies, The Hague. All the contributors have been linked in various capacities with this programme over the years reflecting its transnational feminist links, cultural diversity and international character. The contributors have combined academic scholarship with activist commitment in their lives and work in different geographical and professional locations.

An important figure linking all the contributors has been Professor Dr Geertje Lycklama who retired as Chair of the Women and Development Programme in 1999. All of us have worked with her and this book represents our collective effort to acknowledge her international academic and national political career and achievements, as well as her contributions to the field of women/gender and development studies. As a founding member of Development Alternatives for Women in a New Era (DAWN), Geertje Lycklama's major contributions in the field of WGD rest in her tireless effort throughout her career to promote women's concerns in two key areas. One is women's work and well-being in everyday life in which she has been particularly concerned with women migrant workers. The other area is women organising for change, particularly in the domain of gender policies. Women, work, struggle have been her key words. Her commitment to building women's strength (personal, organisational, and political) and links between women's organisations within and across regions of the world has yielded many benefits to future generations of women, in the Caribbean, Southern Africa and Asia. Her particular concerns for the plight of migrant women workers in the global context, has contributed to an enhancement of their visibility in academic treatises and policy debates. In many ways, her promotion of an interactive relation between the Women, Gender and Development Programme at the Institute of Social Studies and women's organisations and research institutes in the South has contributed to the shaping of a global vision for this field. Her feminism has enabled her colleagues and partners to explore path-breaking research themes and innovative action in many areas. We dedicate this book to her.

We would like to thank all the contributors to this volume and each other for the collective and individual inputs which have made this book possible. We also gratefully acknowledge the first round of editing by Rosalind Melis, the eagle-eyed copy editing by Ratna Sahai and of course Ritu Menon for support and friendship.

Introduction: Gender Questions in the Human Security Framework

THANH-DAM TRUONG, SASKIA WIERINGA, AMRITA CHHACHHI

This book engages with the current debate on human security in the context of globalisation, offering a variety of feminist perspectives on some core issues regarding the gender reconfiguration of the state, power/knowledge systems and the implications for people's quotidian security. A key thematic area concerns the intersection between gender—as a domain of power—and human security as a new policy framework based on the intellectual foundations of the capability approach developed by Nobel laureate Amartya Sen and philosopher Martha Nussbaum (Nussbaum and Sen 1993; Nussbaum 2000). The concept became entrenched in development thinking when it was introduced in the 1994 Human Development Report of the United Nations Development Programme. It was there defined as freedom from fear and freedom from want. It was located in seven categories, the economy, food production, health, the environment, the personal and community level and politics. Since then the concept has been widely debated.

Discourses on human security have brought together issues of human dignity, rights and well-being in a comprehensive way. They span a variety of disciplines such as security studies and international relations, international law and organisations, sociology and cultural politics of rights, transnational sociology and economics of human development. Gender issues, although generally present in such discourse, have been approached in a fragmented manner. A consolidation of research findings and theoretical debates on human security from feminist perspectives is urgently needed to ensure effective incorporation of gender concerns in training, research and policy intervention.

The contributions in this book present an integration of a feminist materialist analysis of gender relations with a feminist post-modern approach to gender representation and cultural construction in the era of globalisation. The former approach insists on structural commonality and continuity with regard to the material significance of sexuality, care and work for women's human conditions; the latter resists over-generalisation and argues for a localised understanding of the interplay between ever-changing structures of state, gender and women's social identity and emphasises the significance of discursively embedded power relations. Blending the two approaches and clarifying assumptions on which they are premised can provide a balanced account of how global/local processes have created plural forms of gender power and control, and have shaped new risks and forms of insecurity for women and their communities.

The emergence of human security as an evolving concept expresses a collective search among communities of policy-makers, academic institutions and civic organisations for such ethical and theoretical reasoning as will bring security issues into a new focus. Significant in this endeavour is the ability to comprehend and respond to threats—to human life and dignity—which are outcomes of the interplay between global forces and those forces embedded in national and local structures. The United Nations Commission on Human Security co-chaired by Amartya Sen and Sadako Ogata was mandated in 2001 to provide answers to ways of achieving the Millennium Declaration's goals of attaining freedom from fear and freedom from want for all people. The Declaration was endorsed in 2000 by some 180 states. The Commission's publication of *Human Security Now* in 2003 adopts the definition of human security as the protection of the 'vital core of all human lives in ways that enhance human freedom and human fulfilment'. This definition integrates Human Rights,

Human Development and Human Security as three facets of a common ethical base for the protection of human life and dignity as enshrined in the Universal Declaration of Human Rights (UDHR) and the subsequent Human Rights treaties. Challenges to the Commission to integrate human security concerns in the work of global, regional, and national security-related organisations are many. Most glaring is the fact that the referents of security[1] are not equal, therefore a formula must be found to assess and balance competing needs. Furthermore, experiences of human security are not immune from political, cultural and social shaping. Every dimension of human security involves a direct or indirect mediating role of cultural and religious institutions, spanning from the most local and historically specific experience of individuals and groups to the most global level of disputes over territorial and resource control (Truong 2005a). In the post-11 September 2001 era the world community witnesses the fortification of the state-centric approach to security and a deepening of control over the social body that may override many human rights concerns previously recognised, particularly those emanating from issues of security that have become transnational.[2]

A clear example of the fatal consequences that a predominantly state-centric and masculinist approach to security may have is the 2005 disastrous hurricane Katrina, that destroyed much of New Orleans.[3] This example also demonstrates that all aspects within the security discourse should be looked at from an intersectional perspective, paying attention to issues of gender and race. Again linking the global to the local, it is noteworthy that the slogan of the 'liberation of women' out of the clutches of the Taliban has lost much of its appeal now that it seems clear that in the successor state in Iraq women's security is at stake. In the transition from a secular Iraq to a Shiite-dominated one it is women who stand to lose critical rights.

As pointed out by Hoogensen and Rottem (2004: 156), 'A central problem in defining security outside of state-designated parameters is determining what other parameters could be equally more useful'. They propose gender identity as a significant category through which security needs of individuals (as they identify themselves with particular groups) are articulated. We take this position one step further by arguing for a feminist standpoint which takes as its point of departure the conception of security as the human experience in everyday life mediated through a variety of social structures of which gender is one. In these terms, the referent of security is not just the individual with rights and entitlements but also the social relations that mediate human life in ways that ensure its quality and flourishing—inwardly towards the self and outwardly towards society.

From the perspective of human security as societal security, global and local forces of socio-economic restructuring have led to the withdrawal of the state from social provisioning towards a society characterised by flexible production systems and the informalisation of work, creating conditions of vulnerability and insecurity for working people. The 'crisis of reproduction' highlighted in the DAWN (Development Alternatives for Women in a New Era) analysis of the 1980s debt crisis now spans populations of the North and the South and could well be called a 'crisis of human in/security' (Bakker and Gill 2003; Sen and Grown 1989). This crisis has significant gender dimensions as both women and men are affected in particular ways—the informalisation and feminisation of employment; the lengthening and intensification of women's unpaid labour time and the increase in the 'reproductive tax'; increased burden of the care economy; the 'crisis of masculinity' as men can no longer maintain the myth of the male breadwinner—all these processes not only have implications for security of livelihoods and of well-being but also simultaneously affect the reconstruction, production, confrontation and conflicting interactions of gendered identities (Chhachhi 2004). These in turn have implications for entitlements to enable the transition from capabilities to effective functioning (Sen 1999) revealing the interconnections between political economy and sociocultural dimensions of human existence.

To highlight the intersection between gender—as a domain of power—and human security as a policy framework—we query the notion of 'human' from three angles: 1) the body, 2) the domain of care, 3) the domain of political agency. Starting with Amartya Sen's definition of the minimal account of human security as state provision of a limited set of rights and capabilities by which individuals and groups are able to maintain a threshold of survival with dignity, we suggest that a truly humane security perspective requires the full inclusion of feminism as a constellation of intellectual and social movements attentive to and seeking to redress the historical marginalisation and exclusion of gender-based concerns (Sen 1987, 1999). When gender (as a structural category) is articulated in modes of thinking and social organisations which continue to relate to sexual difference in androcentric manners, this is an epistemic and material violation of humanity. We follow the feminist project articulated in past decades to recover the gendered subject and transform contemporary neutralised 'universalist' discourses.

Using a feminist lens, the contributions in this volume query the framing of politics and economics by international institutions from the perspective of deprivation and vulnerabilities within and across national borders. By making visible the emergence of new 'modalities of being' characteristic of women's experience in different social formations[4] we seek to show how the failure to address the role of gender in the configuration of the political and cultural dimensions of security is related to the existing gender bias in masculine ontology (the centrality of the male subject in determining how and what we should know about humans, economy, politics, environment and societies). The book highlights the need to link a normative approach to human security (the human being as the key referent to the human security policy framework) with an interpretative approach (i.e. which human beings are we talking about, in what context, where and to what effect) that recognises the complexity of the operation of power within and across categories of gender, ethnicity and generation. Feminist engagements in building human security imply addressing the interface between the politics of redistribution and the politics of identity (Fraser 1995). This requires the securing of a normative framework that allows for the recognition as well as redressal of the intersection of relations of inequality with the multiplicity of coexisting, and sometimes competing identities. In this book we explore these intersections through the prism of gender as an axis of power and difference/discrimination/deprivation. It illustrates how the categories of gender, ethnicity and generation and issues of corporeality and human needs are socially situated and politically defined.

Transcending the North-South divide (in content and authorship) the contributions address the gendered implications of transnational processes such as conflict, international migration, human trafficking, the reconfiguring of the state and gender regimes, shifts in gender contracts, changing labour regimes and the erosion of entitlements, the changing boundaries of work and care, environmental degradation, and neo-conservatism and body politics and simultaneously present reflections on reframing strategies and policies for transformation. The contributions highlight the epistemological significance of theorising the human security crisis from the standpoint of those who must bear its consequences. Such knowledge can help foster dialogical solidarity and collective learning between different epistemic communities, thereby eliciting new breakthroughs in theoretical reasoning and practices regarding the gender dimensions of human security.

Human security, gender and the body

Feminist analysis has demonstrated how human bodies are simultaneously personal and political at the deepest levels of being and relating (Butler 1993, 2004; Giddens 1992; Pateman 1988; Lycklama, Wieringa and Vargas 1998; Wieringa 2002). Often regarded as the most 'natural' entity, bodies constitute an arena of constant surveillance and disciplinary practices (Foucault 1980), and can also be regarded as a social field of conditioning and habituation (Bourdieu 1988). Security of bodily integrity is mediated through symbolic inscription on the body itself. As such, the human subject and its body are inexorably linked with the social world of which they are an integral part.

In times of 'normalcy' discursive struggles over the meanings 'inscribed' on the body along markers of gender, class and ethnicity are subtly expressed as non-/conformity to dress codes, norms of sexual behaviour and regulated access. In times of major shifts of power structures, human bodies—particularly female but also occasionally male—have become literal battlefields of broader struggles.[5]

To highlight how women's genderised identities can be used as tools both for state politics and for the politics of resistance—an instrumental approach that may invoke religions, territorial or ethnic boundaries to guard against opposition—Sunila Abeysekera in this volume brings out illustrative evidence from Timor Leste and Sri Lanka of shifting gender norms in the complex terrain of militarised conflicts and post-conflict periods. In conflict situations, the politicisation of women's roles has recoded conventional norms of biological and social reproduction to re-forge women's identity as also combatants and defenders of their 'nation'. In post-conflict situations the reaffirmation of patriarchal norms urges women's return to the family and home—signifiers of 'normalcy' and symbols of self-respect and honour of the community. Such norms and symbols simultaneously ostracise demobilised combatants who have stepped out of traditional moulds in response to the political calling of the 'imagined' community called nation.[6] As noted in other conflict situations changes in *gender roles* do not necessarily translate into changes in *gender relations*. Under conflict resolution and peace-building conditions the participation of women (as required by the United Nations Security Council Resolution 1325) has yet to gain sufficient recognition for their priorities—economic security, integrity of the body, and security from gender-based violence—to be addressed. Abeysekera's analysis of the inversion of gender norms by political forces finds resonance with tendencies in other arenas of cultural and political contestation. For example, at the height of the debate on Asian values, political leaders of Malaysia, Indonesia and Singapore have cast the West as the source of sexual decadence and 'Asian values' as a source of social cohesion—a striking inversion of the old Orientalist definition of the East as the locus of perverse desires and a wantonly eroticised femininity (Said 1978). This invocation of an 'imagined' homogenous set of cultural values housed in the Asian continent has sought to impose particular norms of sexual propriety on a general public that increasingly disregards those norms.

Conservative forces in many locations are united in their aversion to feminism which they regard as the epitome of perversion and licentiousness. Feminism and the women's movement, through analysis and social agitation, have been exposing the abusive practices nonetheless tolerated by hegemonic masculine culture, such as incest, rape, sex trafficking and other forms of sexual violence. Addressing the unity of conservative forces Gita Sen dissects the operation of gender in the international arena of reproductive health. She shows how, under the administration of the United States President, George W. Bush, the significant controls imposed over key levers of state power by religious fundamentalists—together with the harnessing of neo-conservative political economic forces—have undermined the outstanding feminist achievements in the 1990s. Issues of reproductive, sexual health and rights, violence against women, and male responsibility for gender power that have been tabled on global and national agendas of human rights and human development have been obliterated. The implications for a renewal of feminist politics in the international arena of reproductive health, she argues, lie in resolving the core tensions between gender justice and economic justice and the identification of strategic and multiple sites in which gender operates.

The overt tendencies of social control over sexuality suggest that inner forces regarded as most private (such as desires and pleasures) are not exempt from the influence of social power, including the effect of the media. As Appadurai (1990) observes, media—a seemingly free arena—has effectively produced a proliferation of (indigenised) desires through the commodification of pleasures. The 'mediascape'—a term he coins to refer to the fluid landscapes that characterise the process of cultural globalisation—is deeply gendered, and the mass media itself has become a major vehicle for the production, display and explanation of sexualities.

Yet in spite of pluralism, a closer examination of social forms under which sexuality is allowed expression reveals a hierarchical relationship between the different forms. Hegemonic masculinity, built on the subordination of women, is primarily disciplinarian and the most widespread form. Men who exhibit non-hegemonic forms of masculinity and women who refuse subjugation are subjected to a whole range of punitive measures—from covert institutional pressures to overt physical violence (Blackwood and Wieringa 1999; Connell 2001, 2005; Morgan and Wieringa 2005). Violence derived from the need to preserve hegemonic masculine power is most overtly expressed in situations which allow an extension of the power of armed forces over the civil body.

In this volume Imani Tafari-Ama analyses the transaction of 'sex' for material interests in an inner city community in Kingston, Jamaica, to illustrate how women living below the poverty line respond to violence controlled by vigilantes of political parties. She describes women's survival strategies and how their self-realisation tactics are tailored to the cultural dynamics of the urban space they occupy. Intense urban violence has steered their agency in a destructive direction far removed from any ideal of emancipation. The localised reproduction of structural, discursive and gender power dynamics has produced female subjects who internalise and project the overarching masculine practice of violence as their own versions of womanpower. The social promotion of hegemonic masculinity under the conditions of urban violence has resulted in an inversion of ideals of female emancipation. The self-construction of female subjects in the image of the male oppressor may just reflect an ongoing colonisation of consciousness and agency.

Where hegemonic masculinity is not directly expressed by way of physical violence its domination can be felt as and when the existing gender order is challenged by alternative practices. Despite the existence of a wide variety of traditional transgender practices,[7] persons bearing the identities of transgender (males or females), prostitutes or other identities which defy the contemporary hegemonic norms are classified as 'abject' bodies and 'perverse' subjects (Butler 2004). Such a classification often sanctions a variety of forms of violence against them, including zoning and harassment.[8] As Feinberg (1996) points out, transgender 'warriors' have to wage formidable battles at the physical, social, political and psychological levels to be accepted into 'normalcy'.[9]

Joyce Outshoorn analyses the attempt by the Dutch State to neutralise the social tension between morality and sexual identity for a policy of inclusion of 'abject' subjects in the universe of 'normalcy'. After a protracted debate the ban on brothels was repealed in an attempt to regulate prostitution as sex work—thus removing the social stigma—while fighting forced prostitution and trafficking. A highly unusual step by international standards, this move was made possible by the alliance of feminists, secular political parties and local councils.

These contributions highlight the fact that (as an important referent in the human security policy framework) the human being as a subject of analysis must be approached from a variety of angles. S/he is not just an abstract construct of the 'person' as a bearer of rights, but also a body inscribed with cultural mores that shape their mode of being and relating, and a socially-embedded actor whose pursuit of rights and responsibilities in everyday life requires flexible structures of negotiation and resolution of tensions. Security of existence entails security of identity and a sense of belonging. As aptly stated by Yuval-Davis (2003), human security is a terrain in which the sociology of power and the sociology of identity converge.

Human security, work and care

The human security approach which advocates a redirection of policy concerns from a state-based to society-based framework intends to emphasise the significance of quotidian needs and conditions of common people. Care as maintenance is a foundation of the human condition. Care makes the continuity of life and social institutions possible. Unfortunately *Human Security Now* (2003) overemphasises waged work and neglects care addressing it only indirectly at best. Care is either naturalised as women's innate capability, or externalised to cultural fields (Truong 1997; Gasper and van Staveren 2003). Literature on women's work too has tended to emphasise caring labour only as a constraint on women's employment. Recent studies have however led to a broadening of the concept pointing to the importance of caring labour as a particular type of social relation (kin and non-kin based) as well as an ethical and political practice (Gilligan 1982; Tronto 2003; Folbre 2001; Sevenhuijsen 1998; Fraser 1997). Diane Elson (2000) has argued forcefully for integrating caring into economics with the concept of the 'care economy'. Irene van Staveren (2001) has further conceptualised this care economy by positioning it vis-à-vis the market and the state, arguing that each of these three domains are crucial for an economy as well as interdependent, each expressing different values (caring, freedom and justice), and each operating with different forms of interaction (gifts, exchange, and redistribution).

This understanding of caring labour is far more complex than the earlier 1970's and 1980's studies of the opportunity costs of women's unpaid work (often measured as wages forgone). Feminist analysis of care has shown how it is both paid and unpaid, straddles the public and private realms, is subject to cash payments and service provision and could be contractual or non-contractual. The care economy in a sense is a 'mixed economy' involving the state, market, household and voluntary sector. Contemporary processes of economic restructuring illustrate the significance and changing boundaries of institutional responsibilities for care-related provision and services. Earlier literature has tended to focus primarily on developed countries highlighting the withdrawal of state subsidies for the care economy (Chhachhi and van Staveren 2004; Gardiner 1997; Lister 2002). However the recent shift from welfare to 'workfare' with liberalisation in countries of the North as well as erstwhile socialist countries is leading to a convergence with the situation in developing countries where it is employment rather than the state which has provided the primary basis for social citizenship entitlements which include some crucial dimensions of the care economy (Chhachhi 2004; Risseeuw; Truong; this volume).

Carla Risseeuw illustrates how the currently rapid reform in north-west European welfare states involves a major retraction with new criteria of exclusion. The recent shift in the Dutch government policy offers a specific case: portrayed as progressive on welfare provisions, it is unexpectedly coupled with traditional notions of gender and the nuclear family which counter the hitherto gender-neutral concept of citizenship and equality. One result is that the issue of care has become significantly less pronounced as a concern for current policy-making than in neighbouring countries.

Reversals are also occurring in erstwhile socialist countries with a re-negotiation of the 'reproductive contract' (Pearson 1997). Thanh-Dam Truong provides an account of the obliteration of care, which is arranged through institutions, and of its policy implications for national women's organisations in Vietnam. She describes how the concept of gender equality, which was written into the constitution of Vietnam in 1946 and reinforced by a number of additional legal codes and policy directives, has produced a 'working mother' gender contract that purports to alleviate women's care burden. Concerns for the care domain may be considered as a structural tendency rather than a temporal demand by women's organisations. Yet, as the current process of liberalisation deepens, a clear shift of the terms of this contract can be discerned. Policy rhetoric and practices give more emphasis to the combination of household production and motherhood as an efficient means to respond to care needs—justified by a swing towards ethical norms of care which emphasise women's virtue rather than state duty. Unable to reverse this swing, women's organisations now have to battle on three fronts: household livelihood, women's political representation and the claim for state resources to prevent an obliteration of the gender equality policy.

In this regard the human security approach has yet to free itself from the regnant tendency in neo-liberal reforms which tends to apply primarily male norms in valuing and regulating social life, obliterating the significance of arrangements which provide care for the very young, sick and elderly. The resilience of androcentric tendencies in modes of thinking cannot be overstated. For all the pronouncements about women, children and the elderly as social groups vulnerable to human security threats, the global reality—of young men, women, boys and girls being traded as commodities (Dottridge 2004; Truong 2005b), and the elderly being subject to neglect and abuse often without kin support (Risseeuw, this volume)—tells another story, and brings home the message that these tendencies may reflect a deep crisis in care systems worldwide.

The emergence of global 'care chains', with women from Southern countries as care providers, caters to the 'care deficit' in the North and the debt crisis in supply countries. Noeleen Heyzer places the trafficking of women and children—one form in which the global care chain is constituted—within the broader context of human mobility shaped by a congruence of complex social dynamics interacting with structures of gender inequality at every level: national, global, communal and familial. Such interaction has produced gender-based patterns of regional and international migration which channel young women into sexual services, domestic services and intercultural marriages of convenience. Countering such tendencies, she argues, requires a well-coordinated approach that addresses issues of economic security and marginalised identities within the frame of Human Rights.

The gendered relations of labour in care chains, and issues of power, privilege and inequality highlight the intersection of ethnic gender identities in constructing the 'mistress and the maid' and the conditions for value extraction (Young 2001). Rachel Kurian's contribution drawing on cases of Filipina au pairs in the Netherlands, highlights how gender and class hierarchies are fortified through cultural constructs of racial and ethnic prejudices which are subtly deployed in institutions and work practices. Conceptualising this exchange as a 'care chain' that functions within local and international labour markets, she traces the economic value embedded in this chain and offers a framework to assess the gains and losses to the respective sending and receiving countries (see also Yeates, 2004).

The contributions in this volume emphasise the need for feminist scholarship to perform what Youngs (2004: 77) calls 'an act of ontological revision'; to go behind the appearance and examine how differentiated and gendered power constructs social relations that become reality. Such an act focusing on the care domain can help expose plural modes of sustaining life and quotidian security that are vulnerable to policy changes. An understanding of such effects can consolidate the resistance to a formula of gender equality which does not include the necessary term regarding rights and duties in the care domain.

Human security framework: prospects for feminist engagements

Feminist engagements with the human security framework need to open up a new space for constructive thinking and deliberation from which a bridge can be formed between the normative approach to human security (the human being as a bearer of capabilities, rights, entitlements and duties) and the interpretative approach (which human beings we are talking about, in what context, where and to what effect). The former is significant in the matter of recognition of rights and in preventing state derogation of its duties. The latter recognises the complexity of the operation of power within and across the categories of gender, ethnicity and generation. When grounded in realities of deprivation for which a politics of social transformation is required, an interpretative approach to human security can contribute to redressive action more properly suited to the context in which rights are claimed.

Virginia Vargas elaborates on the emergence of a new feminist consciousness that yearns for a critical utopia and an epistemic transformation. She highlights how the dilution of a substantial part of feminist agendas (as a result of gender concerns becoming institutionalised) combined with a backlash associated with a crisis in democracy in many countries, has led to a shift of feminist politics back to a focus on linkages with broader networks and social movements. The active involvement of many Latin American feminists in the World Social Forum (WSF) expresses the conviction that democratic forces can build alternatives through a combination of male and female social actors with multiple forms of resistance. Multiple strategies are thus required based on common orientations—these to be formulated in a process of constant dialogue about differences which is grounded in a commitment to collective struggles for social transformation.

In an attempt to engage with state structures to reform the normative framework of assessing women's empowerment, Saskia Wieringa discusses the usefulness of the Gender Empowerment Measure (GEM), as introduced by the United Nations Development Programme in its 1995 *Human Development Report*. She approaches women's empowerment as a field of operation discernible by its mode of appearance and degree of visibility, and as a process that entails agency and consciousness. Through the intermediate step of the Women's Empowerment Matrix she offers suggestions to improve the assessment of women's empowerment at a global scale by incorporating crucial gender-related dimensions which are missing in the GEM. The construction of the African Gender and Development Index—as an alternative to the GEM—consists of a quantitative and a qualitative part, allowing for the inclusion of some elements of women's lives that have been ignored in previous indices, such as care, sexuality and women's rights.

Adopting the concept of 'citizenship in practice', Amrita Chhachhi elaborates on the emergence and the erosion of its enabling conditions based on a comparison of coexistent gendered labour regimes forged in the pre- and post-liberalisation eras in the electronics industry in India during the 1990s. She addresses issues of citizenship entitlements for social reproduction in the context of contemporary processes of global restructuring and flexible employment. Illustrating how, under specified conditions, women workers have been able to assert collective agency at the workplace and negotiate autonomy within the household she documents how the informalisation of the labour market and a consequent increasing vulnerability of households are leading to their disenfranchisement. The concept of 'citizenship in practice' provides a bridging link to understand the processes and consequences of global restructuring in relation to changes in both the labour market and the household, pointing to the integral connection between economic and social policies for human security.

The need to rethink conventional categories of gender in social policies and how this requires further integration of the private, intimate components of life with broader structural aspects to address the new configurations of the 'gender problem' is highlighted by Patricia Mohammed. In a stream of consciousness she reflects on the metaphor of 'plastic'. It evokes the plasticity of gender constructions and the commerce in the gender industry where 'gender has become plastic, good for credit'. She argues for an approach flowing from this conception: 'of adaptability, convenience, responsiveness, capacity for moulding and remodelling, adapting to different climates and taking on as many colours and shapes as there are people and societies.'

Rhoda Reddock's analysis of the Nariva Swamp in Trinidad— a natural ecosystem—illustrates the interconnections between gendered differences in natural resource use, power relations and governance within households, the community and the state. The limits of technocentrism, ecocentrism and ecofeminism are highlighted bringing out the significance of local knowledge systems which challenge gender stereotypes and point to alternative forms of sustainable development which can ensure human security.

The contributions in this book provide insight into substantive domains of human existence which expand the boundaries of the concept of human security. Significant advances have been made in shifting the referent of human security from the state to people and the individual (see Hoogensen and Rottem 2004). Following approaches that move away from a state-centric, militarisitic, undemocratic and elitist focus, the contributions in this book signal the necessity to deepen the understanding of the 'individual' by constantly posing the question of which individual?

From a feminist standpoint they highlight the structural and symbolic construction of 'the individual' through the intersection of multiple and layered identities which are simultaneously gendered/ethnicised/classed/racialised. By placing issues of the intersectionality of identities, the body, sexuality, and the care economy as central to the quotidian and societal experience of human insecurity, we suggest not only an expansion of the boundaries of the concept of human security but also a deepening of its conceptualisation of the human subject.

The embodiment of cultures and the cultural embeddedness of bodies indicate that the hegemony of the normative white, heterosexual, middle class body far surpasses the level of the personal. Similarly the 'abject', its control and its manifestation, has ramifications not only for the individuals involved but also for the ideological and cultural ontology of societies.

The contributions in this book also show that the interlinkage between the global and the local needs to reach further down to the domains of the domestic/private/personal/invisible gendered spaces where domestic violence links with militarism/communal conflict/war and access to crucial capability enhancing resources such as health, education, income are mediated/negotiated and bargained over in terms of local gendered conceptions of entitlements in the community as well as the household. State-centric concepts of human security as well as 'people's security' approaches typically falter at the door of these domestic spheres of existence and fail to address the interlocking effects of multiple hierarchies of oppression/discrimination and deprivation. The gatekeepers of the citadels of global policy formulations, international institutions, national borders, community boundaries and male power and dominance in the household derive a 'patriarchal dividend' as Connell highlights in resisting the opening of borders, boundaries and bedrooms, to reveal the substructure of gender relations (Connell 2005).

A broader and multilayered conception of human security is implicit in feminist engagements which link the global and the local and align issues of recognition and redistribution as evident in the emergence of transnational feminist networks in the last decade. Linking issues of economic justice with gender justice these transnational alliances have mobilised and presented the political, economic and social needs and demands from workers in free trade zones, informal and home-based workers and sex workers, for sexual and reproductive health and rights and equality for women facing religious fundamentalism in different international, regional and national fora. Working with, within and outside nation state structures and international institutions there is much that feminism has contributed conceptually and practically to a redefinition of existing structures of power and dominance. Such a transnational feminist vision of human security entails linking economic justice with gender justice, as well as justice along the other axes of oppression, such as race and ethnicity, spanning the divide between the political and the personal, between the social and the individual. The concept of human security thus reveals itself to have multiple dimensions. Only a careful intersectional perspective is able to integrate the imbricating layers of the local and the global, race and gender, body and society. The continuation of these efforts and the evolution of new modes of imagining to counter the dominance of the androcentric ontology of neo-liberalism and neo-conservatism requires a deeper incorporation and embedding of feminist perspectives to engender human security towards a more humane security vision.

Notes

[1] The individual, the group, different social institutions such as household, firm, market, and the nation/state.

[2] Issues such as global financial instability; re-emergence of diseases previously eradicated; the appearance of new and fatal viruses; environmental hazards; transnational organised crime networks engaged in drugs, arms and human trafficking.

[3] With all resources, military and financial, turned to the war in Iraq it became clear that the human security of the ordinary citizens, primarily black people and women in general, had been jeopardised. There was insufficient military assistance in the direct aftermath. In the breakdown of

social order that followed many women were raped, the poor community, consisting primarily of black people, were trapped in the heavily polluted and inundated city. From a long-term perspective it became clear that with all resources directed to the 'war against terror' as defined by President Bush, insufficient funds and attention had gone to prevention efforts. Additionally it must be noted that the masculinist image of the heroic male saviour is more popular than that of the serious policy-makers and engineers working on the strengthening of dykes and other prevention efforts.

4 These include: urban violence and transitional justice, the labour process strained by pressures of global restructuring, migratory processes spurred by volatility of livelihood, feminist interaction with governments that no longer are willing or capable to command the moral authority over gender equality and are only insisting on the maintenance of regulatory powers.

5 For instance the cases of the mass rapes of women as a tool of war during the period of ethnic cleansing in parts of the former Yugoslavia in 1994 and Rwanda in the 1990s; mass rape as a tool to annihilate the identity of the other in ethnic conflicts in Indonesia during the eruption of the Asian Crisis in 1998; sexually abusive treatment of the bodies of male Iraqi prisoners in 2004 by the American Occupation Army as a technique to break a person's self-identity and dignity for interrogation.

6 Such history continues to repeat itself with few lessons learned from the experiences of women in the national liberation movements of earlier decades, as the experiences of Zimbabwe, Namibia show. On the other hand the long struggle against the apartheid system has taught South African lawmakers that all systems of oppression and discrimination are linked and that therefore all forms of discrimination must be abolished. To date South Africa has one of the most progressive constitutions in the world.

7 See also the testimonies to historical forms of non-hegemonic masculine sexual culture in Blackwood and Wieringa (1999) and Morgan and Wieringa (2005).

8 For example, Hubbard (1998) illustrates how the articulation and reproduction of cultural assumptions about the status of commercial sex workers can inscribe moral values on to the topography of the city and produces a spatial order based on notions of moral pollution, placing street sex workers in marginal sites. Similar notions of purity and pollution have been deployed in the carving of the boundaries of the nation/community as seen in the recovery and rehabilitation operation of abducted women in the aftermath of the partition of India and Pakistan (Menon and Bhasin 1998; Butalia 1998).

9 This 'normalcy' has been revealed as heterosexual, middle class and white. It has been deconstructed from various sides, notably from postmodernist and queer scholars (Binnie 2004; Cruz-Malavé and Manalansan 2002).

References

Appadurai, Arjun. 1990. 'Disjuncture and Difference in the Global Cultural Economy'. *Public Culture* 2. pp. 1–24.

Bakker, Isabelle and Stephen Gill. eds. 2003. *Power, Production and Social Reproduction*. Basingstoke/New York: Palgrave Macmillan.

Binnie, Jon. 2004. *The Globalization of Sexuality*. London: Sage.

Blackwood, Evelyn and Saskia E. Wieringa. 1999. *Female Desires, Same-Sex Relations and Transgender Practices Across Cultures*. New York: Columbia University Press.

Bourdieu, Pierre. 1988. '*The Logic of Practice*'. Oxford: Polity Press.

——. 1998. *Practical Reason, On the Theory of Action*. Stanford: Stanford University Press.

Butler, Judith. 1993. *Bodies that Matter, on the Discursive Limits of 'Sex'*. New York: Routledge.

——. 2004. *Undoing Gender*. New York: Routledge.

Butalia, U. 1998. *The Other Side of Silence: Voices from the Partition of India*. New Delhi: Viking, Penguin India.

Chhachhi, A. 2004. 'Eroding Citizenship: Gender and Labour in Contemporary India'. PhD thesis. University of Amsterdam.

Chhachhi, A. and Irene van Staveren. 2004. 'Work and Care: Brief overview of recent developments'. Document prepared for Staff Group 3 profile ISS. January. The Hague: ISS.

Commission on Human Security. 2003. *Human Security Now*. New York: United Nations.

Connell, Robert W. 2001. *The Men and the Boys*. Berkeley: University of California Press.

——. 2005. *Masculinities*. 2d edition. Berkeley: University of California Press.

——. 2005. 'Change among the Gatekeepers: Men, Masculinities, and Gender Equality in the Global Arena'. *Signs: Journal of Women in Culture and Society*. 30. no. 3.

Cruz-Malavé, Arnaldo and Martin F. Manalansan IV. eds. 2002. *Queer Globalizations, Citizenship and the Afterlife of Colonialism*. New York/London: New York University Press.

Dottridge, Mike. 2004. *Kids as Commodities: Child Trafficking and What to do about it*. Basel: International Federation Terre des Hommes.

Elson, D. 2000. 'The Social Content of Macroeconomic Policies'. *World Development*. 28.7. July. pp. 1347–64.

Feinberg, Leslie. 1996. *Transgender Warriors*. Boston: Beacon Press.

Folbre, Nancy. 2001. *The Invisible Heart: Economics and Family Values*. New York: The New Press.

Foucault, Michel. 1980. *The History of Sexuality*. vol. I: an Introduction. New York: Vintage Books.

——. 1997. 'Society Must be Defended: Lectures at the College de France 1975–1976'. New York: Picador.

Fraser, Nancy. 1995. 'From Redistribution to Recognition? Dilemmas of Justice in a 'Post-Socialist' World'. *New Left Review*. no. 212. pp. 68–93.

——. 1997. *Justice Interruptus: Critical reflections on the 'Post-Socialist' Condition*. New York/London: Routledge.

Gardiner, Jean. 1997. *Gender, Care and Economics*. London: Macmillan.

Gasper, Des and Irene van Staveren. 2003. Development as Freedom—and as what else? *Feminist Economics*. 9.2–3. pp. 137–61.

Giddens, Anthony. 1992. *The Transformation of Intimacy; Sexuality, Love & Eroticism in Modern Societies*. Stanford: Stanford University Press.

Gilligan, Carol. 1982. *In a Different Voice*. Cambridge, MA: Harvard University Press.

Hoogensen, G. and S.V. Rottem. 2004. 'Gender Identity and the Subject of Security'. *Security Dialogue*. no. 35. vol. 2. June. pp. 155–71.

Hubbard, Phil. 1998. 'Sexuality, Immorality and the City: red-light districts and the marginalisation of female street prostitutes'. *Gender, Place and Culture: A Journal of Feminist Geography*. vol. 5. no. 1. pp. 55–76.

Lister, R. 2002. 'The Dilemmas of Pendulum Politics: Balancing Paid Work, Care and Citizenship'. *Economy and Society*. 31.4. November. pp. 520–32.

Lycklama á Nijeholt, Geertje, Saskia Wieringa and Virginia Vargas. eds. 1998. *Women's Movements and Public Policy in Europe, Latin America and the Caribbean*. New York: Garland.

Menon, R. and K. Bhasin. 1998. *Borders and Boundaries: Women in India's Partition*. New Delhi: Kali for Women.

Morgan, Ruth and Saskia Wieringa. 2005. *Tommy Boys, Lesbian Men and Ancestral Wives*. Johannesburg: Jacana Press.

Nussbaum, M. 2000. *Women and Human Development: The Capabilities Approach*. University of Cambridge. New Delhi: Kali for Women.

Nussbaum, M. and A. Sen. eds. 1993. *The Quality of Life*. Oxford: Clarendon Press.

Pateman, Carole. 1988. *The Sexual Contract*. Cambridge: Polity Press.

Pearson, R. 1997. 'Renegotiating the Reproductive Bargain: Gender Analysis of Economic Transition in Cuba in the 1990s'. *Development and Change*. October 28.4. pp. 671–705.

Said, Edward W. 1978. *Orientalism: Western Conceptions of the Orient*. London: Penguin.

Sen, Amartya. 1987. *On Ethics and Economics*. Oxford: Blackwell.

——. 1999. *Development as Freedom*. New York: Oxford University Press.

Sen, G. and C. Grown. 1989. 'Systemic Crises, Reproduction Failures and Women's

Potential' in *DAWN Development Crises and Alternative Visions: Third World Women's Perspectives*. London: Earthscan Publications. pp. 50–77.

Sevenhuijsen, Selma. 1998. *Citizenship and the Ethics of Care: Feminist Considerations on Justice, Morality and Politics*. London: Routledge.

Staveren, Irene van. 2001. *The Values of Economics. An Aristotelian Perspective*. London: Routledge.

Tronto, Joan. 2003. 'Care as the work of citizens: a modest proposal' (draft Paper prepared for 'Dialogues on Care' Conference. Bergen, Norway. October.

Truong, Thanh-Dam. 1997. 'Gender and Human Development: a Feminist Perspective'. *Gender, Technology and Development*. vol. 1. no. 3. pp. 349–69.

———. 2005a. 'Human Rights and the Human Security Agenda' in *The Essentials of Human Rights*. eds. Rhona K.M. Smith and Christine van den Akker. London: Hodder Arnold.

———. 2005b. 'Poverty, Gender and Human Trafficking in Sub-Saharan Africa: Rethinking "Best Practices"' in *Migration Management*. Paris: UNESCO.

Wieringa, Saskia. 2002. *Sexual Politics in Indonesia*. Houndmills: Palgrave Macmillan.

Yeates, Nicola. 2004. 'Global Care Chains: Critical Reflections and Lines of Inquiry'. *International Journal of Feminist Politics*. vol. 6. no. 3. pp. 326–91.

Young, Brigitte. 2001. 'The "Mistress" and the "Maid" in the Globalized Economy' in *Socialist Register: Working Classes Global Realities*. eds. Leo Panitch and Colin Leys. London: Merlin Press. pp. 264–76.

———. 2003. 'Financial Crises and Social Reproduction: Asia, Argentina and Brazil' in *Power, Production and Social Reproduction: Human In/Security in the Global Political Economy*. eds. I. Bakker & S. Gill. Basingstoke/New York: Palgrave Macmillan.

Youngs, Gillian. 2004. 'Feminist International Relations: A Contradiction in Terms? Or: why women and gender are essentials to understanding the world "we" live in'. *International Affairs*. vol. 80. no. 1. pp. 75–87.

Yuval-Davis, Nira. 2003. 'Human Security and the Gendered Politics of Belonging'. Paper presented at the Symposium on Justice, Equality and Dependency in the Post-Socialist Conditions. The University of Warwick: Centre for the Study of Women and Gender.

PART I

Human Security, Gender and the Body

Gendering Transitional Justice
Experiences of Women in Sri Lanka and Timor Leste[1] in Seeking Affirmation and Rights

SUNILA ABEYSEKERA

Civil wars and internal conflicts create an intensified crisis of human security especially for civilians caught in crossfire and rendered homeless and displaced. Between 1990–2000, there were 118 armed conflicts taking place in different parts of the world, largely in the southern hemisphere. Over six million people are estimated to have died in these conflicts; it is also suggested that almost 75 per cent of conflict-related deaths are of civilian non-combatants (Skjelsbaek and Smith 2001). The historical and systematic discrimination experienced by women due to patriarchal structures is enhanced during a conflict. Social and political factors that create women's economic dependence, inhibit their mobility, restrict their participation in the public sphere and deny them decision-making power within the family make them especially vulnerable to a range of abuses and injustices during a time of conflict. Issues of human security are central to any discussion on the specific impact of conflict on women and girls. (UNIFEM 2002; Coomaraswamy 2001; UN 1995: para 135). Although in earlier years, violence against women in conflict situations was largely framed within the rubric of 'outrages upon personal dignity', the understanding of violence and abuse against women in conflicts has, in recent years, become far more sensitive to the complexities of the situation.

This chapter explores the processes of conflict and post-conflict reconstruction on the lives and situation of women who have been directly and indirectly affected by conflict, focusing on the experiences of women in Sri Lanka and in Timor Leste.[2] It examines the strategies and experiences of women and women's groups to affirm their right to participate in and define the content of armed political struggle and its aftermath in terms of gender equality and human security. The moment of transition, at the start of a process of conflict transformation is critical, since it creates an opportunity to consolidate some of the more positive social changes that occurred due to the conflict. This is especially important in relation to the opening up of new spaces of life and work for women, and also for members of marginalised communities including the landless poor and 'low' caste or tribal/ indigenous groups and communities. The 'abnormal' conditions created by war fracture traditional structures of control and dominance and enable the emergence of more socially just, alternative gender relations and structures that have the potential to enhance human security. The challenge then is how to transform these changes into substantive reforms in law and policy so that they become a part of 'normal' life in post-conflict societies.

Much contemporary writing on the position of women in what Cynthia Cockburn and Dubravka Zarkov call 'the post-war moment' focuses on the challenges of maximising the gains of conflict in a post-conflict scenario (Cockburn and Zarkov 2002). Institutional responses, such as the adoption of Resolution 1325 by the United Nations Security Council in October 2000[3] affirm that women and children account for the vast majority of those adversely affected by armed conflict and call for increased representation of women at all decision-making levels working for the prevention, management and resolution of conflict. This chapter looks at two specific areas of such a post-conflict moment in Sri Lanka and in Timor Leste: the participation of women in formal political structures and their capacity to push for institutional and structural commitments to the elimination of violence against women.

There are some critical differences in the two countries which make comparison difficult. Timor Leste is now an independent country engaged in a process of reconstruction and reconciliation as a new nation, with those who led the struggle for national liberation occupying positions of power and decision-making. In Sri Lanka there is an ongoing struggle for greater autonomy within one nation state, in which a fragile ceasefire keeps the process of conflict transformation in a state of limbo. The prevailing situation of insecurity makes any moves towards a sustainable peace and towards long-term reconciliation and healing extremely difficult.

However the experiences of women in the two countries during the period of occupation and control by military forces, as well as during the period of transition exhibit some similarities. In both countries women suffered greatly through years of militarisation and conflict, as victims of violence and displacement, and as combatants as well as heads of household. The consequent changes wrought in their lives affirmed women as independent decision-makers and actors in their own right in the post-conflict phase. As the war and direct conflict ceased and processes of resettlement, reconstruction and rehabilitation set in, women in both Sri Lanka and Timor Leste have been involved in various initiatives to have their voices and opinions heard and reflected in decision-making regarding these processes.

The emergence of identity-based politics, conflict and militarisation in Sri Lanka and Timor Leste

Sri Lanka

In the post-colonial period after 1948 in Sri Lanka the ethnic minorities including the largest, the Tamils, had to renegotiate their hold on political power vis-à-vis the majority Sinhala community. From the 1950s onwards, there were non-violent protests against acts of discrimination in terms of language, in access to higher education and in the distribution of state resources including land. In the 1970s this evolved into a militant Tamil nationalism calling for a separate state of Tamil Eelam. The Liberation Tigers of Tamil Eelam (LTTE) emerged in the 1990s as the most predominant of the militant Tamil groups, through a process of physical annihilation of its opponents and heavily militarised political consolidation. The LTTE has its own women's wing, Suthanthira Paravaihal (Birds of Freedom), with its own women's brigades within the armed forces of the LTTE.

Throughout the 1980s and 1990s, the conflict has escalated, and grown in intensity and ferocity. The most recent attempts at resolution of the conflict through a negotiated political settlement have been facilitated by the Norwegian government, and led to the signing of a Ceasefire Agreement (CFA) in February 2002 between the two main protagonists, the government of Sri Lanka and the LTTE.

The heavily militarised and extended nature of this conflict has had an extremely damaging impact on civil society organisations in the affected areas. In the mid-1980s there were many different voices to be heard in the majority Tamil areas, especially in the Jaffna peninsula. Women's groups, such as the Women's Education Circle, street theatre groups, literary discussion groups all occupied a critical ideological and political space. However, with the LTTE's assertion of its supremacy over all other voices, and as a consequence of its strict hegemonic control over ideological space as well as political and military control over geographic space, their influence has been consistently eroded. University Teachers for Human Rights, in its pioneering work, *The Broken Palmyra* (Hoole et al. 1990) laid bare the terrible realities of human rights abuse in this conflict.

Timor Leste[4]

In December 1975 Indonesian troops launched a brutal invasion of East Timor.[5] The conflict led to over 100,000 deaths,[6] and the devastation of forests and villages resulted in a famine which caused the deaths of tens of thousands more. Although this occupation was condemned by much of the international community including the United Nations, Indonesia remained in control of the country until 1999. On 30 August 1999, following an agreement between Portugal, Indonesia and East Timor, the UN Transitional Authority in East Timor (UNTAET) conducted a

Referendum in which the people voted resoundingly in favour of independence. In response, Indonesian troops and the East Timorese militia that had supported them through the years of occupation went on a rampage of destruction. Elections were held under UN supervision in 2001 and on 14 April 2001, the charismatic leader of FRETILIN, Xanana Gusmao, became the first elected President of independent Timor Leste. In May that year it became the 191st member of the United Nations. Today, it is engaged in a major process of reconstruction and reorganisation of all its social, economic and political frameworks. At the same time, the nation is engaged in a process of healing and reconciliation, partly facilitated through the Commission for Reception, Truth and Reconciliation (CARV) established in 2001.

A key role in the history of women's resistance to the Indonesian occupation in Timor Leste was played by the Popular Organisation of Women of Timor (OPMT), the women's wing of FRETILIN. Many women actively supported FALANTIL (the armed wing of FRETILIN) throughout the conflict period. In addition the cause of independence was also supported by women from exile.

Militarisation, masculinity and gender

Many identity-based struggles and movements define their goals in idealistic terms, and profess to be for 'the greater good' of their people. However, the use of violence as a strategy and as a tactic generates its own dynamic including the committing of inhumane and barbaric acts that target unarmed civilians and public spaces. This creates an environment in which hitherto unacceptable restrictions on human rights are rendered legitimate by the state, in the interests of meeting the threat to 'national' security. Thus, for both state and non-state actors, there is an erosion of democratic practice and human security, as well as a lack of accountability and the prevalence of impunity.

In addition, the intensive militarisation of society as a whole that is an inevitable part of any conflict leads to changes that often have a negative impact, especially on sections of society that lack

7

political and economic power. The process of militarisation has been described as one that enables 'the growing dominance of the military over civilian institutions with a simultaneous decline in democratic institutions and the freedoms and rights of citizens' (Chenoy 2002). Many feminist activists and scholars over the past years (Abeysekera 2003; Butalia 2002; De Mel 2001; Gautam 2001; Manchanda 2001; Rajasingham-Senanayake 2001; Samuel 2001) have examined and critiqued processes of militarisation from the perspective of the reinforcement of patriarchal structures and the role that they play in the production and reproduction of masculinist ideologies and paradigms. The glorification of war and of those who go to war, cults of 'martyrdom', the proliferation of war toys, the glamourising of the 'military' uniform, the entry of military terms into the common vocabulary, are all a part of this phenomenon. Most critical is the political and social acceptance of violence in all its forms as a legitimate and just means and method of conflict resolution. Building on the work of feminist scholars such as Yuval-Davis (1997) and Enloe (1989), other scholars have examined the role of women within armed conflict as members of armies and fighting forces and have documented the changing roles of women in society as the conflict challenges and transforms many traditional norms and social/cultural practices.

The impact of nationalism and identity-based politics on women

In his path-breaking work on nationalism, Anderson (1983: 14) has posited what he calls three 'paradoxes' of nationalism: the objective modernity of nationalism as opposed to its subjective antiquity; the formal universalism of nationality as a socio-cultural concept as opposed to the irremediable particularity of its concrete manifestations; and the 'political' power of nationalisms as opposed to their philosophical poverty and incoherence. The work of feminist scholars who have continued this interrogation of nationalism and nationhood have pointed to what Cockburn and Zarkov (2002: 11) describe as the 'interaction between nationalism, militarism and patriarchy' calling them mutually supportive 'brother' ideologies. Ivekovic and Mostov (2004) refer to the gendering of political discourse and the sexualising of concepts related to issues of nation and nationalism, pointing out that, 'Gender and nation are social and historical constructions which intimately participate in the formation of one another; nations are gendered and the topography of the nation is mapped in gendered terms'.

Operating within the nexus between gender and nation, processes of nation building generate extreme forms of nationalism that valourise the reproductive roles, both social and biological, of women. Women are called upon to be both the material producers of future generations of the 'nation/community' as well as the symbolic representatives of the community's/nation's dignity and honour. 'National mythologies draw on traditional gender roles and the nationalist narrative is filled with images of the nation as mother, wife and maiden. Practices of nation building employ social constructions of masculinity and femininity that 'support a division of labour in which women reproduce the nation physically and symbolically and men protect, defend and avenge the nation' (Ivekovic and Mostov 2004). Sanctions on raising issues of injustices done by men to women within the community are inevitably a part of this scenario. Since the pursuit of the community's rights and dignity is identified as the most critical issue of that moment, women are called on not to raise issues that would 'divide' the community from within. As Butalia (2002) points out, 'In the hierarchy of violence … the "external" violence of conflict somehow comes to acquire much greater significance than the "internal" violence of domestic strife … to everyone, the male is the hero, whether as an army man, or a militant, or simply someone caught in conflict.'

The dilemmas and tensions of being located at the intersection of these two categories of 'nation' and 'gender' make life in conflict situations extremely complex for women. Bunch (2002) has described 'three manifestly gendered elements of war: mobilisation into armed forces, the catastrophic disruption of everyday life and the brutalisation of the body in war'. In the experiences of women in both Sri Lanka and Timor Leste, all three of these elements are clearly present. Women were mobilised as combatants, engaging in direct combat as well as playing key roles in communication and dissemination of information. As daily life was disrupted by the conflict, in both Timor Leste and Sri Lanka, women assumed primary roles as caretakers and heads of household as well as of communities in displacement. They had to face extreme forms of violence including sexual violence as a consequence of the conflict, whether as direct participants in the struggle or indirectly affected by devastation and displacement. At the same time, they had to deal with patriarchal domination within their own communities.

Conflict as a catalyst for change

In both Sri Lanka and Timor Leste, the conflict took place in a context in which the majority of women were underprivileged and discriminated against at every level. In Timor Leste, the largely rural population suffered under intense neglect and under-development; patriarchal norms that restricted women's freedom combined with social and cultural practices to deny women their right to education, to health care, to proper nutrition. In 2002, the female literacy rate in Timor Leste was 36 per cent. In Sri Lanka, the physical quality of life for women was higher than in many so-called developing countries. However, there were a range of restrictions on women's independence rooted in patriarchal beliefs and attitudes; there were also regional disparities which showed low health and education indicators for women of certain minority communities.

The participation of women in decision-making was at a low level in Sri Lanka, with not more than five per cent women in the national Parliament and low figures for female representation in local government. In Timor Leste, the population did not get an opportunity to exercise free adult franchise until the referendum of 1999. Labour force participation rates for Sri Lankan women were concentrated in the more labour-intensive and lower paid sections of the industrial and agricultural sector, and since the 1980s many women migrated for work as domestic workers and factory workers. In Timor Leste, the intensity of the repression carried out by the occupying forces meant that most women remained workers within the domestic sphere.

In both countries, patriarchal social structures place many restrictions on women's autonomy, on their freedom of movement, choice of marriage partner and reproductive and sexual choices. Patriarchal laws deny women the right to own and control resources, especially land, and to engage in economic activity. In many cases, the impact of conflict on women who are already in a subordinate and disadvantaged position serves to exacerbate the difficulties of their situation. However, as the conflict renders women more visible in certain arenas, it is important to remember that, 'there are also important continuities in the experience of women' (Gautam, Banskota and Manchanda 2001).

The period of conflict: Timor Leste during Indonesian occupation: 1975 to 1999

Although not many women of Timor Leste were involved in the conflict as direct combatants in FALANTIL, many were active members of the resistance launched by FRETILIN and played an indispensable role in the clandestine networks that sustained the resistance through the years of occupation. Some women were active in the diaspora, lobbying in the international arena for international intervention in their country.[7]

Radhika Coomaraswamy, the UN Special Rapporteur on Violence against Women observed in her report (Coomaraswamy 1998) that the Indonesian military and the local militias in East Timor used rape as a method of torture and intimidation against the local population. Female relatives of political opponents of the regime were raped as a form of revenge and in order to force the men out of hiding. Several girls (below 18) and women testified about extensive torture, rape and sexual slavery during 1980, and about the creation of entire communities of widows. Women spoke of being raped in front of their families and communities. Others referred to the problems they faced within their communities as a consequence of bearing children as a result of rape. Several women's organisations and networks that had worked somewhat autonomously from political parties, including the East Timor Women's Communication Forum (FOKUPERS)[8] and the East Timorese Violence against Women network (ETWaVE)[9] have also gathered information about violence during this period. FOKUPERS reports that 'many of these acts such as abduction, rape and sharing women like chattels, were planned'.[10] In 1999, they documented 165 cases of gender-based violence including 46 cases of rape.

The widespread use of violence against women as a military tactic in East Timor has also been documented by the international media. In December 2000, the *International Herald Tribune* reported the abduction of 16-year-old Juliana dos Santos following the massacre in the Suai church on 6 September 1999.[11] In March 2001, the *New York Times* carried a story on the problems faced by East Timorese women who bore children of rape.[12] The story highlighted the stigma and discrimination faced by women who had been forced to serve as sexual slaves by the military while living in refugee camps in West Timor and their reluctance to return to Timor Leste. The Indonesian Commission for Human Rights (KPP Ham) in a report released in April 2001 spoke of the high incidence of violence against women including torture, public sexual humiliation, sexual slavery, forced prostitution and rape including mass rape. In August 2001, a La'o Hamutuk Bulletin (of the East Timor Institute for Reconstruction Monitoring and Analysis) focused on the situation of women in East Timor, pointing to the critical role played by women in the struggle for the independence of their country and speaking of the abuse and violence they had suffered, such as forced sterilisation, rape and sexual slavery.

In April 2003, 20 women including 14 women survivors testified before the CARV[13] of violence and abuse they had faced during the conflict. While most of the testimonies related to abuse by members of the Indonesian army and the local militia that supported them, there were also women who reported on their rape and violation by members of FRETILIN, the main resistance movement, as well as by members of the UDT, a group that split from FRETILIN in the mid-1970s. Olga da Silva Amaral and Beatriz Guiterrez testified about their experiences of being held in military sexual slavery for extended periods. Amaral spoke of the situation of vulnerability and slavery that arose when all the men of their village were arrested. Guiterrez, who has three children by three different Indonesian soldiers, spoke of the social problems she encountered within her own community as a result of being perceived as the 'local wife' of the enemy.[14] Forced pregnancy was also an issue, as women were forced to carry to full term and give birth to the children conceived as a result of rape by the Indonesian military.

Sri Lanka: the north and east during the years of conflict: 1977 to 2002

In Sri Lanka the first reports of violence against women from the conflict-affected areas were documented during the period in which the Indian Peace Keeping Forces (IPKF) were in the north and east by the University Teachers for Human Rights in Jaffna (UTHR-J). The first report by them (Hoole et al. 1990)[15] defined 'the worst period' as the months of November and December 1987 and January 1988 when 'there were reported an increasing number of cases of rape, molestation and theft by men from the IPKF.' The cumulative effect of this situation was that women spent their days and nights living in a state of terror. In addition, the intensifying conflict led to many men leaving their homes in order to join the militants or go into exile, leaving women behind to take on the responsibilities for families, the elderly and the young.

Incidents of sexual violence and abuse of women were also reported during the sittings of the Fact-Finding Commission organised in 1997 in the north-central and eastern parts of the country where there were mixed populations of Sinhala, Tamil and Muslim people and where militarisation was intense as a response to large-scale massacres of civilians that had taken place during the 1990s. Testimonies submitted by the Citizen's Committee for the Right to Life of the Border Villagers[16] spoke of a range of violations that occurred because of the location of military posts within villages, usually in the school, and the interaction between the security men stationed there and the village, which often had a coercive element to it. The creation of civilian defence squads (Home Guards), in which one male from each house in the village was recruited for guard duty at night at different points on the perimeters of the village, made the women of these areas extremely vulnerable to sexual abuse on the nights that their menfolk were at work. In addition, there were reports that men from the security forces would indulge in liaisons with women from the village on the promise of marriage and then disappear. The system of transfers within the army and police facilitated this situation and most families complained that they were unable to trace the man concerned because of the complicity of senior officers in hiding his identity[17] and because of the prevailing tensions.

Most incidents of acts of sexual violence against Tamil women in the north and east that were committed by the Sri Lankan security forces have been reported in the 1990s. Several key cases received a great deal of publicity, such as the rape and murder of Krishanthi Kumarasamy, her mother, her brother and a neighbour in 1996 and the murder of Koneswary in 1997. In addition, during the years of the conflict, both the LTTE and some Muslim militant groups operating in the north and east have at different times issued codes of conduct for women including a dress code, and have publicly shamed (by shaving their heads and public display) and even assassinated women accused of 'poor' moral conduct.

Seeking affirmation in the aftermath of conflict

In both Timor Leste and Sri Lanka, the stories of sexual assault and abuse, and of heightened vulnerability to such violations as well as the testimonies of displacement and of sexual harassment and exploitation during and after flight demonstrate the similarities of the experiences of women during the period of armed conflict.

14

Similarly, the period of transition after the cessation of military conflict leads to the opening up of many opportunities for participation in processes of reconstruction, resettlement, rehabilitation and reconciliation, and for raising issues that particularly concern women. In Sri Lanka, during the first years of the ceasefire, women combatants of the LTTE moved into civilian and administrative roles, at the local and district levels. In Timor Leste, some women who worked with FRETILIN at the higher levels moved into senior levels of government. Years of involvement and engagement with the conflict have given these women, in both Timor Leste and Sri Lanka, a wealth of expertise in combat and military/security activities and some recognition of their contribution to the struggle as well as of their right to a presence in the formal arenas of decision-making. The critical discussion at present is whether this expertise and recognition will be reflected in political and legal structures that will strengthen women's equal status and position in society and eliminate violence and discrimination against women.

Involvement of women in the peace process

In Timor Leste, although women played a critical role in terms of the political lobbying and advocacy work that took place at the international level, the inclusion of women in the negotiations was a slow process. In the early 1990s, only one out of a team of 30 negotiators was a woman; over a period of six years, it changed very slowly until in 1997 there were four women on the team. The role played by women from Timor Leste who went into exile in Portugal, Mozambique and Australia was extremely critical in keeping the issue of Timor Leste on the international agenda.

In the Sri Lankan case, there have been various attempts at resolving the ethnic conflict over the past 20 years.[18] In none of these were women a part of the process; nor was there any discussion as to their absence or lack of participation. At the level of civil society, women's coalitions working for a peaceful and negotiated settlement of the conflict[19] performed a bridge-building role between women of the different ethnic communities caught up in the conflict. As the present peace process began in 2002, and especially after the signing of the Ceasefire Agreement (CFA) in February 2002, independent and autonomous[20] women's groups throughout the island began to organise around the issue of inclusion and participation. At the first round of peace talks, the only woman participant was Adele Balasingham, wife of LTTE ideologue Anton Balasingham, who was designated as Secretary to the LTTE delegation.[21]

In October 2002, in an initiative coordinated by the Women and Media Collective, five teams comprising 16 Sri Lankans and six others travelled to various conflict-affected areas of the country. At the end of the visit, the team submitted a Memorandum to the President, Prime Minister, the LTTE and the Norwegian Ambassador in Colombo, calling for the inclusion of women and women's concerns in the peace process. This report paved the way for further lobbying by women's groups (Women and Media Collective 2002). There is no doubt that the decision to establish a Sub-Committee on Gender Issues (SGI) to advise the parties to the peace process on gender issues was at least in part due to these efforts.[22]

Participation of women in the political mainstream and in formal structures of governance

After the Referendum and independence in Timor Leste in 2000, women have gained a fair degree of representation within the formal political structures. However, the process of gaining political space has been difficult and as the La'o Hamutuk Bulletin for August 2001 points out, women are often 'pushed aside in political discussions' despite their leaderships skills and experience.

The process of holding elections in Timor Leste in 2002 brought to the fore some critical issues regarding women's participation in decision-making and the attitude of the post-conflict regime to the equality and equal status of women. In the process of consultations regarding the Constitution, 40 per cent of the Constitutional Commissioners were women. Of these, 24 women (26 per cent) were a part of the Constitutional Assembly that met in October 2002 in order to organise the elections and future government of Timor Leste. In 1999, women's groups created a network, REDE, to lobby for the representation of women in the national and district level decision-making bodies. In 2002, REDE brought forward a proposal for the inclusion of 30 per cent women candidates in the national Parliament, which was rejected by the Assembly. Women activists allege that UN electoral officials colluded with their more traditional male political leaders to defeat the proposal. However, the UN Special Representative offered incentives to political parties that fielded more women candidates; for example, parties with women candidates for senior positions in government would get more broadcast time. In addition, a network of women's groups known as Kaukus went into action providing support and training for women candidates.

In the actual elections, 27 per cent candidates were women. REDE fielded three independent women candidates at the national level; none of them was successful in securing a seat in Parliament. Only 24 women were elected, all of them from the dominant mainstream political parties. In establishing the government, FRETILIN which secured the majority of seats appointed two women to head two key Ministries, those of Finance and Justice, in contrast to many other countries in which women usually were allocated posts linked to the welfare of women and children, and in sectors such as health, education and social welfare. In addition, a woman was appointed Deputy Minister for Internal Administration. In September 2001, the government also positioned women in two key advisory posts to the Prime Minister, one on Human Rights and the other on the Promotion of Equality. The Office for the Promotion of Equality (OPE) works on four platforms: democracy, human rights, effective development and poverty reduction. Its mandate is the promotion of equality between men and women, and the advancement of women through legal reform, formulation and implementation of government policies and programmes and establishment of linkages both within and outside the country.

This process was widely supported through a countrywide

campaign which started off in June 2000 with the holding of the first national Women's Congress in Dili. Attended by over 200 women from various parts of the country, the participants decided on a Women's Plan of Action which contained in it the main elements for which the national networks of women's groups would lobby during the election period. By September 2001, this group had submitted a Women's Charter of Rights with 10,000 signatures to the Special Representative of the UN Secretary General in East Timor; following this, the Charter was also submitted to the Constitutional Assembly. The three key points that were put forward in the Charter were:

- the effective equality of opportunities between men and women;
- commitment to the principle of non-discrimination on grounds of gender;
- guarantees of equal rights for men and women in all areas of life including in the family and in marriage.

In Sri Lanka, the involvement of women in Tamil militancy is an extremely significant factor in the history of the struggles for self-determination of the Sri Lankan Tamils because traditional Tamil society and culture prescribes extremely restricted roles for women in the public sphere. The women's wing of the LTTE has expanded and developed in the years since its inception in 1986, and is known to have a fairly autonomous existence in terms of decision-making regarding its own daily affairs.

Within each district in the north and east that comes under the control of the LTTE, the Women's Wing has its own Political Affairs leader as well as others in charge of civilian liaison. The LTTE's media unit is largely operated by women, and within the LTTE's judicial system, there are two women judges on the Court of Appeal and several women judges in the lower courts as well as many women advocates. The LTTE police also has women police officers and operates Women's Desks at several police stations. Within its fighting forces there are several women's brigades. In addition, women play a key role within the Black Tigers Unit from which suicide bombers emerge. The women cadres who are killed in battle are elevated to 'martyrdom', and each year on 10 October, the LTTE celebrates Women's Reawakening Day, in honour of Malathy, the first woman LTTE cadre to be killed in battle.

Following the Ceasefire Agreement of February 2002, the LTTE established political offices in some areas of the north and east under government control. This led to some shifts in the strategies adopted by the LTTE in its interactions with the civilian populations not living under its control. Members of its second rank, both male and female, have been pushed into administrative operations, and into interaction with local communities regarding matters of their daily existence. This informal and almost unregulated process of 'reintegration' of former armed cadres into civil society has posed a challenge to the LTTE because many of them have little skill or experience that would enable them to carry out these tasks efficiently. In addition, since LTTE cadres have gone through years of separation from 'normal' life, and are now embedded in families and communities, they have also had to develop skills in social interaction that are unfamiliar to them. In spite of these difficulties, female LTTE cadres have emerged as local administrative officials and the southern media, in the first months after the ceasefire, was quick to pick up on this transformation. However, within the decision-making hierarchy of the LTTE, women still do not play a significant role, and major political decisions are still taken by a male hierarchy.

One phenomenon that may reflect an aspect of consolidation of the political gains of the conflict period is the inclusion of women in formal political structures. The first parliamentary elections to be held after the CFA took place in April 2004. The TNA (a broad coalition of Tamil political parties supportive of the LTTE), and the Eelam People's Democratic Party (EPDP, an anti-LTTE group) nominated women candidates for the north, while the TNA also nominated two women from the east. This was the first time that mainstream Tamil political parties had fielded women candidates who were not family members of a male Tamil politician. The two TNA candidates from the east were elected, both entering mainstream politics with a background of long-term engagement with civil society issues in the context of conflict. Batticaloa MP Thangeswari Kadiraman garnered the highest number of votes cast for individual candidates.

Jaffna MP Pathmini Sithamparanathan has been closely involved with a number of women's initiatives in the north over the years of the conflict. Commenting on her participation in the elections, she pointed out the difficulties she faced, in balancing the general political demands for autonomy and self-rule for the north and east, which are priority issues for the TNA, with the more specific demands of women who had suffered as a consequence of the conflict.[23] In an interview after her victory, MP Kadiraman spoke about her experiences in the political arena and stressed the need for women to move out of their homes and into a broad social life in order to become better equipped for politics. The second woman candidate for the Jaffna District was Maheswary Velayuthan, a human rights lawyer, who contested from the EPDP, a party that conducted its campaign under grave pressure from the LTTE. In discussing her role within the Tamil political arena, Maheswary has commented on the oppression and subordination women have to face in society as well as within their own political parties. She also has pointed to male biases in the media which result in male candidates receiving far more coverage for their campaign and political activities than the women.

At present there is a lobby for legal change calling for stipulations that one-third of candidates at local government elections are women and that one-third seats within the institutions should be set aside for women. This proposal was among the issues discussed at the initial meetings of the Sub-Committee on Gender Interests of the peace process, at which a southern member reported that the women representatives of the LTTE were for proposing a 50 per cent representation.[24]

Challenging domestic violence and violence against women

Under UNTAET administration, a Gender Unit that undertook a range of tasks aimed at raising awareness regarding women's issues, and in particular of violence against women, was set up in East Timor. This Unit was particularly responsible for the setting up of Vulnerable Persons Units in the civilian police. The focus on violence against women continued after independence with the support of local and international NGOs as it became clear that the phenomenon did not disappear in the post-conflict phase. The extent of the problem is borne out by many reports, for example one by Milena Pires in 2000 in which she stated: 'After years of a cruel and brutal conflict, the violence learned by the revolutionaries has now been turned on their women'.[25] In 2001, Health Minister Dr Sergio Lobo was arrested for beating his wife and then released by the Dili District Court which declared that 'a man has the right to control the actions of his wife'. The public debate that took place around this case showed that at least some sections of Timorese society were unwilling to accept the situation in which violence against women was 'normalised'. In January 2002, Jose Ramos Horta, Foreign Minister, speaking at a meeting of the UN Security Council clarified the government's commitment to the eradication of violence against women, stating that 'in numerous gatherings around the country many of us have appealed to the communities to seriously reflect on this heartbreaking reality in our country and join efforts to put an end to this'.

The fact that domestic violence and sexual assault were very high on the list of priority issues affecting the entire society of Timor Leste is borne out by a number of research studies done during 2002 and 2003 by diverse non-governmental agencies such as the International Rescue Committee (CIDA/UNDP 2003) and OXFAM, the National and District-Level Consultations on Domestic Violence organised by the OPE in collaboration with UNFPA[26] and various reports from the Sexual Assault Training Programme of Caritas Australia. All reports pointed to a high prevalence of domestic violence at all social and economic levels, with inadequate responses by the law enforcement, medical and judicial agencies. For example, in the period from January to July 2002, the VPU of the Dili District Police received 352 complaints of which 274 were related to domestic violence. At the second

National Congress of Women of Timor Leste held in Dili in August 2004, attended by over 500 women, the issue of violence against women was discussed at length. The shortcomings of the criminal law in dealing with domestic violence and sexual assault, tolerance of violence against women due to customary practices such as 'belarque' (bride price), traditional modes of dispute resolution at the community level that reaffirmed patriarchal norms, acceptance of polygamy and adultery by men[27] were among the problem areas addressed.

What becomes clear in analysing this information is that patriarchal norms, supported by indigenous and religious customs and by tradition, make violence against women in Timor Leste a normal and acceptable act, and militates against any interventions. With regard to the bride price, for example, many people I spoke to said that when men gave 'belarque', they and their families felt they had 'purchased' the woman and could do whatever they wanted with her including act violently towards her. In addition, the fact that they had received the bride price made the woman's family feel that they had no further rights over the life and future of their daughter/sister and led to reluctance to intervene even in situations where they knew the woman was facing violence and abuse. Although many people across the country identify bride price as a social and cultural tradition that creates problems for young men and women, there was no decisive debate on the issue of 'belarque' within the context of social transformation at present under way in Timor Leste.[28] With regard to traditional forms of dispute resolution, which were especially utilised in cases of sexual assault, the negotiations take place between the chief of the village (male) and the male heads of the families of the women involved. The voice of the woman who has suffered the violence and abuse is almost never heard in these proceedings.

In 2002–2003, women's groups, other civil society groups and international agencies working in Timor Leste collaborated with the Office for the Promotion of Equality to draft domestic violence legislation and conduct district-based consultations regarding this new proposed law. Raising awareness and building support among traditional village leaders and the church as well as among lawyers, members of the judiciary and among the law enforcement agencies was also a part of this campaign. In 2003, the draft Bill was presented to the Cabinet and was due to be passed into law. The draft Bill of 2003 defined 'domestic relations' very broadly to include intimate sexual or social relations as well as the relations between employers and servants in the household, and understood marriage to mean legal, religious and traditional or customary marriage. The concept of 'violence' as set out in the draft included physical, psychological, sexual and economic, with rape, incest and forced prostitution being included under sexual violence. The draft Bill also validated the role of social workers, counsellors and community members in cases of violence against women, and called for expeditious trial procedures in cases of domestic violence. In terms of penalties, the draft Bill allowed for restrictive measures, dealt with maintenance and allowed for the inclusion of civil claims for compensation and so on within the criminal case proceedings. The draft Bill has been widely discussed and publicised and there has been a great deal of support for this initiative from all concerned groups and institutions. It has been accepted at Cabinet level and now needs to go before the national legislators. The final form of the Bill is of course subject to changes at this phase, but the process has been inclusive and participatory and has created a high level of public awareness regarding violence against women in Timor Leste.

In the Sri Lankan case, women's groups have been active against violence towards women in many different ways since the mid-1980s. However, there is a fundamental difference between the north and east, and the south of the island in terms of responses to the issue, from the women who are the victims and survivors of violence and the formal structures for justice and redress. This is because of the control exercised by the LTTE in certain areas of the north and east which render the national structures of law enforcement and justice untenable.

In the late 1990s, southern women's groups began an active campaign for the criminalisation of domestic violence, drawing on the 1993 Women's Charter, which is the articulation of state policy on women,[29] in which violence against women was identified as a critical issue. Reforms to the Penal Code in 1995 criminalised sexual harassment and introduced minimal mandatory sentencing for rape. Proposals to de-criminalise abortion and to criminalise marital rape were rejected. A report published by the Women and Media Collective in 1999 stated that 1106 incidents of violence against women in the national newspapers published in all three national languages were recorded.[30] Among the categories taken into consideration were murder, attempted murder, assault, rape, attempted rape, molestation and sexual harassment. By 2002 there was a draft Bill on Domestic Violence which had emerged out of a series of broad-based consultations organised by women's groups and that drew on the framework for model legislation on domestic violence elaborated by the UN Special Rapporteur on Violence against Women in 1996.[31] In 2005, the Bill was passed by Parliament after many substantive changes which render it in effect a Bill that provides for Protection Orders to be issued by Magistrates in cases of complaints relating to domestic violence. The Bill has a broad definition of what constitutes the 'domestic' arena, and focuses on the protection of victims.

In the LTTE controlled areas of the north and east over the past 10 years there is evidence that the LTTE has taken a strong position on violence against women, and against the consumption of liquor, since most women who are victims of domestic violence cite alcoholism as one of the main causes for the violence against them. In 1994–1995, Adele Balasingham embarked on researching cases of domestic violence that were being reported to the LTTE police. Among the issues that she highlights, other than daily beatings and abuse, was the 'reality of marital rape in the lives of Tamil women' (Balasingham 2001: 306).

The LTTE devised its own Penal Code in the mid-1990s and at the time, for example, the penalties for rape were higher than those stipulated in the Penal Code of Sri Lanka. In addition, the LTTE law enforcement agency, the Tamil Eelam Police Force, was reported to be taking strict measures against domestic violence and violence against women. Rajasingham-Senanayake (2001) speaks of coming across the existence of a de facto policy against domestic violence adopted by the LTTE in 1999. In Trincomalee in 1999, she recorded an interview with a young woman activist who said that women brought complaints of domestic violence to the LTTE who 'took appropriate action'. The male offenders were given a first warning; if the violence persisted, they were fined; if this still did not prevent the violence from taking place, the men were sentenced to periods of imprisonment in an LTTE jail. Looking into the situation of women who had been displaced because of the conflict in Vanni in 2002–2003, Elek (2003) reports being told that LTTE cadres take a pro-active stance against incidences of violence and abuse of alcohol within the home. Each village reportedly has a 'good conduct unit' which reports on illegal and criminal activities within the village to the LTTE. 'Once identified, perpetrators are taken into LTTE custody, given "moral education" and, subject to the nature of their crime, sentenced to time in prison or community service. They are then encouraged to rejoin their family'. However, conversations with women in the Eastern Province tell a different story, of lethargy and unwillingness by the LTTE police and courts to pursue cases of domestic violence and of maintenance.[32] Thus it may well be that, just as in the government controlled areas, in the LTTE judicial system too the burden of pursuing justice for women through the formal legal system leaves much to be desired and places too much responsibility on well-intentioned individuals.

The shared problematic

When we compare the experiences of women in a post-conflict situation in Timor Leste and in a transition phase in Sri Lanka, it is clear that despite the many historical, political and cultural differences there are some similarities that create a space for reflection on the obstacles women face in advancing their independence and autonomy within a framework that demands independence and autonomy for their society and people as a whole.

Above all it is clear that patriarchal attitudes and frameworks are deeply embedded in culture, custom and tradition in each of these cases and impinge on the rights of women and circumscribe their daily lives. Thus, although during a conflict women have played a critical role not only in the political militancy of their community but also in ensuring the survival of their families and communities, as the situation changes and the conflict comes to an end, even for a brief period, dominant ideologies of male domination and female subordination once more affirm their primacy in society.

In both Sri Lanka and Timor Leste the status of women as reproducers and bearers of tradition and honour allocates particular roles for women within the community. During the conflict women became vulnerable to a range of sexual violations and abuse which not only caused them pain and suffering but were meant to bring 'shame' and 'dishonour' to their communities. The silence that prevails within families and within communities regarding sexual and physical abuse and violence against women in the context of the conflict is a shared experience across the world. On the one hand women and their families are intimidated by the nature of the power the perpetrators have over them, and fear to make complaints. On the other hand there is the social silence and denial of rape and other forms of sexual abuse due to the patriarchal values that consider women who are victims and survivors of abuse to have been devalued by the act. These attitudes prevail even in so-called 'normal' times; a conflict situation only exacerbates their power and their impact. Families and communities maintain a silence about the issue of rape and sexual violation of their sisters, daughters and wives due to social pressure and the fear of stigma. This further victimises the women and pushes them to an isolated and alienated existence. *The Broken Palmyra* quotes one woman as saying: 'The soldiers destroy us once but the village destroys us a thousand times' (Hoole et al. 1990: 319).

In cases where the women entered into what is described as a 'consensual' relationship with men from the military, as happened both in Timor Leste and in Sri Lanka, one can only accept the term 'consensual' if one ignores the imbalance in power between the two persons concerned. The women in the villages of eastern Sri Lanka could not scream or protest or lodge a police complaint because they were themselves caught up in a web of circumstances in which their silence and complicity in such sexual 'adventures' carried out by the military or the police would secure safety for their men and for their families. The 'temporary wives' of Indonesian military personnel in East Timor were motivated by the same fears of insecurity; if you were known to be the 'wife' of one army man then you were saved from harassment and abuse by the others. Trying to identify 'consent' or 'choice' in such circumstances remains a futile exercise.

In 'normal times' in both Sri Lanka and East Timor women's primary roles were those of mothers, wives and homemakers subordinate to the male head of household. Practices such as dowry and bride price meant that marriage was a property issue often settled by negotiation conducted between families and communities. Women's self-expression through dress and adornments was circumscribed by dress codes that would identify her as a member of the community. Her freedom of mobility was restricted by social norms that ascribed a secondary and subordinate role to her in society and that made a woman's 'purity' and 'chastity' a measure of masculine prowess. Within this context, incidents of violence against women within the family or from the community—including incest and rape—were often downplayed because preserving the unity and integrity of the community was the primary consideration. The conflict served to exacerbate these conditions.

The conflict also created situations in which women were left to care for themselves, the children, the elderly and the sick when villages were abandoned and communities displaced due to fighting; when male family members were arrested or disappeared; when entire communities of women, men and children became the target of attack and abuse by the 'enemy'. In these circumstances women were thrust into the position of head of household and had to hold the social fabric together in often hostile circumstances. They also had to negotiate with those in power for justice and redress for the damage and injuries done to them—building small islands of safety and security in the midst of chaos and uncertainty. 'Crossing the barriers into public space' through an often involuntary process gave many women a degree of self-confidence and a sense of their independent and autonomous personhood that would perhaps not have been possible in times of peace (Samuel 2001). As internally displaced women in Sri Lanka and in East Timor, they developed strategies of engagement with camp authorities, both national and international, that affirmed their status as heads of household and brought material benefits to them and their families.

These processes have led to an erosion of social taboos and barriers to women's public social existence. In the present contexts of both Timor Leste and Sri Lanka we observe women moving into positions within political and administrative structures and creating spaces within which they may consolidate some of the indirect gains of conflict that have transformed their situation as women in their societies. In addition, through their work on violence against women, we see that women of Sri Lanka and Timor Leste are using the experience and expertise gained during conflict periods to bring about changes in social attitudes and values regarding women in their societies.

However, they meet with resistance and opposition from almost every sector of society in both these countries. The reluctance to accept large numbers of young women, in particular, in roles that are new and that challenge existing stereotypes of femininity is widespread. For example, women who are demobilised as a part of any ongoing peace process need programmes for rehabilitation and reintegration into society. Yet their reception by families and communities poses a grave challenge to this process. In Timor Leste, there were few programmes that addressed the specific reintegration needs of women members of FRETILIN who have returned to their homes and villages after years of exile. Some women I spoke to also expressed their frustration at not being given recognition, at being treated as if the sacrifices they made were not actually valued in post-conflict Timor Leste.

There are no formal programmes for demobilisation in Sri Lanka though there has been a great deal of international and national pressure on the LTTE to halt its conscription of children. During the years of the ceasefire there have been some cases in which children recruited by the LTTE, and by the splinter faction led by 'Karuna', have been sent back to their homes with little preparation or monitoring. Observers have reported unwillingness on the part of parents and communities to accept women and girls who have been actively engaged in militancy back into their homes and families. The resistance on the part of schools and other public institutions to welcome these girls back into their original communities was a factor contributing to the rejection on the part of the families. As a consequence, for example, in Sri Lanka there were reports of marriages being arranged for girls and boys below the age of 16, with no consideration for their wishes.[33]

The conflicts have also meant that many women and girls in Sri Lanka and in Timor Leste suffer from mental health problems and psychosocial problems. They have become more at risk of exposure to HIV and other sexually transmitted infections as a consequence of the conflicts. Health problems related to sexual violence and assault and complications during pregnancy and childbirth are often further exacerbated during a time of strife due to the lack of security and breakdown of health services. In 2002 a UNIFEM report observed that 'women's reproductive health problems during conflicts may range from having no sanitary supplies for menstruation to life-threatening pregnancy-related conditions, from lack of birth control to the effects of sexual violence' (UNIFEM 2002: 37). Among critical areas that require focus in any health care interventions designed for women in the aftermath of a conflict are the need for psychosocial support and reproductive health services to be an integral part of emergency assistance and post-conflict reconstruction. The special health needs of women who have suffered from war-related injuries, amputations, sexual violence etc. including treatment for sexually transmitted infections is also critical. The recognition that 'the human rights of women include their right to have control over and decide freely and responsibly on matters relating to their sexuality, including sexual and reproductive health free of coercion, discrimination and violence' (UN 1995) and attention to several recent international documents that have emphasised the rights of women in conflict and post-conflict situations with regards to health care[34] must be the framework within which such interventions take place.

The participation of women in decision-making processes at every level of the post-conflict phase is extremely critical for the success of the reconstruction, rehabilitation and resettlement exercise as a whole. However, as Radhika Coomaraswamy (2001) has pointed out, 'Although women make up the majority of heads of household in most post-conflict situations, their families and their needs are rarely adequately factored into international donor and reconstruction programmes or the distribution of humanitarian aid'.

What becomes clear on a closer examination of the situation is that many of the changes in women's position that are due to the conflict are quite tenuous and fragile. There have been few legal or policy changes that have actually acknowledged the changing role of women in the context of the conflict, and fewer formalised changes in actual administrative practice in terms of recognition for female-headed households and single-parent families. Social attitudes towards women who have been victims of sexual abuse, or who have been widowed or abandoned in the course of the conflict remain locked within traditional patriarchal moral codes. The apparent resolution of the conflict may, it seems, result in no lasting changes in the position of women in these societies, in spite of their contribution to the struggle for self-determination.

Retention of some of the gains made in terms of women's increased mobility and independence during the conflict period remains a challenge in the post-conflict and transitional phases. Commitments to bringing back 'normalcy' ring hollow in the ears of women for whom normalcy means subordination, economic dependence, vulnerability to violence and lack of autonomy. The cases of Timor Leste and Sri Lanka point to the fact that if women emerging out of a conflict situation are to retain some of the autonomy and decision-making power that they gained during the conflict, and if the societies they have contributed so much towards are to garner the benefits of the social changes that have occurred during the conflict period, there needs to be serious commitment on all sides to making this happen. Militant movements face the challenge of dealing with the traditional patriarchal and hierarchical conventions enmeshed within their structures. Governments and other national and international agencies engaged in supporting processes of transition and transformation must design and implement programmes in gender-sensitive ways and in ways that allow the voice of women who have been a part of the conflict to be heard. Civil society organisations, and especially women's groups, that have been active during the conflict period must engage in a tremendous lobbying and campaigning exercise to ensure that the positive changes wrought in women's lives during times of conflict are recognised and valued and become a part of the post-conflict reality of these societies.

Notes

[1] The name by which the people of East Timor now refer to their country and their nation.

[2] In Sri Lanka, the island nation of south Asia, members of the Tamil minority community took up arms in a struggle for a separate state in the late 1970s and an uneasy ceasefire brokered by Norwegian facilitators in 2002 has survived for over two years. East Timor, the eastern part of the island of Timor, in the Indonesian archipelago, launched a struggle for self-determination and independence from Indonesia in the mid-1970s and became an independent nation in 2001.

[3] UN Security Council Resolution 1325 (2000).

[4] Much of the discussion on Timor Leste is based on information and documentation I gathered during my visit there in late 2003, supported by Caritas Australia for which I am grateful, and give special thanks to Anna Cody for her insights.

[5] In 1974, accompanying political changes in Portugal, East Timorese political

movements engaged in agitation for independence. The main ones were the Timorese Democratic Union (UDT) with close links to Portugal, the Revolutionary Front for Independent East Timor (FRETILIN) and the Association for Integrated East Timor (APODETI) favouring integration with Indonesia. The years 1974–1975 saw internal fighting between the different political groups, and by September 1975 FRETILIN had gained ascendance.

6 Nadiah and Kamal Bamadhaj, *Aksi Write: Word Wizards*, Rhino Press, Petaling Jaya, Malaysia, 1997.

7 Emily Roynestad, 'Are women included or excluded in post-conflict reconstruction—a case study from Timor Leste', UN Division for the Advancement of Women, November 2003.

8 Founded in 1997, FOKUPERS organised the first-ever Conference of Timorese women in Dili in November 1998 as well as the first public demonstration against violence against women in Dili on 25 November 1998.

9 Founded in 1998, as *Gertak*.

10 FOKUPERS Bulletin, 1999.

11 Mark Dodd, 'A family on East Timor grieves for a daughter', *International Herald Tribune*, 22 December 2000.

12 'Children of Rape', *New York Times*, 1 March 2001.

13 See CARV report on www.easttimor-reconciliation.org.

14 The situation of military sexual slavery is not new to the women of East Timor. The island was occupied by the Japanese imperial army during World War II and there is a record of almost 1000 women who were held as sexual slaves by the Japanese army during that time. See Report of Women's International War Crimes Tribunal on Japanese military sexual slavery, in Tokyo, December 2000.

15 *The Broken Palmyra—The Tamil Crisis in Sri Lanka: An Inside Account* by Rajan Hoole, Daya Somasundaram, K. Sritharan and Rajini Thiranagama; Sri Lanka Studies Institute, Claremont, CA: April 1990.

16 'Border' villages because of their existence on the borders of the actual arena of conflict.

17 Personal testimonies heard during the Border Village Commission of which I was a member; this remains unpublished information in the possession of the Border Villagers' Committee.

18 An All Party Conference in 1984; the talks held in Bhutan's capital, Thimpu, with all Tamil militant groups present in 1986; the Indo-Lanka Peace Accord of 1987; the ceasefire of 1990; a cessation of hostilities in 1994; and so on.

19 Among them are the Women's Action Committee (1982–1986)), Women for Peace (1984–1990), Mothers and Daughters of Lanka (1990–present). For further information see S. Abeysekera 1995.

[20] In this context, the term 'autonomous' is used to refer to women's groups and organisations that do not have any link with any mainstream political party.

[21] Adele Balasingham, of Australian origin, has been actively and intimately involved with the LTTE from the early 1980s and has played a key role in formulating the positions of the LTTE regarding women's role within the struggle.

[22] The government and the LTTE nominated five women each to this Sub-Committee; the government appointed four women from the south with an active record of engagement with issues of peace, human rights and democracy and one woman professional from the east. The LTTE candidates were from their women's wing, holding leadership positions in five districts with large areas under their control.

[23] For further information on women and the elections of 2004, see *OPTIONS*, journal in English, published by the Women and Media Collective, Issue 1, 2004.

[24] Kumudini Samuel, personal communication, Colombo, October 2004.

[25] Report made to CIIR (Catholic Institute on International Relations), London, 2000.

[26] Final Report on Workshop and District Consultations for Domestic Violence Legislation: Office for the Promotion of Equality (OPE), Timor Leste, July 2003.

[27] 'Polygamy serves as one of the root causes of domestic violence in Timor Leste', quoted in Domestic Violence Legislation Policy Paper, OPE, Timor Leste, 2003.

[28] For example, although the prohibitions placed on dowry in India have not actually eliminated the practice, there is at least far more judicial and legal sensitivity to issues of violence against women due to dowry related issues as a consequence.

[29] Drawn up by the state in 1993 after a process of national consultation with women from all parts of the island and representing all sectors.

[30] Women's Rights Watch: Year Report 1999, Colombo, Women and Media Collective, 1999, p. 7.

[31] United Nations Commission on Human Rights (UNCHR) document E/CN.4/1996/53/Add.2; 2 February 1996.

[32] Based on private communications.

[33] Information gathered on visits to Batticaloa in June 2004.

[34] For example, see the 1999 report of the ICPD+5 (International Conference on Population and Development, Cairo, 1994) meeting which recognised the need to ensure reproductive rights and provide reproductive health care in emergency situation, especially for women and adolescents.

References

Abeysekera, Sunila. 1995. 'Organizing for Peace in the Midst of War: Experiences of Women in Sri Lanka' in *From Basic Needs to Basic Rights: Women's Claim to Human Rights*. ed. Margaret A. Schuler. Washington DC: Women, Law and Development International.

———. 2003. 'Maximising the Achievement of Women's Human Rights in Conflict Transformation: The Case of Sri Lanka'. *Columbia Journal of Transnational Law*. vol. 41. no. 3.

Anderson, Benedict. 1983. *Imagined Communities: Reflections on the Origins and Spread of Nationalism*. London: Verso.

Balasingham, Adele. 2001. *The Will to Freedom: An Inside View of Tamil Resistance*. London: Fairmax.

Bamadhaj, Kamal and Nadiah. 1997. *Aksi Write: Word Wizards*. Petaling Jaya, Malaysia: Rhino Press.

Bunch, Charlotte. 2002. 'Feminist Conceptualizations of Peace, Human Rights and Women's Peace Activism'. Draft paper presented at international conference on Conflict, Women and Peace Building. Colombo.

Butalia, Urvashi. 2002. 'Introduction' in *Speaking Peace: Women's Voices from Kashmir*. ed. Urvashi Butalia. New Delhi: Kali for Women.

Chenoy, Anuradha M. 2002. *Militarism and Women in South Asia*. New Delhi: Kali for Women.

CIDA/UNDP. 2003. 'Prevalence of Gender Based Violence in Timor Leste'. Research Report. Canadian International Development Agency and UN Development Programme. July.

Cockburn, Cynthia and Dubravka Zarkov. eds. 2002. *The PostWar Moment: Militaries, Masculinities and International Peacekeeping: Bosnia and the Netherlands*. London: Lawrence and Wishart.

Coomaraswamy, Radhika. 1998. 'Report of the UN Special Rapporteur on Violence against Women, its Causes and Consequences'. Mission to Indonesia and East Timor on the issue of violence against women. UN Doc. E/CN.4/1999/68/Add.3. 21 January 1999.

———. 2001. 'Report of the UN Special Rapporteur on Violence against Women, its Causes and Consequences'. UN Doc. E/CN.4/2001/73. Geneva: United Nations.

De Mel, Neloufer. 2001. *Women and the Nation's Narrative: Gender and Nationalism in Twentieth Century Sri Lanka*. New Delhi: Kali for Women.

Elek, Sophie. 2003. *Choosing Rice over Risk: Rights, Resettlement and Displaced Women*. Colombo: Centre for the Study of Human Rights. University of Colombo.

Enloe, Cynthia. 1989. *Bananas, Beaches, Bases: Making Feminist Sense of International Politics*. London: Pandora.

Gautam, Shobha. 2001. 'Women and Children in the Periphery of People's War'. Kathmandu: Institute of Human Rights Communication.

Gautam, Shoba, Amrita Banskota and Rita Manchanda. 2001. 'Where There Are No Men: Women in the Maoist Insurgency in Nepal' in *Women, War and Peace in South Asia: Beyond Victimhood to Agency.* London/Thousand Oaks/ New Delhi: Sage Publications.

Hoole Rajan, Daya Somasundaram, K. Sritharan and Rajini Thiranagama. 1990. *The Broken Palmyra—The Tamil Crisis in Sri Lanka: An Inside Account.* Claremont, CA: Sri Lanka Studies Institute.

Ivekovic, Rada and Julie Mostov. 2004. *From Gender to Nation.* Ravanna: A Longo Editore.

Manchanda, Rita. 2001. 'Introduction' in *Women, War and Peace in South Asia: Beyond Victimhood to Agency.* eds. Shoba Gautam et al. London/Thousand Oaks/New Delhi: Sage Publications.

Office for the Promotion of Equality. 2003. Final Report on Workshop and District Consultations for Domestic Violence Legislation. Timor Leste. July.

OPTIONS. 2004. Special feature on Women and the Elections of 2004. Colombo: Women and Media Collective. Issue 1.

Rajasingham-Senanayake, Darini. 2001. 'Ambivalent Empowerment: The Tragedy of Tamil Women in Conflict' in *Women, War and Peace in South Asia: Beyond Victimhood to Agency.* ed. Rita Manchanda. London/Thousand Oaks/New Delhi: Sage Publications.

Roynestad, Emily. 2003. 'Are women included or excluded in post-conflict reconstruction—A case study from Timor Leste'. UN Division for the Advancement of Women. November.

Samuel, Kumudini. 2001. 'Gender Difference in Conflict Resolution: The Case of Sri Lanka' in *Gender, Peace and Conflict.* eds. Inger Skjelsbaek and Dan Smith. Oslo: PRIO. London/Thousand Oaks/New Delhi: Sage Publications.

Skjelsbaek, Inger and Dan Smith. eds. 2001. *Gender, Peace and Conflict.* Oslo: PRIO. London/Thousand Oaks/New Delhi: Sage Publications.

United Nations. 1995. Beijing Platform for Action.

———. 2002. 'Women, Peace and Security'. A Study submitted by the UN Secretary General pursuant to Security Council Resolution 1325.

UNIFEM. 2002. *Women, War and Peace.* UN Development Fund for Women.

Women and Media Collective. 2002. 'Women's Concerns and the Peace Process'. Findings and Recommendations: International Women's Mission to the North East of Sri Lanka 12-17 October. Colombo.

Women's Rights Watch. 1999. Year Report 1999. Colombo: Women and Media Collective.

Yuval-Davis, Nira. 1997. *Gender and Nation.* London/Thousand Oaks/New Delhi: Sage Publications.

2

Reproductive Rights and Gender Justice in the Neo-conservative Shadow

GITA SEN

Introduction

The decade of the 1990s was an outstanding one for bringing issues of reproductive and sexual health and rights, violence against women, and male responsibility for gender power relations, to the centre of global and national debates on human rights and human development. This was the product of a complex and contradictory set of forces as well as diverse actors and alliances. It was the result of several phases of activism by feminists and their allies even during this relatively short period. From the early struggles to move beyond the neo-Malthusian population control paradigm that had dominated policy-making for over half a century, the terrain of struggle for women's human rights has moved on to later and more complex phases. Sexual rights and the HIV/AIDS pandemic on the one hand, and the political economy of globalisation and economic restructuring on the other have become central to this terrain, even as population 'controlistas' continue to fight rearguard actions.

These newer scenarios had already posed major dilemmas and tensions for women's rights activism during the Clinton presidency in the United States, and prior to 11 September 2001. The strong support of the economic North for women's reproductive and sexual rights stood in uncomfortable juxtaposition to their intransigence in global economic negotiations on world trade, financing for development, and debt repayment. This created major problems for those concerned to promote women's human rights in *all* dimensions. It made it particularly difficult in global negotiations to have an integrated and clear stance against cultural relativism wearing the guise of religion and tradition, and to build stable political alliances for women's human rights.

The work of feminist and other scholars and activists following the conferences of the 1990s showed clearly that security of livelihoods and an enabling economic environment are an important basis for moving forward to meet reproductive and sexual health needs through well-functioning health systems. Yet some of the very countries that were most vocal in their support for sexual and reproductive rights were also the most hard-nosed in South-North economic negotiations. These tensions came to the fore in the 'plus five' reviews for the Cairo and Beijing conferences. Nonetheless considerable advances were possible on reproductive and sexual health and rights during the 1990s because of the limited control over state power by religious fundamentalists.

This scenario has undergone a major change during the administration of George Bush Jr. in the USA with much stronger control over key levers of state power by religious fundamentalists on the one hand, and the rise of neo-conservative political economy on the other. The first years of the century have seen significant and tangible evidence of this in key conferences on HIV/AIDS, Children, and Population, as well as in many other sites. This chapter builds on previous analyses of the earlier phase (Correa and Sen 1999; Francisco and Sen 2000; Sen and Madunagu 2001; Sen and Correa 2000) to draw implications for the current phase in which feminists and their allies are struggling to maintain hard-won gains and move forward. It also steps back to provide an analytical frame to explain the core of the tensions between gender justice and economic justice,[1] and the strategic implications of the multiple sites in which gender relations operate; and suggests how forward movement can be made.

37

Multiple sites of gender relations—strategic implications

Recognition that gender relations of power are not simply located in a single site of human interaction has been incipient during much of the debate within women's movements and organisations during the late 19th and 20th centuries. This recognition became particularly focused in the third wave of the global women's movement from the late 20th century on.[2] It is during this period that the debates about 'public' versus 'private' spheres, nature versus culture coalesced into clarity about the distinctions and linkages between two important sites where gender relations are played out. Feminist anthropologists and economists have used the language of production versus reproduction, viz., subordination within households (based on relations of inheritance/property, the division of labour, the 'care economy', sexuality, childbearing and rearing, and personal autonomy) versus gender relations in communities, labour markets, and political and legal systems. In both sites, the chief focus has been on power relations and hierarchies between women and men, i.e., gender relations as we usually understand them.

But this recognition has not sufficiently addressed the third site in which women are oppressed, viz., as members of oppressed economic classes or castes, or on grounds of race, ethnicity, sexual orientation, or nationality. This third site and its strategic implications have not been adequately analysed within the women's movement. This constitutes a gap in feminist theorising because subordination and oppression/exploitation in all three sites are linked and constitute the lived realities of women's existence. Typically we tend to think of the first two sites as the loci of gender relations while the third is left hanging conceptually. Understanding the need to overcome and transform power relations in the first two sites was itself partial and somewhat ad hoc in the earlier waves of the women's movement.[3] The current third wave has a clearer conceptual understanding of the first two sites but inadequate theorising about the connections to the third site has left us without effective political tools in key struggles at both global and regional/national levels.

Women's political movements have had to address the tensions of struggling for gender justice (in the first two sites) while addressing the implications of women's presence in struggles as members of oppressed classes, castes, races, etc.[4] These tensions have been present within women's movements and between women's organisations and other organisations. An often cited example is the tension between the birth control movement of the early 20th century in the USA and anti-racism struggles. Key founders and members of the feminist birth control movement were suspected of being ambiguous in their relation to the racist eugenicists of the time (Chesler 1992). Another well-known example is the hostile attitude of many male-dominated labour unions to the presence of women workers in modern industry, and their attempts to relegate women to the sphere of unpaid work in the home (Hartman 1981). A third illustration is the attitude of male leaders of nationalist movements who, while being eager to draw on the presence of women in their struggles, have been also enthusiastic votaries of sending them back to the home once the movement's goals have been achieved. This has also been true of many situations where women have been called out of the home to fulfil their patriotic duties in times of war or armed conflict, only to be sent back to the arena of domesticity once the conflict ends.

Women's attempts to secure gender justice and parity with men within social movements have all too often been resisted on the grounds of not creating divisions within the movement. They have in many situations been met with the promise that issues of gender justice would be addressed as soon as the other (and more important?) issues of economic or social justice have been dealt with. At the same time, women's movements that have not addressed other social or economic justice issues, have often been limited in their efficacy. *The main question is how to address the subordination and oppression of women on account of gender relations of production and reproduction on the one side, and as members of oppressed classes, nationalities, races etc. on the other.*

Women's organisations and other social movements have, in

practice, given a variety of responses to this central question. Women's organisations have sometimes cooperated with dominant classes or races as in the case of some of the birth control pioneers and the eugenicists; the resulting alienation from the struggles of oppressed classes or groups have created a wide divide between struggles to change gender relations and other struggles. At other times, and especially (but not exclusively) during critical nationalist, anti-racist, or anti-caste struggles, women have acquiesced to putting gender justice on the back burner. Within the most progressive sections of the women's movement, there is a tacit understanding that the ideal line to take runs between these two extremes, viz., women should ally with movements for social justice, but struggle within them to change gender practices and understanding.[5]

This is often easier said than done. Anti-feminist beliefs and practices are rife within many social movements, and transforming these to where the movement becomes genuinely supportive of gender justice can be a long drawn out and exhausting struggle.[6] In addition, social movements are built through processes of internal consolidation as well as external alliance building. While a movement's own gender practices may not be too problematic, its allies may be much worse on gender justice. For instance, the movement to cancel the 'odious' debts of South countries often works in alliance with the Catholic Church whose current hierarchy is vehemently opposed to gender justice. While debt cancellation may improve the national economic autonomy of some South countries, making it possible for their governments to better address some of the livelihood and basic needs of both women and men, putting gender justice on the back burner may also have serious negative consequences for women.

Thus the tension between economic justice and gender justice may be more deep-rooted in practice than women's organisations have recognised to date. The hard fact of the matter is that there is no simple congruence between the three sites of women's oppression. Being on the side of the oppressed along one dimension does not guarantee an equally progressive approach to other dimensions of oppression. Being in favour of economic justice does not guarantee that one is supportive of gender justice or even understands what it entails. Conversely, being in favour of gender justice certainly does not assure support for economic justice.

At the political level, the varying pace and direction of different dimensions of the current global environment and changes since the 1960s certainly means there is no automatic linkage between gender and other changes. Alliances have become more complex. The progressive (in gender terms) sections of most social movements are not the strongest. Too many social movements find it convenient to 'use' women for their ends without addressing gender relations. For women, the biggest challenge is one of political identity—which identity should they choose as their primary one? And how is the choice linked to a feminist social project?

Women's movements—the struggle for self-definition

Androbus and Sen have described the three phases of the international women's movement.

> Reference is often made to 'three waves' of the international women's movement: the first wave in the late 19th to early 20th century, the second covering the mid-20th century, and the third the late 20th century and on. Although these three waves are often depicted as distinct, we believe it is instructive to look at the connections between them.
>
> The first wave had three distinct sources. One source was in the colonised countries with the emergence of social reform movements that had as their primary focus the transformation of cultural practices affecting civil laws, marriage, and family life. While these reform attempts mobilised possibly as many or more men as women, they were an important early strand in the transformation of social discourse and practice affecting gender relations. A second source was the major debate within the social democratic and communist organisations of the late 19th and early 20th centuries, which then carried forward into the debates in the Soviet Union on the 'woman question'. This strand of debate was the most explicit about the connections between the institutions of private

property, the control over material assets, and women-men relations within families and society. A third source was the liberal strand that combined the struggle for the vote with the struggle to legalise contraception; this strand existed mainly though by no means exclusively in Europe and North America.

It is worth recognising the presence of these different strands in the very first wave of the women's movement because they delineate in an early form potential strengths as well as tensions that characterise the international women's movement right until today. The presence of multiple strands from early on has made for a movement that is broad and capable of addressing a wide range of issues. But the potential tensions between prioritising economic issues (such as control over resources and property) or women's personal autonomy or bodily integrity existed then and continue to exist now.' (Antrobus and Sen 2005)

The United Nations conference in Nairobi in 1984 marked the end of the Decade for Women. It also marked a major turning point in women's understanding of their relationship to the twin issues of equality and development. Clearly represented by the basic proposition of the DAWN[7] group that 'women do not need a larger share of a poisoned pie' (Sen and Grown 1987),[8] the view that *gender justice without economic justice* would not address women's concerns took hold. Integrating women into an unjust economic order or struggling for gender equality by itself began to be seen as partial. The global climate of growing economic inequality among and within nations, and the model of structural adjustment based on the Washington Consensus created the environment for these views to grow.

The pendulum swung in the other direction through the UN conferences of the 1990s, especially Vienna, Cairo and Beijing. Growing recognition of the enormous global deficit on women's human rights brought to the fore issues such as violence against women, and reproductive and sexual rights. Gender justice in reproduction and production became central to the debates of the 90s; struggling for *economic justice without gender justice* seemed as limited as its converse. By the time of the Beijing conference in 1995, there was a growing consensus in the global women's movement that economic justice and gender justice need to go hand in hand. Not all members share equally in this understanding, but it would be fair to say that it is now the dominant view within the movement. Despite this, how to convert this understanding into practical politics remains a major challenge for the women's movement. It is also the case that women's movements are light years ahead of many other political actors—states and social movements included—in this understanding.

Globalisation and anti-women fundamentalism: women's challenges in the 1990s[9]

The challenges facing feminist attempts in the 1990s to link gender justice with economic justice at the global, national, and local levels came from two directions. On the one hand, complex and poorly regulated processes of globalisation appeared as the new form of a free market juggernaut creating deep and growing inequalities of wealth and income, and in which rising numbers of impoverished people, especially women, were being marginalised from access to secure livelihoods. On the other hand, one set of reactions to globalisation was the strengthening of national, religion-based, ethnic or other identities in which the assertion of 'traditional'[10] gender roles and systems of authority and control was central.

These contradictions meant that women's struggles for greater personal autonomy did not mesh easily with their concerns and demands for a more just and equal economic order. The challenge for women, therefore, was how to assert the need for both economic justice and gender justice in an increasingly globalised and fundamentalist world. This core challenge conditioned the potential and actual roles of civil society organisations and social movements as much as of agencies and governments.

The conferences of the 1990s were a key forum where these challenges were addressed and where new possibilities for bridging gender justice and economic justice began to take shape. They were also the first significant occasions when 'women's issues' came forward from the margins of women-only conferences to the mainstream global agenda. The Cairo consensus of 1994 represented a major paradigm shift in this regard. But agreements reached in Cairo with respect to gender and reproductive rights were built upon agreements regarding women's human rights that had already been reached the previous year at the human rights conference in Vienna. The Beijing Platform for Action of the Fourth World Conference on Women expanded on the Vienna agreements on women's human rights, the Cairo recommendations on reproductive and sexual health and reproductive rights, and the macroeconomic agenda of the World Summit on Social Development in Copenhagen in 1995.

These agreements were fraught with controversy although no more so than many other global issues, and probably less than some such as world trade. What was striking was the extent to which a small minority of religious conservatives and their allies could hold the negotiations to ransom. Their opposition continued through their attempts to reverse the Cairo and Beijing agreements during the 'plus five' reviews. What accounted for the conservatives' ability to have so much 'voice' in global negotiations despite being a relatively small minority?

In the 1970s and 1980s, political factors conditioning UN negotiations were characterised by the harsh tensions of a bipolar global order. These tensions had to be negotiated carefully by feminists because in terms of gender the socialist bloc of the time had made a number of key advances. Cuba, for instance, was one of the earliest countries to enact a law regarding domestic work, even though its attitude to lesbian, gay, bisexual and transgender (LGBT) issues was less than exemplary. In 1985, just before the Nairobi women's conference, a group of Latin-American feminists visited Havana to convince Fidel Castro of the relevance of gender equality and its correlation with macroeconomic issues. Subsequently, Cuba took progressive positions regarding women's rights at the United Nations.

But the climate of the unipolar 1990s was different. First

World versus Second World conflicts were replaced by South versus North tensions in many arenas. While some protagonists maintained their old positions, others began to change. In the Beijing +5 negotiations, the positions of the Cuban delegation were not predominantly motivated by its historical commitment to gender equality, but governed by South-North economic tensions as exemplified particularly by the US economic blockade. While the principal text of these negotiations appeared to be women's rights, the critical sub-text[11] was the continuing South-North divide.

In this climate, religious conservatives have systematically attempted to emerge as the champions of the South. The hard line positions taken by the North negotiators on every economic issue—the right to development, debt, trade, financing—provided fertile soil for a growing closeness between the Vatican and at least some of the South's negotiators. By the early 1990s, the Vatican under the papacy of John Paul II had all but silenced Catholic liberals and liberation theologians by branding them as proto-Marxists, and filled the Church's hierarchy with prelates who were extremely conservative on both gender and grass roots empowerment of the poor. Nevertheless, the hierarchy appeared to recognise the strategic importance of making common cause with South countries.

The United Nations Conference on Environment and Development (UNCED) in 1992 witnessed one of the earliest major interventions by the Vatican in a speech against global poverty and inequality. From then on the Vatican began to use its growing clout to argue against global economic inequality while opposing women's rights and gender equality in every possible international forum. By the time of the Vienna conference on human rights in 1993, the Vatican had begun to mobilise its forces against the recognition of women's rights as human rights. In Cairo, the Vatican allied itself with Islamic conservatives to resist the adoption of the International Conference on Population and Development (ICPD) Programme of Action, 1994. This opposition continued through the succeeding conferences.

While the conservatives were certainly most vehement in their opposition to abortion and sexual orientation, this was only symptomatic of their core objection to gender equality itself. They fought tooth and nail against all notions of reproductive and sexual health and rights, were adamant in their refusal to recognise the brutality of domestic violence against women in all societies (preferring instead to sanctify the myth of 'the' happy nuclear family), and vehement in their assertion of 'cultural' and 'religious' practices and beliefs, however harmful to women. Very early in the Cairo +5 and Beijing +5 processes, it became evident that the main strategy of forces opposing gender equality and women's human rights was to block the adoption of a final document. Conservative forces were not interested in reviewing the implementation of agreements (the main objective of the +5 review processes); they were bent on undoing the consensus reached in Vienna, Cairo and Beijing.

To some extent these difficulties were because the global economic environment was even more unequal in the late 1990s than in 1993, 1994, and 1995 when the agenda for gender justice and women's human rights was legitimised. Among other issues, the non-level playing field faced by South countries in global trade and finance negotiations was far from conducive for gender justice to get a fair hearing.

Despite these unfavourable conditions, both the Cairo +5 and Beijing +5 reviews ended with the gains of Cairo and Beijing intact, and with further progress on some key fronts. It also became clear through the negotiations that, although South-North economic struggles provide fertile ground for the surfacing of other tensions, many of the hard core governments opposing women's human rights would have done so regardless of economics. In this light, the political progress observed in the 1990s conferences must be credited to the strategic capacity of global feminist networks to navigate between the Scylla of religious conservatism and the Charybdis of the North's economic agenda.

To do this, women's organisations and networks had to overcome their own internal disagreements and build strong coalitions across global divides. In the 1970s and 1980s, tensions were at play among feminists, particularly on the differences between the North's and South's women's agendas. In the 1990s, these tensions were gradually resolved through sustained efforts at building alliances, and the agenda for gender justice was articulated and legitimised at the global policy level. This global feminist consensus was anchored in the indivisibility, integral character, and universality of human rights as agreed at Vienna, and the notion that an enabling political and economic environment (economic justice in short) is a prerequisite for fulfilling women's rights.

Women's organisations continued to play multiple strategic and tactical roles during Cairo +5 and Beijing +5. The extremely important role played by women's organisations and activists within and outside government delegations during the original conferences of the 1990s had given them considerable experience and credibility. However, women had to work strategically to analyse the political direction of the negotiations during the 'plus 5' reviews, and to support the building of key coalitions among governments. One such crucial coalition that emerged was SLACC (Some Latin American and Caribbean Countries), a negotiating group that began to distinguish itself from more conservative positions within the Group of 77. Although SLACC itself may have been a short-term tactical phenomenon, its emergence was a signal of major importance. For the first time, a significant bloc of South countries was willing to stand as a bloc for more progressive positions on *both* global economic justice and gender justice.

The neo-conservative era: a clash of civilisations?

The rise to power of the protagonists of 'a new American century' has drastically altered the global geopolitical environment that is the ground on which economic justice and gender justice are negotiated. Mainstream discussions have described this as the rise of a new era where long held norms of Westphalian national sovereignty are as much at risk as recently negotiated agreements around global warming. The gender blindness of some of this analysis can lead to serious errors in political understanding as I will argue.

The geopolitics of a unipolar world encompasses the rise of a new imperial ambition, using the 'war against terror' as an excuse, and intent on strategically reshaping the global polity to suit its interests. The following elements appear to be central to this agenda.

Externally:

- Military force will be used to counteract US economic weakness, and reshape the US relationship to traditional economic allies ('old' Europe) and the new emerging economic challenger (China);

- A small set of regional satrapies will be strengthened to create and maintain a new global order under the US imperial umbrella; Britain and Israel appear to be in this set, but the identity of other key vassals is still unclear;[12]

- The role of the UN will be further downgraded so that it does not become a barrier to imperial ambition; at best the UN will play a 'janitorial' role of cleaning up the messes created by the imperial power or its regional satraps;[13]

- The 'war against terror' supplemented by the fearsome modern armoury of the Empire—depleted uranium bunker-buster and daisycutter bombs, tactical nuclear and chemical/biological weapons[14]—will be used to terrorise and keep the mass of countries in line with US economic and strategic interests;

- US corporations will therefore be ensured free rein to access materials and markets, and flout painstakingly negotiated environmental, labour, and social agreements.

Internally:

- Further dismantling of welfare and workers' rights and environmental standards in the name of improving US competitiveness;

- Giving free rein to US corporations;

- Shifting the public debate from livelihoods, employment, social security, rising poverty and inequality to 'terror' threats, zygotes and stem cells, and sexuality;
- Continuing support for de-secularising the political space, supporting the anti-women storm troopers, and shifting the blame for social ills to feminists and LGBT people.

Ideologically:

- Suppressing internal dissent and moving towards a more closed society in the name of the 'war on terror';
- Positing ideological oppositions externally and internally not so much in the traditional terms of democracy versus dictatorship, or secular versus theocratic, as in the primal language of good versus evil;
- Replacing gender equality and liberal freedoms by the norms of the patriarchal family and heterosexuality.

The 'neo-con' agenda is certainly not without challenge, nor without its own internal tensions. Major world powers such as 'old' Europe and Russia are not falling easily into the grasp of the new imperium, nor is China. Despite all its internal fissures, the economic South (through its dominant countries such as Brazil, India, South Africa leading the G-20) has been able to have some impact on global trade negotiations. And at the ideological level, American popular culture itself is considerably at variance with the preferred neo-con ideology of patriarchal family and heterosexuality.[15] American television, movies and print cannot easily return to the mores of the simpering 1950s; too much has changed culturally. Popular culture is full of sexuality, varieties of families, and LGBT relationships; the genie is out of the bottle! And furthermore has been globalised to distant corners of the world.[16] Motivating young American men to join the imperial legions through the promise of subservient wives and domestic domination will no longer be as easy as it may have been in an earlier era.

But the neo-con agenda also has some factors in its favour.

First, despite differences, there is still very little tension among different factions of the North on economic issues. Where US corporations lead, European and Japanese corporations still happily follow (or lead!). Second, in relation to the creation of regional satrapies, internal US opinion is not widely divided. Nowhere is this is more evident than in relation to Israel, Palestine and the current war in Iraq. The Democratic Party has traditionally been the strongest supporter of Zionism, and this still shows in its refusal to seriously oppose the neo-con agenda being implemented by the Israeli Ariel Sharon regime. In relation to Iraq as well, opposition to the Bush administration has been muted, and challengers in an election year have preferred to focus on the tried and tested call to 'bring the boys home' rather than take on the core of the neo-con agenda. Nonetheless, there are two import ant places where there are clear and sharp differences between neo-cons and Democrats—protectionism vis-à-vis trade, and gender.

The gender blindness of mainstream discussions of neo-conservatism results in an overweening focus on one aspect—the attempt to move beyond the Westphalian institutions of national sovereignty. The other and equally critical aspect is the attack on gender equality, women's human rights, and LGBT sexuality. This second aspect is essential to the neo-cons because it provides both the organisational basis and the ideological content of their agenda.

Globally, what we are witnessing today is no 'clash of civilisations', and nowhere is this clearer than in Iraq. Before the world's bemused gaze, the secular state of Iraq where women were educated and social development prioritised is being transformed into a theocratic one.[17] In the 1970s, in neighbouring Iran a revolution led by the religious hierarchies and supported by progressive forces overthrew a US-supported government, and proceeded to sharply control women. In Iraq, to the contrary, a theocratic state that will proceed to bring in stricter adherence to Sharia and subordinate women will very likely replace the government that has been overthrown by the US.

Global institutions and negotiations on reproductive and sexual rights

There is no 'clash of civilisations' on reproductive and sexual rights and gender equality between the neo-cons and religious conservatives. This has become very clear during the first three years of the Bush administration. It has also become clear that the payoff to the religious right wing within the US for its loyal electoral support to the Republican Right is made through strong and direct support and pressure from the White House itself on domestic issues and in global negotiations. These years have seen the US administration promote abstinence as a major method to handle the HIV/AIDS pandemic, to place parental control over the rights of adolescents even at the cost of the health of young people, and to take over the Vatican's role as mobiliser and strategist against gender equality, and reproductive and sexual health and rights in global negotiations.[18] A major move is currently afoot to gain legitimacy in the UN for the patriarchal, nuclear family, and thereby to broaden the base of support within governments of the South.

What this has meant is that supporters of women's human rights now face a formidable combination of religious conservatives (Christian and Muslim) and the US government. However, governments have not simply caved in to the pressure in the current discussions around ICPD +10 and Beijing +10. This became evident first in the Asian regional conference on population and development hosted by the United Nations Economic and Social Commission for Asia and the Pacific (ESCAP) in late 1992. With initiative and strategic and tactical support from women's organisations, Asian governments (with strong leadership from the larger countries)—together with key European donors, Japan, Australia and New Zealand—turned back a major conservative assault on the ICPD Programme of Action. This has been succeeded by similar action in the recent sub-regional meeting in Latin America. What is heartening is that, however limited or partial the implementation of ICPD may have been, many governments (or at least their health ministries) appear to have internalised—at least to some extent—the paradigm shift of Cairo.

For a small country, however, contradicting the Vatican is one thing; standing against the US is entirely another. The capacity of UN agencies to withstand pressure is uneven; the conservative attempt to isolate and weaken the UN's Population Fund (UNFPA) continues with renewed force. And while ICPD +10 activity at least has the capacity of a large organisation like UNFPA behind it, Beijing +10 has only the limited capacity of the UN's Division for the Advancement of Women (DAW) as backstop. All the difficulties faced by women's organisations during the 'plus 5' reviews are present in heightened form thanks to the takeover of the US administration by the neo-conservatives.

A key question here is whether, in light of the ESCAP and sub-regional Latin American experiences, the previous pitting of South versus North along the lines of economic justice versus gender justice has changed. At one level, there is some movement in this direction. Liberal governments in the South and the North (minus the US) made common cause in favour of gender justice in ESCAP. On the other hand, in recent and ongoing meetings of the Commission on Population and Development, of the Commission on the Status of Women, and of the Commission on Human Rights, the US government, the Vatican and Islamic conservative governments have worked closely together regardless of the ongoing bloodshed in Iraq and Palestine. These moves appear to indicate a more straightforward opposition of gender liberals versus gender conservatives, independent of economic or geopolitical issues.

But there are also fissures and tensions within the liberal camp. The attempt to create a strong bloc out of the G-20 to confront the economic North in trade negotiations may weaken support for reproductive and sexual rights within some progressive South governments. Women's organisations will need to mobilise strongly to prevent gender justice from being sold down the river yet again. In doing this they will have to strategise consciously and build on the opposition to the neo-conservative agenda of the American imperium.

And they cannot do it alone.

A final word to other development NGOs and networks. Unfortunately, there are still far too many global and other levels whose commitment to gender equality is weak, and whose beliefs and political practice are fraught with patriarchy. But for too long, the tendency among even the more progressive development NGOs is to leave gender equality to be struggled over by women's organisations alone. It is high time they recognised that women's struggles for gender justice, economic justice, and participatory democracy are central and may be key to the energy, strategic thinking, and innovative wisdom this era of globalisation and fundamentalism demands. (Sen and Madunagu 2001)

Notes

[1] Ideally gender justice ought to include elements of economic justice, and vice versa. However, proponents of economic justice between nations, classes or other groups often ignore gender; supporters of gender justice also sometimes ignore the environment of economic inequality and injustice within which gender is located. In doing so both sides leave out key aspects of the lived experience of women's lives.

[2] Reference is often made to three waves of the international women's movement: the first wave in the late 19th century to early 20th century, the second covering the mid-20th century, and the third the late 20th century and on (Antrobus and Sen 2005).

[3] Antrobus and Sen (2005) has a longer discussion of this issue.

[4] In this paper we conflate women's oppression as members of subordinate classes, castes, races etc. under the term 'economic justice'. Strictly speaking this is incorrect because the struggles of oppressed races, castes etc. include important non-economic elements just as gender does. However, in the specific political conjuncture addressed in this paper, the main problem we are focusing on is between economic justice and gender justice.

[5] The engagement of women's organisations with the structures and practices of the World Social Forum and the attempt to transform them provides one contemporary illustration.

[6] A similar problem exists with regard to movements for justice on grounds of race, caste or nationality.

[7] Development Alternatives for Women in a New Era is a network of women scholars and activists from the economic South who engage in feminist research and analysis of the global environment and are committed to working for economic justice, gender justice and democracy. It was formed in 1984

and put forward a path-breaking critique of global development from a southern feminist perspective in 1987.

8 This proposition and the analysis on which it was based caught the imagination of many feminists because it was a succinct representation of what they were already thinking and experiencing.

9 This section draws extensively from Sen and Correa (2000) and Sen and Madunagu (2001).

10 'Traditional' customs and beliefs are often not traditional at all, but are customs of recent vintage created for the specific purpose of controlling women.

11 This sub-text needs to be read with some care. There is sometimes a tendency among anti-globalisation forces to cast South governments as the champions of a more just global order. While the clout of North governments in global negotiations clearly became greater in the 1990s as compared to the 1970s, this is due at least in part to growing disparities among South countries themselves. These disparities appear to have eroded the capacity and political will of the South to negotiate effectively together against the North on economic issues. Sharply increasing inequality within many countries has also created powerful supporters of globalisation within South countries. Nor are these economic struggles simply over national sovereignty; they are also a mixed bag of battles over exclusion from globalisation, or over its spoils.

12 Which Asian (Pakistan or India?), Latin American, or African countries will be picked to play this role is not obvious.

13 As it is currently being called upon to do by the US Democrats in Iraq.

14 In short, weapons of mass destruction and devastation.

15 The religiosity of Bush and British Prime Minister, Tony Blair, may be genuine, but this is hardly true of the neo-cons generally. US Vice President, Dick Cheney, is known to have an openly lesbian daughter who campaigned for him in the election, and who was carefully protected from both left and right.

16 The real transformations in family relationships and popular practices vis-à-vis personal life, sexuality and gender in the North and in growing parts of the South has been one of the strongest basis of support for reproductive and sexual rights in the global norm-setting arena.

17 The end outcome in Iraq is not obvious, but certainly religious authorities will be hard to put down in any future state.

18 Key negotiators for the Vatican in the UN conferences and reviews of the 1990s have simply moved over to official positions on US delegations.

References

Antrobus, P and G. Sen. 2005. 'The women's movement' in *Claiming Global Power: Transnational Civil Society and Global Governance*. eds. Srilatha Batliwala and David L. Brown. Bloomfield, CT: Kumarian Press.

Chesler, Elle. 1992. *Women of Valour: Margaret Sanger and the Birth Control Movement in America*. Random House Inc.

Correa and Sen. 1999. 'Cairo +5: Moving Forward in the Eye of the Storm'. *Social Watch*. no. 3. pp. 81–86.

Francisco, F and G. Sen. 2000. 'The Asian Crisis: Globalisation and Patriarchy in Symbiosis'. *Social Watch*.

Hartmann, H. 1981. 'The Unhappy Marriage of Marxism and Feminism: Towards a More Progressive Union' in *Women and Revolution: A Discussion of the Unhappy Marriage of Marxism and Feminism*. ed. L. Sargent. Boston: South End Press.

Sen and Correa. 2000. 'Gender Justice and Economic Justice, reflections on the 5-year reviews of the UN Conferences of the 1990s'. Paper prepared for UN Development Fund for Women (UNIFEM). *Dawn Informs* 1/2000.

Sen, G and C. Grown. 1987. 'Development, Crises and Alternative Visions: Third World Women's Perspectives'. *Monthly Review Press*. New York.

Sen, G. and B. Madunagu. 2001. 'Between Globalisation and Fundamentalism: Gender Justice in the Cairo +5 and Beijing +5 Reviews'. *Dawn Informs*. November.

3

Gender Power Dynamics in Jamaica's Ghetto Trap[1]

Southside

IMANI M. TAFARI-AMA

The underbelly of Jamaica's outwardly cosmopolitan body is not as alluring as its public relations agents desire and make it out to be. This has sorely affected the island's political health and public image. In recent years the international media have emphasised that this popular tourist destination is somewhat less than pristine because of the extreme violence stalking some of the inner city streets of Kingston. And because the fickle tourist industry is currently the number one foreign exchange earner, the local authorities have deliberately and continuously tried to sanitise the literally bloodied streets of its capital city in an effort to convince visitors that this beautiful Caribbean island is safe. They succeed—to whatever extent they do—only because the all-inclusive tourist activities take place on the showpiece North Coast, well away from the flying bullets and the mayhem in inner city enclaves of Kingston.

With most of the local population, this public relations gambit has enjoyed variable success (if any at all). Jamaica is a very class-stratified society so it is quite possible for the elite—just like the tourists—to avoid all contact with the danger areas, except from the safe distance between the real world on the television screens and their securely gated properties—or security guard patrolled resorts. However, people living in inner city communities cannot avoid the harsh reality of their streets. Jamaica generally is like a powder keg waiting to explode, and for those living below the poverty line the danger is not merely televised, it is live and direct. The law of the urban landscape is 'blood for blood' and 'fire for fire'. Hence, for poor city residents, violence is embedded in their past, pervades their present, and threatens to overrun their future.

Against the backdrop of complexities that attend the intersection of poverty and violence in the inner city environment it is paradoxical that, generally speaking, Jamaica stands out for the resourcefulness of its people and for the country's many positive achievements, particularly in the areas of culture and sports. However, as elsewhere in the world, the problems of urban poverty and violence pose tremendous threats to national security and the personal well-being of the population as a whole.

> Jamaica has traditions of caring and warmth, notably in rural peasant communities. However, the past 30 years have seen an escalation of community violence; in 1962, a total of 65 persons were murdered island wide, as compared with an all time high of over 900 persons murdered in 1996. The result is an increasing number of victims, co-victims, witnesses, and perpetrators of violence, especially in urban communities with problems of urbanisation: unemployment, inadequate shelter and sanitation facilities, inadequate child care and supervision facilities, informal or illegal ways of survival, dependence on political handouts, neglect of social service agencies, segregation from the more privileged neighbourhoods (Sobers 1997: 3).

The material and symbolic disadvantages attending the lives of people in Jamaica's inner city areas are compounded by over three decades of gang warfare. These deadly conflicts started in the late 1960s and can be attributed to the increased partisanship of the political parties and the manipulative style of clientilism that politicians practised (Edie 1991). The system encourages men to become party thugs (Stone 1986), compete against oppositional party factions and prove their (masculine) superiority or hegemonic masculinity (Connell 1995: 77) by the use of extreme violence.

This dominant discourse of violent hegemonic masculinity has resulted in the construction of its corollary: subordinate femininity. However, not all women subscribe to this contrived dichotomy. Sometimes women themselves use their bodies to acquire income, influence, protection and prestige or to exercise power—through force—against one another. On the other hand, their bodies are seized by force by men as a prize of conquest in the ongoing turf wars and political confrontations, underlining the gender differentiation that reifies hegemonic masculinity and its expression in violence, and some women's acquiescence. Such expression of the multiple workings of hegemony is a tragic irony that becomes more extreme and explicit below the poverty line, but of course, is not necessarily limited to the inner city.

Because of the fearsome authority that they embody, the Rude Boys, as the gangsters are called, have become the villain-heroes of the inner city. However, we have to distinguish between the political dons or party thugs, and the Rude Boys, men who express their power through violence and criminality without necessarily being affiliated to a political faction. The politicised Rude Boys manage to straddle the social gulf between the elite class that the politicians embody and the urban grass roots where they reside. However, they also function as a law unto themselves (or more correctly, as flouters of the law) and therefore constitute the proverbial thorn in the flesh of the local security forces.

Poverty and violence thus constitute a dialectical constellation in the structure of Jamaica's political economy. This is hardly surprising because the inner city has become an international motif for poverty and violence. It is a fact that state-controlled structures of power actually facilitate the persistence of the social injustices which result in these indicators of urban marginality (Castells 1983). Explaining this dilemma, Connell argues that

> [t]he state both institutionalises hegemonic masculinity and expends great energy in controlling it. The objects of repression, e.g. 'criminals', are generally younger men themselves involved in the practice of violence, with a social profile quite like that of the immediate agents of repression, the police or the soldiers. However, the state is not all of a piece. The military and coercive apparatus has to be understood in terms of relationships between masculinities: the physical aggression of front-line

troops or police, the authoritative masculinity of commanders, the *calculative rationality* of technicians, planners and scientists (Connell 1987: 128–9, emphasis added).

Anthony Harriott locates the current dilemma in which Jamaica finds itself firmly in a nexus of (state) violence, the international drug trade and the specific expression of hegemonic masculinity that these authors are describing.

[T]he levels of organisation of the gangs have become more complex particularly those involved in international drug trafficking. *Their success is largely related to their linkages to the formal business sector (particularly in entertainment and other hospitality services), the state and party system, a significant measure of public approval*, and the material resources (and social capital) with which to buy immunity from the law (Harriott 2000: 18, emphasis added).

It goes without saying, therefore, that in Jamaica, expressions of the inner city motif of 'blood for blood, fire for fire' have become a social hazard for a number of reasons. They pose a threat to society in general and particularly to those residents who have no recourse but to live with this state of affairs. However, the possibility of a political domino effect, if the reputation of Jamaica as prone to violence results in the destabilisation of the tourism-dependent economy, is considered by some to be a more important consideration. From whichever side this contradiction is viewed theoretically, its practical threat for the persons who live in communities like Southside cannot be denied.

Barry Chevannes' analysis of the crime figures in the late 1990s emphasises the crisis proportions of the violence, poverty and hegemonic masculinity nexus.

Despite heterogeneity, women and men have had to be extremely resourceful in devising survival strategies to deflect some of the effects of the poverty and violence that they encounter in their everyday lives. Such transactions include women exchanging sexual favours both for material advantage and, in some cases, the social security linked to this practice.

Arrests for Major Crimes in 1996 and 1997 by Age and Type

Age	Murder		Robbery		Rape		Shooting	
	1996	1997	1996	1997	1996	1997	1996	1997
<16	8 (2.0)	8 (1.6)	68 (2.9)	30 (2.2)	51 (6.2)	19 (2.9)	11 (1.3)	6 (0.8)
16–20	77 (20.2)	111 (22.5)	430 (18.2)	67 (19.7)	140 (16.9)	79 (11.9)	238 (27.1)	195 (29.6)
21–25	143 (37.4)	141 (29.1)	860 (36.5)	416 (30.7)	210 (25.4)	165 (24.8)	326 (37.2)	260 (36.8)
26–30	76 (19.9)	125 (25.3)	710 (30.1)	338 (24.9)	180 (21.8)	144 (21.7	132 (15.1)	145 (20.5)
31>	78 (20.5)	109 (21.5)	290 (12.3)	306 (22.5)	228 (29.7)	358 (38.7)	170 (19.3)	101 (12.3)
Total	382 (100.0)	94 (100.0)	2358 (100.0)	1357 (100.0)	826 (100)	65 (100.0)	877 (100.0)	07 (100.0)

Source: Chevannes 1999: Table 12.

Selling sex

Sex sells. Sex is used universally by the advertising media, to shape and influence the fashions, desires, lifestyles and minds of mass millions. Obviously then, sex and the gendered bodies which are inscribed with sexual identities are all central elements in everyone's lives—regardless of race, nationality, gender, class or religion.

Sex and the human body form a tonic nerve that interconnects with all other facets of human life in many ways. Therefore, precisely because of interconnection, what is said about sex and the embodied meanings ascribed to sexualised words make good tools for analysis of societal problems in Jamaica. A detailed examination of this multifaceted and intriguing subject—sex—is necessary for an accurate theoretical deconstruction of the many delicately nuanced binary oppositions operating within and affecting lives of most ordinary inner city Jamaicans.

By and large, the government and local churches turn a blind eye towards the hedonistic behaviour of White visitors and the naked exhibitionism that abounds and is encouraged within the confines of the north coast resorts. Only when outrageous pictures appear in the newspapers do we hear cries of condemnation. Otherwise it is business as usual. One of the most lucrative businesses in the north coast tourist circuit is selling and buying sex: selling the charms of Black bodies to White buyers for their sexual satisfaction.

In this scenario, race, gender, complexion, age and nationality all matter and all mean something tangible to both the buyers and sellers of sex. But it is important to remember that sex and sexuality for and with White tourists vacationing in north coast hotels is a world apart from sex and sexuality for and with Black inner city residents living in Kingston. The social meanings and body language of the interactions are basically all the same in both worlds, but the rules and results are very different. Sex in the tourist world involves escapism of one form or another for everyone. But in a perverse inversion, sex in the inner city world only ensures temporal survival in the vicious ghetto trap from which few of the buyers or sellers escape. The politics and economics of sex in this inner city ghetto environment, far removed from the tourist resorts, is where my central focus lies.

The ghetto trap

Southside, an inner city community in Central Kingston, is a typical example of the *garrison community* phenomenon in Jamaica. Percival 'Ites Man' Caldwell, football coach from that community, recalls that this name was given in the early 1970s because some footballers decided that they would call themselves Southern Ethiopia to counteract the designation of the contiguous area of Dunkirk as 'Biafra' to reflect the poverty conditions that were akin to the notorious Nigerian situation. Over time this was shortened to South and when the press caught on to the name they added the 'side', hence Southside. The 6,000 residents of the community are, characteristically, poor people of predominantly African descent who are for the most part unemployed. Some are self-employed while a minority is wage earning. These residents live in poor housing and socio-economic conditions and exist under the constant threat of violence, due to the activities of the gangs, security forces and itinerant criminals.

In a very real sense, the disadvantaged residents of inner city enclaves like Kingston's Southside are caught in an economic and social trap not of their own making. This ghetto trap of poverty, violence and crime is a vicious cycle of disenfranchisement and immobility. To get to the root of precisely how this evolved over the past few decades we first have to talk to old-timers in the community, like Ras Carlie.

> The real changes came in the late sixties; after those business people started moving out, the politics set in. This displaced a large number of people because of the fear of political violence that escalated by 1967 when one man was shot and killed inside a dance hall called Goldfinger Lawn at 34 Fleet Street. A Chinese family that owned that property used to live in that area until they moved out. As far as I know, it started there. That was the first time that I can recall seeing gun violence in

politics. It lulled for a time and then it started again in 1972. In 1969 when Macka, a member of the Maxi Gang lost his life, it caused a split between youths in the area. Politicians came in and labelled one set as Spanglers and one set as Skull. As far as I could understand it, it was people who lived beyond Gold Street at that time, going west, who were the Spanglers while the people on the eastern side of Gold Street were the Skull. From that time until this time, the battle has not ended.

In my view, most of the youths that were involved in the conflicts at that time had nothing to do with politics. It would have faded out if politics had allowed it to and made the youths solve their problems. The youths were youths that grew together. The press presented Spanglers as PNP and Skull as Labourite but as I said before, most youths weren't dealing with anything political. It was a press hype to print things and say they were so when they weren't so. In a way, the election in 1976 was not as hostile as in the earlier seventies. This was because of the state of emergency and things like that. I can only recall two detainees from here; the two are deceased now. You had Foreign Pants and Rock-I who was more recently killed. People did not fear them because normally, what they did was not something that involved all of the people, just a number of youths who had conflicts among themselves.

You had the Peace Truce in 1978 and that continued through the rest of the seventies until 1980. Then in 1980, during a political campaign by one of the parties, it started again. You had some shooting and some people got injured. That died down, then you had the Gold Street massacre.

Things got out of hand from there on then. From such time to this time, things have not changed. Or I should say, it has changed from better to worse because everything from sixties, seventies and even the early part of the eighties was better than now. The nineties are way out of control; you have a divided community right now. One time you could go to any corner, any hours. You could go anywhere freely without fear. Now it is divided up into different gangs who are fighting themselves for reasons unknown. It is only the Almighty that can settle this. I think this is beyond man's control because of how people are thinking now. Most of the youths nowadays, it's like they have been turned into killers. It is hardly likely that they can be reformed. It seems as if better days might come but I know that better ones have passed. The kind of joy and happiness that used to exist in the community no longer exists. Before, it was a twenty-four-seven community. Now, I think that we have been reduced to six hours; everyone is living in fear because no one is sure of what is going to happen next. Who might be the next victim? (Ras Carlie, Laws Street)

If we examine Jamaica's evolution as a nation, we note that the formation of the political parties and their style of personality-driven leadership followed directly from power games played out in the colonial experience. Since Independence in 1962, those who control the state and its apparatuses have used force as an organising principle—a tactic fundamental to the British modus operandi of divide and rule. The two main parties in Jamaica today, the Peoples National Party (PNP) and the Jamaica Labour Party (JLP) are always the main contenders for the 60 parliamentary seats, leaving political novices not versed in the art of partisan politics to struggle to recoup their deposits.

The watershed event signalling the use of violence in politics came in 1966 when Tivoli Gardens, the first *garrison community,* was constructed by the JLP on the ruins of the bulldozed and burnt out homes of the previous residents of the infamous Kingston ghetto known as 'Back-o-Wall' or 'Dungle'. This bulldozing operation was organised by the Minister of Housing Edward Seaga, currently Leader of the Opposition JLP. In the three decades which followed the Foreshore razing, politicians from both sides of the divide constructed many other garrisons. Residents were allowed to live unmolested in these politicised areas based on party affiliation while, in a clientilist exchange, party loyalists were rewarded with scarce benefits like housing, labour contracts and phallic prizes of deadly weaponry—the modern archetype of masculinity.

By instigating the partisan violence, politicians in effect primed the ghetto trap and provoked a vicious cycle of reprisals, the original cause of which many in today's Southside can't even remember. Gang feuds have been reinforced by feelings of revenge

64

arising out of the human losses that families have suffered during the years of conflict. The syndrome of revenge is also fraught with gender power dynamics, since those who perceive that they have been injured, lash out in turn on those who lack guns and whom they recognise to be weaker and without the phallic authority connoted with weaponry. The legal system is also so corrupt that many injured parties do not perceive it as a viable avenue through which to achieve justice; and as a popular international slogan points out: 'No justice—no peace!'

Ballistic affairs

When the political battle lines were drawn in the quicksand of urban poverty, Southside was on the side of the JLP, an identity which was established when party opponents were forcibly removed or 'roped out' of this community in the run-up to the 1980 General Election. This pattern of disembowelling communities in the name of partisan pursuits has resulted in the separation of family members and splintering of community relations—the main causes of the present syndrome of citizen insecurity. Although the JLP has been the more influential party in Southside, they 'never really did anything much for the people of Southside,' Edward Seaga, the party leader, confessed to me in a telephone interview.

Despite the dominance of JLP loyalties in Southside, some amount of support for the PNP persists, resulting in the evolution of partisan allegiances that cut across family and geographical lines. The bizarre reality is that clashes have occurred on contiguous corners between party supporters, with members of the same family falling on opposite sides of the battle lines. Although the family provides a cultural buffer in the midst of all the instability created by the partisan tactics of divide and rule, family loyalties are often in fact the root cause of the cycle of revenge killings.

The pain suffered by relatives who lose loved ones to gun violence fuels the reprisals, invariably enacted by male family members. A man who perceives that he or a member of his inner circle has been *dissed* or disrespected in any way, often feels obliged to retaliate with violence in order to save the perceived family honour. This revenge motive feeds the cycle of ballistic warfare as enacted by corner crews or the individual *bad man*.

Although the doom and gloom currency imposes limits on the speech of many residents, there have been instances when representatives of the power structures have attempted to implement social welfare programmes. In the 1970s Prime Minister Michael Manley was Member of Parliament for the Central Kingston area, and Southside was used as a test case for the PNP's attempt to improve the lives of women and children by providing support for households as a whole. Alicia Taylor,[2] who played a vital part in this experiment, recalled that this project, funded by the Bernard van Leer Foundation in the Netherlands, was fraught with political contradictions from start to finish. It was finally hijacked when the government changed in 1980. This hiatus in political development and direction (and even reversal in some cases), compounded the stagnation in the national economy. The subsequent two decades were distinctive for the steady decline in standards of living for people of all classes across the board, but particularly for inner city residents like those in Southside. In the meanwhile, those few men behind the cold barrels of the state-of-the-art guns, which are all too readily available in these areas, highlight the fact that citizen security is one of the most pressing development problems in these enclaves in particular and in the country as a whole.

It is significant to note that the formation of the Central Kingston Task Team (CKTT) is associated with the recent dramatic decline in gang violence and criminal activities in the Central Kingston area.[3] The CKTT initiative, financed by The Grace and Staff Foundation, a corporate institution on the seafront border of the Southside community and facilitated by its General Manager, Frances Madden, includes the traditionally warring contiguous communities of Southside, Tel Aviv, Rae Town and Spoilers. Gang and area leaders hold fortnightly discussions with representatives from the community and state, non-governmental, and other corporate institutions under the theme 'Gone too Soon: Stop the

Violence.' The peace which has held since the launch of the Task Team has brought the hope, to this and other communities, that with increased social consciousness and through cooperation of the victims, the discourse of violence can be challenged. The CKTT encourages protagonists in the violence dramaturgy to take responsibility for effecting this change in values, attitudes and behaviour. They in turn have accepted the challenge to erode chronic victim behaviour by acting to overcome the obstacles of underdevelopment that have shaped their lives.

Despite the heroism of this local development, the problems affecting inner city communities have nonetheless to be placed in the larger framework of the world political and economic systems. The ballistic weapons of the political dons and the Rude Boys proclaim the downside of Jamaica's location in the proverbial backyard of North America. The island's proximity to South America is another threat since the Colombian dons now control the drug trade on the streets of Kingston. Thus, in more ways than one, the discourse of violence in inner city garrison communities like Southside is now out of the control of the local security forces; indeed the latter are also regarded as a clear and present danger because of their penchant for illegal 'law enforcement', corruption and outright criminality.

Adding salt to these wounds, American cable channels are now available to the most deprived households and as a result inner city residents have received deep doses of cultural penetration by foreign values and lifestyles. Pre-programmed values are reinforced through representation—for example, of violent men as heroes.[4] Ironically, the phallic themes which run through people's lived experiences and which are institutionalised in the entire social fabric, serve to portray ballistically violent manhood as sexy. That this cultural association has captured the imagination of some Jamaica's inner city youth, is evident in the lyrics of some artists who perform in the genre of dance hall music—a classic example of art reflecting society and being the mouthpiece for enunciating the everyday prescriptions for social practices.

Rude Boys

Out of this murderous milieu emerged Jamaica's now infamous Rude Boys who became grist for the murder mill. As a cultural icon, the *hot-stepping Rude Boy* was constructed in the popular culture discourses of the late 1960s, and the identity idiom was transmitted via the music and translated into a designation of a *real man as a badman*, who was as fearless as he was feared.

As Hebidge notes, the Rude Boy phenomenon can be traced back to as early as 1962, when

> Roland Alphonso released an early Ska record ... which dealt with the Rude Boys. However, it wasn't until 1966, when the Wailers produced the track 'Rude Boy' for Clement Dodd, that the cult [sic] really took off inside Jamaican pop music (Hebidge 1987: 73).

Other releases from an outstanding array of artists who exemplified the notoriety of the Rude Boy phenomenon included The Wailers' 'Rule Them Rudie' [and 'Steppin' Razor'], Derrick Morgan's 'Tougher Than Tough' and Prince Buster's 'Too Bad'. The latter song boasted, 'Rude Boys never give up their guns, no one can tell them what to do' (Hebidge 1987: 73), an assertion that foretold the defiant fearlessness of the present-day version of the Rude Boys personae, the Shotters, who have come to dominate the gangs of today.

The popularity of the Rude Boys extended to the Reggae era, which started in 1968. The paraphernalia of the idiom—the dark (mafia) glasses, the *bopping* walk, the dapper dress styles and the characteristically phallic symbols of ratchet knife, motorbike and guns, have also persisted as part of the identity gears of the Rude Boys—or Raggamuffins as they were known in the 1980s. Nowadays the more affluent sport tinted Toyota Deportees or other imported vehicles, plus the ubiquitous cell phones, as necessary technological 'tools' of the trade. This array suggests that meanings of violence and sexuality are intertwined in prevailing notions about how to enact a space-specific definition of real manhood.

A few politicians, in typical opportunistic mode, courted

some of the Rude Boys to act as their clients in the urban grass roots. Not all the men who became party thugs were Rude Boys, and not all Rude Boys were seduced by the scarce-benefits-and-spoils practices of persuasion, but the insertion of the Rude Boys into the partisan political project of inner city turf contestation had pronounced implications for the social security of the country as a whole.[5] The rise to power at the subaltern level of the politicised Rude Boys was reflected in the late 1960s in the proliferation of warring gangs. Terry Lacey's summation of the main gangs that operated in the West Kingston area between 1966–7 is still relevant although the socio-political order has changed dramatically and the number of names have burgeoned way beyond this estimate.

> Trench Town, Denham Town, Back O' Wall, Moonlight City—these names of parts of Western Kingston conveyed images of youth gangs, political gangs, Rastafarians, of Prince Henry's gang, the Max gang, the Blue Mafia, the Dunkirk gang, the Phoenix gang, the Vikings, or the Roughest and the Toughest. These gangs symbolised the latent power of the lumpen proletariat. In the period 1966–7 many were armed to provide the 'soldiers' for a battle between the PNP and JLP in Western Kingston. After this short introduction to politics within the system, some of the gangs reverted to ordinary criminal activities, others turned to more revolutionary politics and used their newly-acquired guns to terrorise the rest of society (Lacey 1977: 32).

The type of consciousness required for the revolution suggested here is certainly not reflected in the spraying of blood, bullets and bodies all over the urban landscape. And while a number of killings can be traced back to gang conflicts and politics there is still an element of itinerant criminality connected to the drug trade and dominated by ongoing revenge dynamics, making people throw up their hands (regarding possible revolution) and say 'It can't done!' In other words, those below the poverty line often feel there is virtually no escape from the death trap in which they are caught.

Here we should be careful not to 'lumpen proletariatise' the youth, as this would avoid the necessary interrogation of a political system whose experiment is long out of control. Ever since the introduction of the discourse of violence into political divide and rule practices in the late 1960s general elections have been marked by a dramatic escalation of political violence in Jamaica's inner city communities.

The peace treaty

The most intensely contested elections were held in 1967, 1972, 1976 and 1980. Mirroring the apparent heroics of cinematic protagonists, local gangsters like Claudie Massop (JLP) and Bucky Marshall (PNP) emerged as the stars of the inner city dramaturgy, which was all the more tragic because this bizarre production of real manhood was no fiction but harsh reality. The blood, bullets and bodies were all real. The various roles that the politicians and security forces have played in this war effort identify them as co-villains whose autographs have been written in and with the very blood of the pawns in their political power game of bourgeois democracy.

> The level of political violence in the run-up to the 1976 elections got so high that the Prime Minister declared a State of Emergency. A Gun Court was set up in the centre of Kingston and a law was passed whereby anybody found carrying a gun could be immediately arrested and detained for an indefinite period... The situation only began to improve when Claudie Massop and Bucky Marshall, the Rude Boy gunmen for the two political parties in Kingston's slums, signed a truce and decided to work together to improve local conditions... This move was started by the Rastafarians. The shift from violent to peaceful solutions to Jamaica's problems was reflected in the next phase of the island's pop history— Reggae (Hebidge 1987: 74).

During the 1970s hard core Claudie Massop controlled Tivoli Gardens, the JLP-identified area of Western Kingston, while the equally tough Bucky Marshall dominated the PNP stronghold of Kingston Pen.

The battle had been bloody. Bucky's PNP boys had powered in hard and wiped out a lot of Massop's JLP boys, and not just no-hopers, they got a few ranking party members as well—and Massop's boys had come back with a vengeance late in the day and massacred entire households of PNP supporters, until it seemed like there was no stopping the epidemic of political violence and nobody even tried very hard (Thomas and Boot 1982: 85).

In the midst of this chaos the stabilising influence of Rastafari became unmistakable. Rastafari reclaimed race as the site for struggle and resistance (to violence) and thereby provided a direct foil to those men who choose to express their identities in the idiom of violence. In the late 1970s the Rastafari refrain of 'peace and love' politics found resonance with the gangsters who, after all, grew up among members of that home-grown and Afro-centric *livity*.[6] Touched by the Black Consciousness energies that flowed in the seventies, grass roots man and man[7] realised that the practice of Black man killing Black man must stop. Rastafari provided the spiritual *grounding*[8] that is eschewed in the political realm, but which was so crucially needed to put the internecine conflicts on pause.

Leading inner city Rastafarians persuaded the political gunmen from both sides to share ganja 'peace pipes' with each other; and while the marijuana-filled water-filtered chalices were passed from hand to hand, the Rasta-led reasoning about the bread-and-butter and life-and-death issues at stake took place. After evaluating the ways in which they had, senselessly, been fighting against each other, the top-ranking political gunmen decided to call a halt to hostilities in order to cool down the heat in the inner city.

Much to the astonishment of the politicians, the contested enclaves themselves and the society at large, the warlords decided to heed the Rastafari call to 'cease fire,'[9] and came together in a determined effort to end the bloodbath that had been unleashed on the inner city communities. In the immediate aftermath of the signing of the Peace Treaty the street fighters wanted Bob Marley to lead a special concert to mark the occasion. Marley had himself been shot and injured in a politically motivated 'Ambush in the

71

Night', as he dubbed one of his many hit songs, just prior to the 'Smile Jamaica' Concert which heralded the 1976 general election. In order to avoid further political entanglement, Marley had left the island and resided in England for a few years but agreed to return to perform at the politically unprecedented Peace Concert, when personally invited to do so by Claudie Massop. Officially entitled 'The One Love Concert', the Peace Concert—as it was popularly known—was held at the National Stadium in April 1978 and featured a Who's Who list of prominent Reggae artists. The historic event brought together opposing political leaders Michael Manley and Edward Seaga, as well as the gang leaders who had agreed to relinquish the warfare.

However, not even the spiritually loaded shot in the arm of Rastafari philosophy and pragmatic politics could cause inner city peace to hold; the phantom proved easier to broker than to maintain. Those advocating peace were swimming against the tide of blood left behind by those cut down 'for reasons unknown', as a baffled Ras Carlie put it. In the aftermath of the highly successful concert, despite—or maybe because of the boldness of the gesture of the peace pact brokered by the gangsters themselves—the leaders of the said peace effort were unceremoniously and brutally eliminated by the security forces, bringing the notoriety they had enjoyed to an abrupt end. In their determination to promote peace, that generation of gang leaders had unfortunately also demonstrated their redundancy to the entrenched political parties and to the traditional political leadership in the island.

Claudie Massop's ambush and brutal murder (he was shot 54 times by the police) sent shock waves over Kingston's inner city communities for quite a long time. His was only one among a series of legally sanctioned high-profile eliminations, a trend which prompted noted Reggae artist Peter Tosh to pen the sardonic lyric, 'all who signed the Peace Treaty now resting in peace in the cemetery'.[10] Massop's legacy is still felt in the centralised form of leadership, which has been retained in the West Kingston area and is strikingly different from the amorphous style of turf leadership that characterises other communities such as Southside.

After the elimination of the peace advocates the gang feuding in the conflicted areas (somewhat naturally) intensified—as demonstrated by the proliferation of rival gangs.

Gunmen gone wild

The level of violence which has washed over the inner city areas since 1980 has taken a cruel toll on an entire generation. When noting the collated statistics it is frightening to think of the proportion of men per capita in a little island of two and a half million people who have died. In 2003 the number of persons killed was 1138, and at the end of March 2004 over 270 had died violently, outside Central Kingston, since the start of the year. These figures are set against a backdrop of at least two decades of mayhem that have claimed over 12,000 lives.[11] Taking a retrospective glance into this brutal history, Hanif notes that

> in 1993, 45 young men aged 13–18, 182 aged 19–25 and 157 aged 26–30 were killed. Although the numbers get lower after this age group, they are not insignificant. In over half of the cases one man shot another. Figures for 1994 are even more staggering: 197 men between the ages of 19–25 were murdered, and 82 died aged 13–18. Male on male violence for just one month was 579 and of course, this is an under-reported number (Hanif 1995: 4).

The chances of identity recovery for the subordinated, under the double-barrelled circumstances of poverty and violence, are extremely limited. Many youths are sucked into the maelstrom through the systematic social lack and exclusion that leave them with no other recourse than to react in the codes that they create to deal with this experience of dehumanisation. To make matters worse, some men perceive 'menial' work to be unbecoming for a *man*. On the other hand, being the predominant heads of households circumscribe the options that women are able to choose from in their strategies to survive.

Attempting to gain materiality through the patronage style of politics only reinforces violent masculinity, which ultimately has devastating effects on those who use this means of achieving selfhood and simultaneously strengthens the more dominant and deadly violence of the privileged class as represented by the state and its apparatuses. The sub-text of this dialectic, therefore, is that the subordinated subalterns (i.e. inner city residents) perform the project of the hegemonic order, while internalising the notion of acting in their own interests (Gramsci 1957; Lukes 1986).

Climbing out of the bottom of the barrel is easier said than done as far as the 'gun man' is concerned. Having grown accustomed to surviving by the fear caused by his 'tool', many do not know how to be powerful without it. Some women also define themselves as powerful by being violent. They fight *matey wars*, usually over the possession of a man. So many men have died, are in prison or are abroad, as a result of the cyclical conflicts that fewer and fewer men are available to women. The rivalry between mateys is also enacted in the dance hall environment in practices locally called *modelling* or showing off. Modelling entails competitions among women and is expressed in material and symbolic terms.

The insidious influence of the political economy is again evident in this symbolic and sometimes physical form of violence. For example, one gains ascendancy by being able to out-fight one's rival, dress more expensively and dance more creatively—especially in a sexually explicit fashion suggestive of superior sexual expertise, which is more capable of capturing the man who might be the object of competition. These competitions ultimately reinforce the prevailing patriarchal norms in which men's desires are given central place and consequently also preoccupy the women who are interested in them.

Subordinated women

An inevitable outcome of a system of male domination based on violence is the subordination of women. Despite diversity, women can become particularly disadvantaged in the inner city scenario when their bodies are literal battlefields in the reproduction of structural, discursive and gender power dynamics. Subjects to the didactics of hegemony and the dominant discourse of violent masculinity, some women living in inner city communities have internalised such method of expressing power and perform it as if it were their own.

The violence they display towards each other in contests over men reflects a choice but also displays the extent to which women's identities are a function of this prevailing discourse. Located at the fulcrum of this power paradox, poor and disadvantaged Black women attempt to resolve the conflicts that insinuate their larger problems by the use of a range of weapons—acid, machetes, ice picks, their bodies, words—in an odyssey of *modelling* against their adversaries. These power dramas erupt into fights with such monotonous regularity that people who witness the performances—especially children—cynically treat them as everyday street entertainment. They choose sides to see who will win, cheering on the opponents as they would boxers in a ring. Thus, as a result of the 'routinisation' (Scheper-Hughes 1992) of violence as an expression of power, many people have become increasingly desensitised to the danger posed by such an enigma so deeply embedded in everyday aspects and attitudes.

Interestingly, the women do not usually tackle their male partners on the issue of their infidelity. A subliminal imperative of this patriarchal discourse impels some women to attack other women who seize the prize of 'their man.' This other woman is as disadvantaged as the attacker in the larger power matrix and is therefore more vulnerable than the 'strong man' in the triangle— being the one who wrote the script and directed the production. In power games the strong invariably seek ways to disadvantage those weakest in options and choices.

Some women may also choose to be in a relationship with a man who is violent because he can provide her with social security and money that he might procure from criminal activities. She feels safe because she has acquired the social value of being protected by association with a man who is feared and respected in the community. The Rude Girls I encountered in Southside embody the host of contradictions intertwined in women's display of competitive violence and preference for relationships with Rude Boys.

Rude Girls

I sat on the sidewalk on Foster Lane one day reasoning with a group of women about this phenomenon. These women actually call themselves Rude Girls—an example of women appropriating the dominant male discourse of violence, and refracting male constructs of power onto their own identity landscape for their own definition and reference of being and acting. One of the women teased another that her matey[12] sat on her[13] when they were fighting. She defended herself by saying,

> I bit her on her breast. She pulled my hair and did a lot of things to me. I defended myself by telling her that I refuse to fight over man. She is the one who is fighting over a man because, as she says, the man wants her.

Another woman said that if she had a man and a woman took him away, she would 'beat her and chop her in her head.' This opinion clearly reflected the internalisation of the dominant 'blood for blood, fire for fire' discourse popularised by the Rude Boys. The vicious cycle of violent hegemonic masculinity is oiled by the widespread assertion that some women choose to have relationships with the men who are engaged in violence because of the sexy innuendoes connoted by the *thug* image. The other two women demurred, saying that they would defend themselves if a woman attacked them but they would not take the initiative to fight over a man since it was a man's prerogative to pursue a woman and not the other way around.

The Rude Girls agreed, though, that when women fight over men it is a weak victory for the winner and mainly serves to boost the ego of the man in question. 'They (the men) love it' was the enthusiastic consensus. A healthy discussion ensued when it was suggested that although it was public knowledge in the community which men and women are sexual partners, some women persist in the practice of forcing themselves onto men who are otherwise engaged. The irony is that such competition is intensified because the violent conflicts among men which steadily decreases the number of available adult males, make it difficult for women to secure 'single' sexual/material partners.

'I have to beat the woman if she is with my man,' one woman insisted, 'because you know that you can't fight a man.'

One woman in the group of five said that she would walk away rather than give the man the satisfaction of seeing her fighting another woman over him. Another response was that some of the men are to be avoided because their encouragement of the competition among women demonstrates their own investment in these violent disagreements.

Although many women in the inner city areas like Southside might tolerate sharing their mate for the sake of maintaining the relationship with the man, many of them are not happy with this situation. They demonstrate in no uncertain terms the extraordinary lengths they will go to in order to keep a man. In the matey tradition, the more powerful perceives herself to be number one in vexed if not violent competition with her mate or matey, whose shortcomings are gauged based on various matriculation criteria.

The cultural acceptance of monogamy for the woman but not for the man is a schizophrenic value system that allows men to have multiple partners and promotes a political economy of contested relations between women who do not subscribe to this practice. On the other hand, women who have multiple relationships with men are stigmatised as *sketels*.

Conclusion

Although crime and violence often appear to be the only way out of their situation for those seemingly marooned below the poverty line, this is but a contradictory illusion which causes more suffering and pain and provides no real solutions to the ingrained poverty. Bullet-ridden encounters and the continued subordination of women are only reinforced by the gunmen-gone-wild kind of lifestyle. Gang/criminal violence, partisan/political violence and domestic/family violence do not provide Southside residents with tools or avenues to escape their entrapment in debilitating social conditions. Rude Boys or Rude Girls may experience a short-lived boost to their ghetto-fabulous status and may enjoy a transient increase in their economic solvency, but ultimately most of them remain caught up and entangled in the ghetto trap of poverty and violence. Most observers will agree: it is a literal vicious cycle perpetrating yet more blood, bullets and bodies.

Notes

1 This chapter based on my (2002) PhD thesis is discussed in my forthcoming book, *Blood, Bullets and Bodies: Sexual Politics Below Jamaica's Poverty Line* to be published by the University of the West Indies Press. It also features two of my supervisors of that study, Professor Geertje Lycklama à Nijeholt and Dr Saskia Wieringa.

2 Interview in February, 1999 when Ms Taylor was lecturing at the University of Technology in Kingston.

3 In 2002, there were 73 murders in this area; in 2003, this declined to 39 murders and in 2004 no one had been killed till the end of March.

4 Increasingly, violent policemen are also the avant-garde heroes, again suggesting a definition of masculinity that correlates desirability with violence.

5 For historical accuracy, I must distinguish between Rude Boys as a cultural construct for masculinist identity and the men who provided the 'hard core party support' (Stone 1986: 49). Although some Rude Boys are party activists, most function independent of direct party affiliation. However, as Stone's analysis shows, backed by the activism of the party thugs, popular support for the political parties 'fluctuates between an estimated bottom line of 90,000 to 110,000 and grows as large as 150,000 to 160,000 when the party's fortunes are on the ascendancy'.

6 See Murrell et al. (eds.), 1998 for a comprehensive exposé on Rastafari.

7 Men is used to describe homosexuals in local parlance hence the plural term 'man and man'.

8 Used here in the metaphoric electrical sense, this word also speaks to the Rastafari expression for *reasoning* in a group.

9 Bunny Wailer, who was an original member of the Wailing Wailers, sang a powerful and didactic hit in this era called 'Cease Fire', of the conflict-ridden tenor of the day.

10 The CKTT peace initiative, is reminiscent of this earlier peace experience. Optimists are hoping however, that the contemporary architects of peace will not suffer the same fate as their predecessors.

11 CVM television newscast, 30 March 2004.

12 The other woman having a relationship with the man she is also in a conjugal partnership with.

13 In addition to being a literal allusion to a decisive moment in the fight, this is also a symbolic reference to someone who attains dominance over another.

References

Castells, M. 1983. *The City and the Grassroots: A Cross-Cultural Theory of Urban Social Movements*. London/Australia: Edward Arnold.

Chevannes, B. 1999. *What we Sow and What we Reap: Problems in the Cultivation of Male Identity in Jamaica*. Kingston: The Grace Kennedy Foundation.

Collins, P.H. 1990. *Black Feminist Thought: Knowledge, Consciousness and the Politics of Empowerment, Perspectives on Gender*. vol. 2. London: HarperCollins Academic.

Connell, R.W. 1987. *Gender and Power*. Cambridge/Oxford: Polity Press.

——. (1994), 'Gender Regimes and the Gender Order' in *The Polity Reader in Gender Studies*. Cambridge/Oxford: Polity Press. pp. 29–40.

——. 1995. *Masculinities*. Cambridge/Oxford: Polity Press.

Edie, C.J. 1991. *Democracy by Default: Dependency and Clientilism in Jamaica*. Boulder/London: Lynne Rienner Publishers. Kingston: Ian Randle Publishers.

Gramsci, A. 1957. *The Modern Prince and Other Writings*. New York: International Publishers.

Hanif, N.Z. 1995. 'Male Violence Against Women and Men in the Caribbean: The Case of Jamaica'. Wand Occasional Paper. CARICOM and the International Planned Parenthood Federation.

Harriott, A. 2000. *Police and Crime Control in Jamaica: Problems of Reforming Ex-Colonial Constabularies*. Barbados/Jamaica/Trinidad and Tobago: The University of the West Indies Press.

Hebidge, D. 1987. *Cut 'N' Mix: Culture, Identity and Caribbean Music*. New York: Methuen and Co., in association with Methuen Inc.

Lacey, T. 1977. *Violence and Politics in Jamaica, 1960-70: Internal Security in a Developing Country*. Oxford: Manchester University Press.

Lukes, S. 1986. 'Introduction' in *Power*. ed. S. Lukes. Oxford: Basil Blackwell Ltd. pp. 1–18.

Murrell N.S. et al. eds. 1998. *Chanting Down Babylon*. Philadelphia: Temple University Press.

Scheper-Hughes, N. 1992. *Death Without Weeping: The Violence of Everyday Life in Brazil*. Los Angeles/Oxford: University of California Press.

Sobers, Y.M. 1997. 'Wholeness for our Children'. Kingston: Bernard van Leer Foundation. mimeo January 30.

Stone, C. 1986. *Class, State and Democracy in Jamaica*. New York/Connecticut/London: Praeger.

Thomas, M. and A. Boot. 1982. *Jah Revenge: Babylon Revisited*. London: Eel Pie Publishing Limited.

4

The New Regulation of Prostitution in the Netherlands

JOYCE OUTSHOORN

A conference room in Amsterdam in the autumn of 2001.[1] Behind the microphones at the tables at the top end are seated representatives from the Internal Revenue Service, the Inspection of Work Conditions, Social Security, the Municipal Health Authority and the Fire and Security Department. In the audience there are spokespeople from the prostitutes' union (Rode Draad: literally, the Red Thread), the Confederation of Dutch Trade Unions (Federatie van Nederlandse Vakverenigingen, FNV) and the Foundation against Trafficking of Women (Stichting tegen Vrouwenhandel, STV). Also present are employers in the sex industry, such as the Association of Pleasure-House Entrepreneurs (Vereniging van Exploitanten van Relaxbedrijven) and the Association of Window Prostitution Owners (Vereniging van Raamexploitanten). There is even a representative from a clients' organisation, the Foundation for Man, Woman and Prostitution (Stichting Man, Vrouw en Prostitutie). They are all involved with the National Platform for Prostitution (Landelijk Platform Prostitutiebeleid). Several interested scholars and journalists make up the rest of the audience. The topic of discussion is the implementation of the highly publicised legalisation of brothels in the Netherlands in 2000.[2]

The conference was a typical manifestation of Dutch corporatism where all interested parties sit round the table to achieve consensus and compromise about policy in a certain area. Prostitution is no longer a controversial moral issue, but is now defined as sex work, provided the work is voluntary. Prostitutes are entitled to social insurance if employed; they also have to pay taxes and can unionise. Sex employers have to observe labour law, health and safety regulations, and pay social insurance and taxes. Brothels are allowed within certain areas and have to comply with local regulations; pimping is no longer a criminal offence. Forced prostitution, often tied to trafficking of women, is to be eliminated. Traffickers can be sentenced to an eight-year prison sentence. The legalisation in the Netherlands is unique; only New South Wales, Australian Capital Territory (ACT) and Victoria in Australia have similarly recognised prostitution as sex work (Sullivan 2004) and recently Austria has set steps in motion to this end (Sauer 2004). What led the Netherlands to this major policy change—one that is highly controversial; the more so given the international 'notoriety' for its liberal drugs policy, the legal possibility of euthanasia and its flourishing gay scene? The question can be answered by looking at the changes in the prostitution world of the 1970s which led to the first political demands to lift the ban on brothels and legalise voluntary prostitution, and examining the political debate and the major actors involved in the political arena around the issue. Finally the legalisation will be discussed in the context of the culture of the Netherlands and the way controversial moral issues are generally solved in this traditionally pluralistic society.

The 'scene'

The orderly scene of corporatism at work is in stark contrast to the reputation the Netherlands has abroad: the red light district of Amsterdam 'with women on display behind windows; sex shops and live sex acts on stage and the special sites (*afwerkplekken*)[3] where street prostitutes deal with customers are world famous. In other towns too the sex industry is usually concentrated in one area which catches the eye with pornographic images. Utrecht, for instance, has a river with canal boats where the clients can cruise along by car or boat to choose a sex worker.[4] In addition there are so-called sex farms in the countryside and pick-up sites along the big highways frequented by lorry drivers and salesmen. Legalisation seems to have enhanced the notorious image; the Netherlands's approach to prostitution is often contrasted to the Swedish abolitionist approach to clean up prostitution by criminalising the client (not the sex worker: she is the target of rehabilitation policies) (Svanstrom 2004).

The prostitution market in the Netherlands is a segmented one, offering a wide range of services. At the top of the hierarchy are the women working in chic clubs for affluent businessmen. Then there are the sex workers based in other private clubs; women working at home; the window prostitutes (a number of whom are self-employed); women in the escort business, and at the bottom end are the streetwalkers and the drug addicts who offer services at rock bottom prices and will work without a condom. Estimates of the number of prostitutes vary widely, and so do figures about the composition of the workforce. During the debates in Parliament MPs usually cited 50,000 to 100,000 sex workers of whom half are assumed to be from outside the European Union. Of the non-EU prostitutes, half are held to be illegal migrants. Researchers are predictably more conservative in their estimates which lie between 20,000 and 30,000 sex workers in 1998, of whom about five per cent are male and five per cent transsexual or transgender (Nationaal Rapporteur 2002: 83). The number who are victims of trafficking is even harder to determine, given its underground nature and the debate about the definition of trafficking. It is often confused with the smuggling of migrants since some of those smuggled can be sex workers wanting to work in Europe. The most recent reliable figure is that there were about 3500 victims of trafficking and forced prostitution in the year 2000, the majority of them from Central and Eastern Europe.[5]

The rise of the new sex market

In the Netherlands prostitution was regulated in the past by state and local authorities for reasons of public order, morality or health.

Even in times when abolition of prostitution was the official policy goal, some degree of condoning the selling of sex occurred. In the course of the 19th century a system of municipal regulation developed which allowed for brothels and imposed compulsory medical check-ups of prostitutes. In garrison towns especially authorities were anxious to stop the spread of sexually transmitted diseases and prostitutes were seen as the major source of contamination. This regulation became the object of attack of a rising abolitionist movement which united evangelical Protestants and feminists in the latter part of the 19th century (de Vries 1997). Their campaigns met with success when the Morality Acts were passed by Parliament in 1911; and homosexuality, abortion, the display and advertising of contraception, brothels and living off the earnings of prostitution became illegal. Prostitutes themselves were not liable to prosecution.

It did not lead to the end of prostitution. In the big ports of Amsterdam and Rotterdam selling and buying sex occurred in bars, streets and private houses in certain working class quarters. Local authorities condoned these as long as there was no disturbance of the peace and some measure of discretion was maintained. The red light district of Amsterdam was quite small in the 1970s, not yet an object of a huge tourist interest; and the Katendrecht quarter of Rotterdam catered mainly to transient sailors. Prostitution was not a political issue and hardly made for crime headlines. Drugs were not yet available and the scare about venereal disease had been subdued by the use of penicillin after the Second World War. Organised crime hardly existed. In popular culture the prostitute was often portrayed as a generous and even motherly figure who lent a listening ear to misunderstood husbands and who called herself a social worker. The scene itself was presented as slightly bohemian and romantic, if perhaps a bit seedy. The occasional murder of a prostitute lent the glamour of danger and adventure.

The 1970s, however, saw a number of fundamental changes in the prostitution business as it turned into a modern sex industry in the Netherlands. As sexual mores loosened in the 1960s and

1970s—leading from a highly regulated sexual life to far reaching sexual liberty and openness in a relatively brief period of time—sexual wishes and desires also underwent a transformation. With the rise of prosperity in the Netherlands (and the rest of Western Europe) sex tourism boomed. Sex entrepreneurs in South-east Asia who were left with slack on their hands after the United States army departed from Vietnam, were able to attract Western male tourists as the new consumers of their services, catering for both hetero and gay men. The home scene also underwent a drastic revolution. Sex telephones, sex clubs and escort services proliferated, catering to the new demands of the increasingly affluent Dutch male (hetero and gay). At the same time, and for the same reason (rising living standards), the supply of prostitutes in the Netherlands ran low. After the introduction of social welfare in 1964 women no longer had to turn to prostitution when in financial trouble. A rise in the number of foreign prostitutes in the Netherlands was the result: recruited first from the West Indies and Latin America, they later came from Thailand and the Philippines. At the beginning of the 1980s it was becoming apparent that some of the women from these countries were being trafficked and that professional crime networks were involved in this activity. But as late as 1977, repealing the articles on prostitution was explicitly rejected by the incumbent Cabinet after a Commission that had overhauled the Morality Acts recommended leaving things as they were (Outshoorn 2004: 187). The brothel ban was seen as a weapon for local authorities to threaten those brothel keepers who overstepped the (informal) standards: no fights, no minors, no indecent behaviour outside the premises.

In contrast to the small-scale businesses of the traditional red light districts in the big cities, which existed in relatively peaceful coexistence with their working class neighbours, the new sex industry was neither small-scale nor peaceful. Neighbourhood protests against its expanding activities and rowdy clients soon gained in strength. In response to these, local governments attempted to stop the expansion and to relocate the sex industry to areas with fewer inhabitants, such as industrial estates. The City Council of Rotterdam sought a solution in setting up an 'Eros Centre' to relieve the hard-suffering residents of Katendrecht, but the courts struck down its attempts as these contravened the prohibition of brothels of the Penal Code and held that one cannot regulate what is forbidden (van Mens 1992). For Rotterdam, and other municipalities faced with similar dilemmas, lifting the ban became imperative to regulation, and this demand was adopted by the powerful Association of Dutch Municipalities (Vereniging Nederlandse Gemeenten, VNG). It started the lobby for repeal of the brothel ban and framed the issue in terms of law and order. The demand was supported by the De Graaf Foundation (Meester de Graaf Stichting), which was the only interest group organised around the issue at the time and which wanted to legalise all prostitution.

In the 1970s the Netherlands had a highly mobilised women's movement that had gained access to policy-making, leading to the establishment of an office for women's policy within the national bureaucracy, the Department for the Coordination of Women's Emancipation (Directie Coordinatie Emancipatie, DCE) (Outshoorn 1995). Women's groups succeeded in putting sexual violence on the political agenda and at first prostitution and trafficking were regarded as varieties of violence, with rape, domestic violence, incest and sexual harassment. Framed in this way it gained the attention in 1981 of the junior minister for Emancipation, the feminist Hedy d'Ancona of the Labour Party (Partij van de Arbeid, PvdA) and her 'femocrats'—feminist bureaucrats. She organised a conference on sexual violence in The Hague a year later and after some debate prostitution was included in the programme. During the conference there were two competing definitions of the issue. One viewed prostitution in terms of power relations between men and women, in which the woman had to subjugate her sexuality to the man's, turning prostitution into sexual domination (Acker and Rawie 1982). The other held that prostitution was a way of making a living and should be regarded as work. The demand was raised to lift the ban on brothels as a first step in regulating the sex business and improving the working conditions for prostitutes. Trafficking was also acknowledged as a growing problem and was included in the prostitution debate from then on.

Cooperation between the DCE officials (the femocrats) with movement activists, feminist lawyers and researchers, produced a format for a position paper which found its way into official cabinet papers (Nota Bestrijding Seksueel Geweld 1984). A distinction was made between 'voluntary' prostitution, which should be regarded as work and regulated so that the position of the sex worker would improve, and 'forced' prostitution when women were coerced into this practice. Repealing the brothel ban was required to introduce decent business practices in the prostitution sector. Discussions with feminist activists and prostitutes had convinced the femocrats that this would be the best way to improve sex workers' position (Outshoorn 2001a: 161). From then on the defining of sex work entered the political discourse on prostitution. In the women's movement it replaced the sexual domination approach which saw women as powerless victims on whose behalf feminists had to act, and shifted to the notion of a self-assured sex worker who would be able to fight for her rights. The feminists involved in fighting sex tourism were formed into the Foundation against Trafficking of Women, which was financially supported by the women's policy office.

By the mid-1980s there was no powerful women's lobby in favour of abolition, the policy which follows from the concept of sexual domination. It continued to be espoused by radical feminists or by religiously inspired groups; and led to a number of strong and active anti-prostitution organisations in several countries and at the supra-national level. In the Netherlands radical feminism was important and highly influential in the women's movement of the 1970s. However, radical feminists disappeared with the institutionalisation of the women's movement organisations and the state funding of feminist projects in the early 1980s, both of which they vehemently opposed. The underlying reason for their demise is the way in which the political elite in the Netherlands responds to challengers: the latter are invited to participate and express their grievances, thereby splitting a social movement into a moderate and radical part. The radical feminists were partly absorbed into the mainstream and the rest disappeared. Religiously inspired abolitionist groups had all but disappeared, although since the legalisation of prostitution some new groups from orthodox Protestant circles have emerged around the issue.

Legalising prostitution

As the ban on brothels and on pimping were both in the Penal Code, a parliamentary act was required to change the law. Ironically it was the Christian Democrat Party (Christen Democratisch Appel, CDA) which suggested lifting the ban in 1983 during a debate on the modernisation of criminal law, so that municipalities would be able to regulate it. Facilitating prostitution still carried the outdated penalty of work camps for the offenders—though these had been shut down decades before. The CDA had always subscribed to the moral view on prostitution; it was a vice, with fallen women as victims and adulterous men as perpetrators, and which therefore needed to be eradicated (Outshoorn 2001b: 475). The first Christian Democrat/Liberal cabinet with Lubbers as Prime Minister came up with a bill in 1985 which actually went for legalisation.[6] It incorporated the distinction between voluntary and forced prostitution; the distinguishing characteristic is the degree of infringement on the prostitute's right to self-determination. The state should not morally judge or outlaw the selling of sex, but only intervene in cases of excess, i.e. when violence and coercion were employed at recruiting or keeping a woman in prostitution. Voluntary prostitution was to be regulated as sex work; a prostitution deal was seen as a contract between two consenting adults. Repealing the ban on brothels would enable a local authority to set its own standards for health and safety. In the debate the Christian Democrats took the view that prostitution was ineradicable and that the state should therefore regulate it to 'protect' the prostitute, leaving the classic moral view to the orthodox Protestants represented in Parliament. The Left saw prostitution as a form of sexual domination but also accepted the distinction between voluntary and forced prostitution, and came out in favour of legalisation. The Liberals emphasised the sex work discourse, limiting the role of the state to setting standards on working conditions and fighting forced prostitution. The Second Chamber passed the bill in 1987; the vote splitting neatly along the religious/secular divide in the party-system.[7]

But the bill ran into trouble in the First Chamber, as the Christian Democrats here refused to relinquish the role of the state as a moral minder or to regard voluntary prostitution as work; in their view prostitution was always coerced. At the end of the debate a vote was not taken, as there were also legal problems: the definition of coercion in the bill was at odds with a proposed bill against trafficking. The parties agreed to wait for the latter's acceptance in the Second Chamber, after which the First Chamber would debate both in conjunction. This proved problematic since, following a general election in 1989 (a different coalition, now consisting of Christian Democrats and the Labour Party) a new Minister of Justice—a conservative Roman Catholic—produced a draft bill on trafficking that did away with the distinction between forced and voluntary prostitution when 'Third World' women were involved. Prostitutes from poor countries were seen as victims of trafficking per definition. The Socialists in the Second Chamber were furious, but voted in favour as they feared a fall of the coalition cabinet. The First Chamber showed more courage when it debated the repeal ban and the anti-trafficking bill in 1992. It does not have the right of amendment, but by intimating that it would reject both bills it forced the minister to produce several redrafts. It was not sufficient to save the repeal bill!; the anti-trafficking bill—with higher penalties for traffickers and a precise and inclusive definition of the offence—was passed (Outshoorn 2004: 193–7).

The outcome left local authorities with empty hands. The sex industry continued to grow, and increasing citizens' protests against the nuisance was putting pressure on them to act. But as most actors in the policy arena expected that sooner or later a new bill would be submitted to Parliament, the authorities and police of the major towns started to anticipate its likely content: the lift of the ban, with regulation left to the local level. Amsterdam developed its own policy, closing brothels outside certain designated zones such as the red light district, checking illegal migrant sex workers and minors, and closing down sex clubs because of hazards. Brothels with some semblance of decency were condoned. The health authorities had a long-term relation with the prostitution scene and offered voluntary checks for sexually transmitted diseases—the AIDS scare had provided them with new funding. The VNG developed a model ordinance for municipalities on how to regulate the business after the likely repeal of the brothel ban.

Stopping trafficking proved harder. The police did not have it as one of their top priorities and the specialised vice squads who had dealt with it were integrated into the regular police force in the early 1990s. The Foundation against Trafficking of Women kept up its argument and won a concession from the Ministry of Justice when it was decided to give temporary residence permits to victims of trafficking willing to testify against their traffickers (Outshoorn 2004: 193).

In the meantime the social climate had also changed considerably. The ill-fated repeal law had tried to modernise criminal law in the more humanitarian and liberal vein of the 1960s and 1970s. In the 1980s politicians and police worried about the rise of organised crime which was strongly on the increase. The attitude towards migration had changed and prostitution became linked to both the fear of mafia practices and 'floods' of illegal sex workers coming into the country. It also faced international pressure to tackle child sexual abuse after the discovery that child pornography was often produced within its territory. When the first cabinet without Christian Democrats of the 20th century was formed in 1994, the so-called Purple cabinet (Kok I) of Liberals, Social Democrats and Social Liberals came up with a new draft to lift the ban in 1997; it reflected this change of social climate while retaining some of the earlier modern and humanitarian spirit.

The bill promised a 'realistic approach without moralism' to prostitution, limiting the role of the state to eliminating forced prostitution. It aimed to control and regulate the exploitation of prostitution, to fight forced prostitution more effectively, to protect minors from sexual abuse (a new addition) and to 'protect' (not 'improve') the position of prostitutes. Lifting the ban meant municipalities themselves could impose standards and license the sex trade; prostitution would be treated as sex work. Decriminalisation, according to the memorandum to the bill, would lead to its normalisation, control, cleansing and regulation. The bill set an age limit for prostitution at 18 (the normal age of consent is 16). It did away with the ill-conceived idea of regarding all 'Third World' sex workers as trafficked victims; non-EU prostitutes would be able to work in a brothel, but brothel keepers—as all other employers in the Netherlands—would be prohibited from employing illegal workers. Therefore only women with valid papers could work in the sex business; and the cabinet (plus the vast majority of Parliament) had no intention of providing work permits for non-EU sex workers. Nor did they intend to legalise the migrant sex workers already present in the country without papers. (The estimated number of non-EU sex workers was between 10,000 and 15,000).

Parliament debated the bill in 1999.[8] The dominant formulation was in terms of sex work. The secular parties stressed the labour aspect of prostitution; it is hard and exacting requiring a certain degree of toughness and certain skills, but it is also specialised work. A sex worker does not have to deliver her services if she chooses not to do so. The moment she says 'no' her constitutional right to bodily integrity is invoked, and neither client nor employer can force her to agree. Therefore, the cabinet maintained that prostitution can never be 'fitting' work that a woman could be required to do to retain her right to unemployment or social security benefits. The religious parties invoked the question of local autonomy versus the central state in order to allow local councils to reinstate the ban on brothels, but this was countered because the constitution holds that the Penal Code is binding for the whole territory of the Netherlands.

The Second Chamber passed the bill in 1999 with the familiar voting pattern of secular versus religious parties; that same year the First Chamber also voted in favour of the bill—the secular in favour, the others opposed. The only concession the religious parties were able to obtain was that the bill would only take effect by 1 July 2000, a date later postponed to 1 October 2000. This was to give local authorities more time to set up their own regulation and system for licensing, under the pretext they were not yet prepared for the change, despite the fact that the VNG had a model plan for this. This was a success for the Christian Democrats and the orthodox Protestant parties in Parliament, acting on behalf of smaller municipalities who had hoped the bill might fail or that local exceptions would be incorporated by CDA amendment.

Implementation of legalisation

The passing of the bill was not accompanied by any huge public debate; neither had there been on earlier occasions. The media would provide the occasional background story, usually accompanied by suggestive images of blonde girls in a pink boudoir, but the repeal came as no surprise to the interest groups in this arena who had by now organised themselves as corporate actors, or to the wider public that had been expecting this for years. It does not mean it is uncontroversial for those who are actually involved in the policy arena. Many municipalities have by now set up a licensing system for brothels which must comply with labour and safety regulations, but many of them try to limit their number and this is leading to complaints by sex entrepreneurs, including some women who want to run their own club. The municipality of Leiden, for instance, has given licences to the four existing brothels but is refusing new sex entrepreneurs. Others, especially the small towns with orthodox Protestant councils, are trying to circumvent the law by redrafting their urban planning so there are no suitable areas available for a sex business. One of these towns is now being taken to court by the Association of Pleasure-House Entrepreneurs. Some of these entrepreneurs have become creative in escaping the zoning, setting up sex caravans along the provincial highways, but the authorities have intimated that these will not be condoned.

There is also a heated debate about the displacement effect of the new law. Prostitution has always been like communicating vessels; if the authorities crack down on brothels, street prostitution emerges; if streetwalkers are stopped, one gets bar prostitution or massage parlours. Many predicted a similar effect of the repeal: since brothels have to conform to strict standards, untrustworthy entrepreneurs will invest in escort services—then supposedly proliferating in Amsterdam—using sex workers without papers. The number of streetwalkers would also increase. At a conference in May 2003 it was reported there were no signs of this actually occurring in the city.[9]

The passing of the bill also led to the usual debate about the virtues of bringing vice out in the open rather than suppressing it. Social and health care workers pleaded for legalisation to maintain contact with their sex worker clients. Suppression would lead to prostitutes going underground, especially the illegal migrant sex workers, out of reach of the municipal health service or of the women's aid shelters. Interestingly, since the legalisation, the argument is now reversed. Licensing brothels is now said to have the same effect as suppression—supposedly forcing prostitutes underground. For municipalities are active in promoting and monitoring the rules. The mayor of The Hague made headlines by ordering brothels to stick to the same opening and closing hours as pubs (the latter in the Netherlands being 1 a.m. during the week and 2 a.m. at the weekend). Sex bosses complained, saying men prefer to come after having a drink.

What has hardly been contested is the introduction of a law making the carrying of an ID compulsory for a prostitute; she also has to register with the Internal Revenue Service. The idea of all residents having to carry an ID is highly controversial and attempts by consecutive cabinets to introduce this have been strongly opposed, with opponents not eschewing comparison with the measures of the German occupation during the Second World

War. The ID measure does not augur well with the hoped-for effect that repeal would lead to the improvement of the position of sex workers. Some predict that it will lead to them leaving the profession; given the high demand they will then in all likelihood be replaced by migrants without papers.[10]

Overall, it is the question whether after less than two years of its introduction one can already assess whether the law is achieving its goals, such as reducing forced prostitution, as well as other mal-effects, (Nationaal Rapporteur 2002: 205). The first report monitoring the effects cautioned against definitive judgement (Daalder 2002). This warning has been supported by other researchers (e.g. Scholtes and Wagenaar 2002) and those familiar with the grass roots of the 'scene', contradicting the negative reports in the press. They recommend an improved coordination of the implementation and cooperation of those working in the area—i.e. more corporatism.

Accounting for change

There are several good political explanations for the legalisation of prostitution in the Netherlands. For those who fought against the Morality Laws in the 1960s on the platform against state intervention in private life and morals, the brothel ban was the last remnant of state interference still intact, telling citizens it was immoral to provide the facilities for sexual transactions. In the course of the 1980s, the ban was construed as an obstacle to a sensible answer to the endless complaints of neighbourhoods faced with the excesses of the new sex industry and the demand for its repeal had the support of a very strong ally: the VNG—often characterised as the most powerful lobbyist (with Shell) at the national level. The idea of legislation was also helped by the inside access of the women's movement in the national government and legalising sex work to improve the position of prostitutes and combat forced prostitution—through trafficking—became tabled in key policy papers. This idea ran parallel to the market discourse of liberalism, strongly in ascendance in the 1980s and well represented in politics by the two liberal parties, the Social Liberals of D66 (Democraten 66) and the conservative liberals of the People's Party for Freedom and Democracy (Volkspartij voor Vrijheid en Democratie, VVD). The process towards legalisation ran into trouble when a Christian Democrat minister tried to remove the basic distinction between forced and voluntary prostitution; but with a secular cabinet in 1994 with a parliamentary majority, there was no way to stop the repeal. The Christian Democrats could accept lifting the ban and doing away with pimping as an offence for pragmatic reasons, but would not accept the idea of prostitution as sex work.

There were no powerful organised interests opposing legalisation. Radical feminism as a force had disappeared, and the abolitionist organisations who successfully achieved their goals in the 1911 Morality Acts had dispersed even before the Second World War. The orthodox Protestants stuck to the abolitionist position, that the state should preserve morals, but they were a small minority in Parliament and were regarded by their opponents as being hopelessly moral and outdated.

The legalisation of prostitution can be seen as a prime example of the pragmatic approach to moral issues in the Netherlands. This pragmatism, coupled with a tolerance of deviant behaviour as long as it does not threaten public order, has often been linked to the open and cosmopolitan character of Dutch society, a society already highly urbanised in the 16th century; a seafaring and commercial nation, comparatively wealthy, with a regular flow of immigrants ever since. It has also been linked to the absence of a dominant elite, as it has always been a society of many minorities, none of which could dominate the others. To live together without disorder and violence required cooperation and compromise to achieve consensus. This has led to a pragmatic approach to issues touching on different moral values, with a series of strategies to accommodate them, such as delaying action as long as possible, depoliticising the issue by turning it into a technical matter or coming up with procedural solutions (Lijphart 1968).

However, these informal rules for dealing with divisive moral issues were not observed any longer in the 1960s when the system in which they evolved, the older segmented society of the *Verzuiling*—pillarisation—broke down. This paved the way for the legalisation of the issues prohibited in the Morality Acts of 1911: the display and advertisement of contraceptives, abortion and male and female homosexuality. It did not, however, permanently damage the culture of consensus and compromise. A close analysis of the liberalisation of these issues has shown that the new laws which superseded the Acts were in fact also supported by the opposition, even if it first resisted liberalisation (Outshoorn 1986; Kennedy 1995). Political scientist Hans Daalder has pointed out (1966: 219; 1995) that elites, once convinced (often belatedly) of the necessity to take action, will move to arrive at a 'mutually acceptable solution', finding it easier to compromise than to make a definite choice for one alternative. The historian Kennedy, writing on the revolution in morals of the 1960s, maintains that the Dutch create consensus by constructing a self-evident need for change: a paramount cultural value being an acknowledgement of the need to keep up with changing times; social change is considered as both inevitable and good (Kennedy 1995; 2000: 17). He notes that with the crumbling of the old system of *Verzuiling* the Dutch took a consciously anti-moralistic posture on social issues, often finding solutions in procedural rules, purposely leaving matters vague: the state has now abrogated its function as a moral taskmaster (idem 21).

Underlying the pragmatic approach is the conviction of nearly all the political parties that prostitution is ineradicable and that in the long run human nature is hard to reform: mankind will sin. Therefore policy should aim at channelling undesirable behaviour in controllable ways. The term 'realistic' abounds in the prostitution debates: to consider voluntary prostitution as 'sex work' is regarded as a feasible policy; licensing brothels is sensible and it is efficient as it gives the police the time to chase 'real villains'. In no way can the legalisation be interpreted as a libertarian move: it is a policy to bring prostitution activities to the surface in order to make for better control by the authorities. The state may have abrogated its authority to pronounce on moral matters, but it has not relinquished its regulatory powers and in the best corporatist tradition these are always exercised in consultation with other involved parties.

Notes

[1] Conference of The Red Thread (Rode Draad), 1 October 2001.

[2] The law was passed in 1999, but took effect on 1 October 2000.

[3] 'Afwerken' means literally 'to give the finishing touch'. The sites are officially approved and intended both to relieve the neighbourhoods from men cruising in cars and to make work safer for sex workers. There are two such sites, in Amsterdam and Rotterdam, near industrial areas where street prostitutes picked up by clients in cars can deliver their services. At the sites clients can also pick up a sex worker. In recent years they have been frequented by Latin American transsexuals and transgenders as well as East European women without papers accompanied by their pimps. Drug use and violence are rife. The Rotterdam site was slated for closure in 2005 after neighbourhood complaints. The police prefer such concentration of street prostitution as it makes for easier control; it also makes it easier for the women's outreach services to contact and help sex workers.

[4] The terms 'prostitute' and 'sex worker' have been used interchangeably; it is important to note that most women working as such do not identify with either label as they tend to see their work as temporary.

[5] Quoted from: E.M.H. van Dijk (2003), Mensenhandel in Nederland 1997–2000, Zoetermeer: KLPD/NRI, in: Tweede rapportage van de Nationaal Rapporteur, Mensenhandel. Aanvullende kwantitative gegevens, Den Haag: Bureau NRM, 2003, p. 82.

[6] This was due to the fact that the Minister of Justice was a Liberal of the VVD, with an explicit instrumental approach. For the bill: HTK 1985–1986, 18202 (Opheffing Bordeelverbod), nrs 1–3, 24–9–85.

[7] For the debates: HTK 1986/1987, 18202, TK 66, pp. 34783502 (2–4–87), for the final vote: p. 3511 (7–4–87).

[8] HTK 1996–1997, 25437, nrs 1–3. Opheffing Bordeelverbod, 1–7–97. For the parliamentary debates: HTK 1998–1999, TK44, 27–1–99; TK 45, 28–1–99; for the vote: TK 49, 2–2–99.

[9] Conference Vrouwenhandel en Europa, The Hague, 9 mei 2003.

[10] This could be countered by giving sex workers from outside the EU work permits, but this is explicitly prohibited in the Law on Labour by Aliens (Wet Arbeid Vreemdelingen). There is little support for revising it, and the Netherlands also runs the risk of contravening international treaties it ratified if it does so.

References

Acker, Hanneke and Marijke Rawie. 1982. *Seksueel geweld tegen vrouwen en meisjes.* Den Haag: Ministerie van Sociale Zaken en Werkgelegenheid/DCE.

Daalder, Hans. 1966. 'The Netherlands: Opposition in a Segmented Society' in *Political Opposition in Western Democracies.* ed. R.A. Dahl. New Haven/ London: Yale University Press. pp. 188–236.

——. 1995. 'Politici en politisering in Nederland'in *Van oude en nieuwe regenten. Politiek in Nederland.* ed. Hans Daalder. Amsterdam: Bert Bakker. pp. 40– 72.

Daalder, A.L. 2002. 'het bordeelverbod opgeheven: prostitutie in 2000–2–1'. Den Haag: WODC.

de Vries, Petra. 1997. *Kuisheid voor mannen, vrijheid voor vrouwen. De reglementering en bestrijding van prostitutie in Nederland 1850–1911.* Hilversum: Verloren.

Kennedy, James. 1995. *Nieuw Babylon in aanbouw. Nederland in de jaren zestig.* Amsterdam: Boom Meppel.

——. 2000. 'The Moral State: How Much Do the Americans and the Dutch Differ?' in *Regulating Morality. A Comparison of the Role of the State in Mastering the More in the Netherlands and the United States.* eds. Hans Krabbendam and Hans-Martien ten Napel. Antwerpen/Apeldoorn: Maklu. pp. 9–23.

Lijphart, Arend. 1968. *Verzuiling, pacificatie en kentering in de Nederlandse politiek.* Amsterdam: De Bussy. ch. 8.

Nationaal Rapporteur. 2002. *Mensenhandel. Eerste rapportage van de Nationaal Rapporteur.* Den Haag: Bureau NRM.

Nota Bestrijding Seksueel Geweld. HTK 1983–1984. 18452. nrs 1–2; Beleidsplan Emancipatie. HTK 1984–1985. 19502. no. 2.

Outshoorn, Joyce. 1986. *De politieke strijd rondom de abortuswetgeving in Nederland 1964–1984.* Den Haag: VUGA.

——. 1995. 'Administrative Accommodation in the Netherlands: the case of the Department for the Coordination of Equality Polity' in *Comparative State Feminism.* eds. Dorothy McBride Stetson and Amy Mazur. Thousand Oaks/ London/New Delhi: Sage. pp. 168–186.

——. 2001a. 'Regulating Prostitution as Sex Work'. *Acta Politica* 36. 2: pp. 155– 80.

——. 2001b. 'Debating Prostitution in Parliament'. *European Journal of Women's Studies.* 8. 3: pp. 473–91.

——. 2004. 'Voluntary and Forced Prostitution: the "realistic" approach of the Netherlands' in *The Politics of Prostitution. Women's Movements, Democratic States and the Globalisation of Sex Commerce.* ed. Joyce Outshoorn. Cambridge: Cambridge University Press. pp. 185–225.

Sauer, Birgit. 2004. 'Taxes, rights and regimentation. Discourses on prostitution in

Austria' in *The Politics of Prostitution. Women's Movements, Democratic States and the Globalisation of Sex Commerce.* ed. Joyce Outshoorn. Cambridge: Cambridge University Press. pp. 41–62.

Scholtes, Hans and Henk Wagemaar. 2002. 'Legalisering van bordelen ligt op koers' (Legalisation of Brothels is on Track). NRC Handelsblad. 12 November.

Svanstrom, Yvonne. 2004. 'Criminalising the john—a Swedish gender model' in *The Politics of Prostitution. Women's Movements, Democratic States and the Globalisation of Sex Commerce.* ed. Joyce Outshoorn. Cambridge: Cambridge University Press. pp. 225–245.

Sullivan, Barbara. 2004. 'The women's movement and prostitution politics in Australia' in *The Politics of Prostitution. Women's Movements, Democratic States and the Globalisation of Sex Commerce.* ed. Joyce Outshoorn. Cambridge: Cambridge University Press. pp. 21–41.

van Mens, Lucie. 1992. *Prostitutie in bedrijf. Organisatie, Management en Arbeidsverhoudingen in Seksclubs en Privéhuizen.* Delft: Eburon.

PART II

Human Security, Work and Care

5

Combating Trafficking in Women and Children

A Gender and Human Rights Framework

NOELEEN HEYZER*

> *Women and children are trafficked not only for forced prostitution but also for legal and illegal work, legal and illegal marriages, organ trade, camel racing and bonded labour.*[1]

Trafficking in human beings is increasing in both magnitude and in reach.[2] It has become a multi-billion dollar industry run both by individuals and by small and large organised crime networks. It affects vulnerable individuals, particularly women and children, in every region of the world and has become a major human rights concern. A communique from the G-8 countries on combating transnational organised crime identified the phenomenon as 'the dark side of globalisation'.[3]

Human trafficking refers to the recruitment, transportation, transfer and harbouring of persons, by threat of force or deception, for the purpose of exploitation. It involves not only prostitution, debt bondage, forced labour and enslavement of adults and children, but also child soldiering and sexual slavery.[4] The ILO

---

* The framework and recommendations in this chapter draw on the work of the United Nations Development Fund for Women's (UNIFEM) programme to combat trafficking in South and South-east Asia as well as the author's work on international migration of women as domestic workers. See Noeleen Heyzer, Geertje Lycklama à Nijeholt and Nedra Weerakoon, (eds.) *The Trade in Domestic Workers: Causes, Mechanism and Consequences of International Migration*, Zed Books, 1992.

101

estimates that some 12.3 million people are enslaved in forced or bonded labour or sexual or involuntary servitude at any given time.[5] While the nature of trafficking makes it difficult to know the real extent of the phenomenon, an estimated 600,000 to 800,000 persons—mainly women and children—are trafficked across international borders each year. The number of trafficked persons within countries is still unknown. Approximately 80 per cent of those trafficked across international borders are women and girls, and 50 per cent are minor.[6]

It is necessary to examine this trafficking of women and children within a broader context of labour migration (legal and illegal) and the movement of people from conflict zones and crisis situations as refugees and internally-displaced persons. These movements in turn interact with structures of gender inequality at every level—global, national, communal and familial. The analytical and action framework set out here addresses these links in a holistic and coordinated manner.

Globalisation, labour migration and trafficking

From an economic perspective, trafficking should be recognised as but one component in the complex and shifting continuum of population mobility and labour migration.[7] Movements intended to be temporary may later become permanent; movements voluntarily entered into by would-be migrants may later become forced incidents of trafficking; and those who have been trafficked may later choose to remain in the place of destination as a permanent migrant. At the end of the 20th century, there were an estimated 175 million international migrants, nearly three per cent of the world's people. Nearly two-thirds of these, about 104 million, were in developed countries. Approximately nine per cent, nearly 16 million, were refugees. The movements within borders are considerably larger than those across them. Internal displacement from armed conflict is estimated to have affected 25 million people in 47 countries in 2002.[8]

Population movements, whether voluntary or forced, are not new. European colonisation of Africa, Latin America, East and

South-east Asia and the settlement of the 'New World' of North America probably generated greater relative population mobility than that observed today. Many of those movements also involved various forms of trafficking—including slavery, 'state trafficking' of prisoners and political exiles, and the recruitment of forced labour by individuals and countries. However, the 20th century brought about some fundamental changes in the nature of trafficking and in the international norms and standards that govern it.[9]

Until the rise of the modern nation state most forms of migration were essentially voluntary; people moved to escape some form of deprivation in the area of origin or to benefit from some anticipated opportunity in the area of destination. Boundaries of nation states as such did not exist. With the introduction of national boundaries population movement has become regulated, border controls have been set up and travel documents are required. Would-be migrants who fail to meet the entry criteria set by the countries which are their intended destination therefore become illegal, and this has given rise to both people smuggling and trafficking. It is estimated that more than half the 15–30 million illegal migrants in the world have been assisted by smugglers or have been forcibly relocated by traffickers.[10]

Labour migration is now characterised by increasing numbers of women and girls, sometimes described in terms of increasing 'feminisation'. With a few exceptions, migrant flows have tended to be male-dominated, as employers in destination countries sought primarily male immigrants for manual labour. Unaccompanied women and children rarely migrated in significant numbers. In the 20th century changes in both supply and demand factors led to the feminisation of migration flows and a sharp increase in the numbers and proportions of women and children migrating on a short-term or temporary basis in search of work.

One reason for this shift is that migration is often both cheaper and easier for women than for men. The fees charged for women migrating from Indonesia or Bangladesh to the Middle East, for example, are much lower than those for men, owing to the high demand for women domestics and the ease of placement.[11] The education and skills requirements are lower for women than for men, since the increased demand for female labour has been in areas such as household and caregiving work, fast food and other services, and low-wage manufacturing.[12]

Although legal channels have been established for some of these migration flows—for example, from Philippines, Indonesia and Sri Lanka to the Middle East—many women and children move illegally and are thus at risk of being trafficked.[13] Gender inequality in both source and destination areas also increases the vulnerability of women and children, particularly girls, to trafficking.

The dramatic growth in migration and trafficking flows has resulted from a combination of push, pull and facilitating factors. 'Push' factors include uneven economic growth and the breakdown of economic systems, an increase in war and armed conflict, environmental degradation, natural disasters, and high levels of gender discrimination and family violence. The 'pull' factors are the economic growth, relative prosperity and peace in industrialised and newly industrialising countries which are creating increased demand for imported labour. Migrant workers thus form two streams—on the one hand, the highly skilled professionals demanded by new advances in information and medical technologies, and on the other, the far more numerous group of unskilled and less educated workers willing to take the low-wage, part-time and contract jobs that citizens are often reluctant to take. The entry of the former group is welcomed and legitimised by the receiving state; the entry of the latter group is carefully guarded against and hence many of them enter illegally and are therefore vulnerable to exploitation and abuse by employers and officials alike.

Growth in the industrialised economies has been accompanied by a quantum leap in low-cost transportation and communication technologies, which facilitates all aspects of migration and trafficking. But the major facilitating factor is the involvement of organised crime, for whom trafficking is a growing source of profit. The United Nations ranks human trafficking as the third largest criminal enterprise worldwide, second only to drugs and arms; it generates an estimated $9.5 billion each year for the procurers, smugglers, and corrupt public officials who make it possible.[14] Due to coercion and exploitation, however, profits per volume are much greater for trafficking than for smuggling and the financial gains are spread more widely. The magnitude of these gains and the low risks involved for those who stand to make the greatest gain—traffickers, corrupt officials and employers—make its prevention especially difficult.[15]

Changes in both the supply of and demand for female labour, partly due to changes in gender roles in industrialised and developing countries, have also increased the proportion of women and children in migration streams, and therefore of women and adolescent girls being trafficked. On the supply side, would-be migrants may be pushed to leave their areas of origin by poverty or lack of adequate economic opportunity. Globalisation has had both winners and losers, slashing economic opportunities in rural areas and in poor countries that are not competitive in the global marketplace, creating what one expert has called a 'crisis of economic security' in such countries.[16] Market liberalisation and privatisation have created an increasing need for cash incomes to purchase the most basic needs, including those once provided by the state. Often this demand cannot be satisfied in local labour markets, forcing families to send members out into the global workplace. In the poorest countries, such opportunities are likely to be found even in neighbouring countries and further afield.

Especially in the poorest countries, moreover, women and girls may be pushed toward trafficking as an alternative to the drudgery, danger and exploitation that characterises their daily lives. In regions throughout Asia, South Asia and Africa, young women may be running away from the prospects of early or forced marriage and constant childbearing, the risks of maternal and child mortality, and the drudgery involved in fetching fuel and water, caring for their families, and contributing to the family income through labour-intensive agriculture or the other kinds of low-paid and unskilled jobs available locally.

In transitional countries of Central Asia and Eastern Europe as well as Russia, the rapid integration of former socialist economies into the global economy—involving wholesale privatisation of state-owned enterprises, large-scale worker layoffs, the removal of subsidies for basic goods and services (including childcare, food, housing, education and health care)—took place almost overnight before alternative legal and regulatory frameworks could be put in place. The major beneficiaries, besides those with the money to buy up the state properties, have been large criminal networks and organisations which flourish in the climate of poverty and insecurity. While many women initially embraced the prospect of staying at home and caring for their children, the problems of job and income loss, the elimination of nurseries for children of working mothers, the abrupt dismantling of services previously provided by the state—with a dramatic increase in alcoholism, violence, and crime—has resulted in the disintegration of family and community ties and women are looking for new opportunities and new lives elsewhere.

The demand for trafficked labour has also increased. Sex tourism and child pornography have become global industries, fuelled in part by new information technologies such as the Internet.[17] However, globalisation has also created a growing demand for cheap, low-skilled labour in both developed and developing countries in agriculture, labour-intensive manufacturing, food processing, construction and the service sector in general, including domestic service, home health care and sexual services.[18] As industries continually seek to cut costs, some have relocated to low wage economies while others remain 'flexible' through worker layoffs, part-time work and increased use of subcontracting—undermining the power of trade unions to protect jobs, wages and basic rights. The dominant market ideology has also led to a weakening of regulatory and monitoring mechanisms to protect working conditions, minimum labour standards or basic human rights.

Yet the wage and working conditions that may be unacceptable to workers in industrialised countries are often attractive to those from poorer countries where wages are even lower, and there are large numbers of unemployed and underemployed. Since most trafficked workers have low levels of education and may be illiterate in the language of the receiving country, they are usually unaware of the existence of minimum standards or of the means of enforcing them; they are unaware of their human rights or of any means by which they might claim those rights. But even if they are cognisant of these aspects, their status as illegal workers deprives them of the means to enforce minimum wages and working conditions. Young women are in particular demand because they are often regarded as more compliant and less likely to rebel against sub-standard working conditions.

The increasing entry of women into the paid labour force, either full or part-time, has created a huge demand in industrialised countries for the labour and time of women and children, particularly girls, in unpaid household and care work since men in most cases have not increased their share of such work. The wages, traditional low status, and demanding hours of jobs in this sector are such that indigenous women or residents in these countries avoid them if they can, adding to the demand for illegal and trafficked labour.

The nature of work available to migrant and trafficked labour leads to widespread denial of basic human rights, particularly for women and children. Sub-standard practices and the use of undocumented workers means that the employers involved have an interest in concealing these workers which often leads to physical confinement. Domestic workers are particularly vulnerable since their work is physically confined to the employer's household which is generally regarded as a private domain beyond the reach of regulation. The resulting psychological isolation exacerbates the unequal power relations between the migrant or trafficked worker and the employer; in addition to that, gender stereotypes render women and girls especially vulnerable to physical violence and sexual abuse. The low wages paid to trafficked workers, combined with frequent withholding of pay by employers and the high fees charged by traffickers, often forces women trafficked into areas of employment other than prostitution to resort to it, ultimately in order to survive or to repay the debts incurred during the process of being trafficked.

It is not the mere existence of the demand for cheap labour in another country that generates the conditions for trafficking. It is the de facto restriction on the ostensible right respond to this demand that leaves the undocumented migrants vulnerable to trafficking. While the vulnerability of women and girls is significantly increased by the impact of unequal gender relations at every stage in the process, the fundamental issue is the lack of legal channels through which potential migrant workers can access employment opportunities that are theirs by right according to international human rights standards.

Trafficking, armed conflict and state fragmentation

> The breakdown of law and order, police functions and border controls that accompany armed conflicts create an environment in which the trafficking of women has flourished. (UNIFEM: *Women, War and Peace* 2002)

> Trafficking is fostered by transition, instability, poverty, disintegrating social networks, and disintegrating law and order in sending, transit and receiving countries. (United Nations: *Women, Peace and Security* 2002)

Two United Nations studies examining the impact of war and armed conflict on women have documented how armed conflict and trafficking are linked in various ways.[19] Traffickers often use routes through countries that have been engulfed by conflict, since border controls and normal policing are reduced. Both refugees and displaced women and girls are taken as hostages and later trafficked into slavery, forced prostitution and forced military recruitment by way of abduction, or sold into marriage.

In 2001, the United Nations High Commissioner for Refugees reported that there were 19.8 million refugees, asylum seekers, and others of concern, and that women and children constitute 80 per cent of the world's refugees and internally displaced persons.[20] Flight is often triggered by severe forms of gender discrimination and persecution, sometimes combined with ethnic, religious or class discrimination. Refugees, returning and displaced women and girls (as refugees and returnees), often suffer discrimination and human rights abuses throughout their flight, during settlement and on their return. For example, women and girls may be forced to provide sexual services to men and adolescent boys in exchange for safe passage for themselves or their families or to obtain the necessary documents or other assistance. Girl children who become separated from their parents may face the risk of sexual abuse or be forced to participate in military action.

The breakdown of community and family protection mechanisms in settlement camps for refugees and displaced persons leave women and girls vulnerable to 'physical and sexual attacks, rape, domestic violence and sexual harassment'. [21] The loss of social support networks that typically accompanies uprooting means they have less power to escape, defend themselves, or obtain the protection and assistance needed to survive. Lack of security and poorly lit camps leave women and girls at risk of attack both inside and outside the camps.

According to the UN study on women, peace and security, 'Culture has been used to explain away certain crimes, resulting in a failure to address the problems of security and protection.' In some cases, prostitution, alcohol abuse, drug trafficking and other illegal activities have been seen by authorities in charge as 'normal' activities, part of the refugees' culture.[22] Women's inability to obtain basic services or protection takes a tremendous toll on their physical and mental health. Left with few options, many turn to prostitution in exchange for basic survival needs.

The effects of trafficking and sexual slavery are profound, especially for young girls. They face a myriad physical and mental health problems due to rape, sexual abuse, sexually transmitted infections including HIV/AIDS, trauma and unwanted pregnancies.[23] Torn from their families, women and girls who have been brutalised by their kidnappers are then often rejected by their own kin. In some cases young girls who had been abducted by soldiers or rebels spent months searching for family members after escaping from their captors, only to be turned away in disgrace when they did find a relative. In some places orphanages set up for children separated from their families and communities have themselves facilitated trafficking in children, particularly girls.[24]

The trauma that women and girls experience in such situations, as well as their fear of being stigmatised, often leaves them unable to discuss their ordeal, especially as concern victims of sexual violence. This puts them at a disadvantage during asylum proceedings or refugee status hearings, making it more likely their requests will be denied. Moreover, domestic laws and immigration policies that fail to address the differential impact of armed conflict on women may force them to return to their countries—where they risk further violence. Women and girls may be forced to stay in abusive marriages to avoid losing their visas and having to return to countries in conflict.

Gender discrimination in families and communities

In countries with patrilineal family systems daughters are seen as a liability. Their families are obliged to ensure their sexual purity, marry them well, provide substantial marriage expenses and continue to offer material resources to the daughter's marital family on auspicious occasions. Households, especially poor households, cope with this in various ways. If an opportunity arises families may trade undervalued females with little thought for their rights or future well-being, hence sales into prostitution or marriage to men who make no monetary demands—thus predisposing them to trafficking.

Women are manipulated by consumerism and family loyalty to fulfil family needs and consumption in the name of cultural tradition—duty, care, gratitude—even if it means their becoming engaged in pornography or prostitution. This is known to occur in some matrilineal and bilateral contexts, where a daughter's role and status is equal to or valued more than a son's, and where a daughter traditionally provides economic and social security to ageing parents. On the other hand, in contexts where sexual purity is the insignia of ideal womanhood, rape and sexual abuse, or non-conformity to prescribed sexual codes result in stigma and loss of self-worth, which leaves these 'damaged' women and girls vulnerable to trafficking. Vulnerability caused by marital infidelity, alcohol, family violence, desertion by husbands or fathers and divorce also increases the risk of women being trafficked. It is important to note, however, that while trafficked women may see themselves as victims of structural forces at one level, they have also—initially—seen themselves as being able to solve some of the critical problems faced by their families and communities. In some countries pressure from family members is often a factor in trafficking.

Politics and economics have been the cause of build-up of such 'pressures'. Communist China's one-child population policy together with the retained cultural preference for sons has produced the demographic anomaly of imbalanced male/female ratio—there are now more men. Long years of war in Vietnam have skewed the balance towards women. The pressure on Vietnamese women to marry, even as second or third wives, has resulted in a thriving trade in Vietnamese women for the Chinese marriage market. Similar pressures are also emerging in India in response to the dowry system and other pressures for sons rather than daughters giving rise to inter-state movements of girls from states such as West Bengal and Assam to better off states such as Punjab and Haryana to fill gender gaps.[25] The image of Asian women as docile, subservient homemakers has generated another form of trafficking—'the mail-order-bride' system, flourishing now in newly industrialised countries in East Asia as well as Western Europe and North America.[26]

Demand for prostitution has also greatly expanded with the industry becoming globalised. A report on trafficking in South Asia noted that depending on 'age, looks, docility and virginity,' a Bengali or Burmese woman could be sold in Pakistan for US$ 1,500–2,500, and that for each child or woman sold, the police claim a 15–20 per cent 'commission.'[27] In many countries, prostitution is now an integral part of tourism, both domestic and foreign, and some countries are specifically promoted for 'sex tourism'. The growing demand for prostitution may also be linked to the breakdown of the family, and thus the number of divorced, separated and unmarried men with the level of income to buy sex. The commercialisation of women's bodies through pornography, advertising, entertainment and the media also contribute to demand.

A gender-responsive and human rights-based approach to trafficking

To date, the international human rights framework has not fully caught up with globalisation. Although persons are deemed to have an inherent human right to cross-border mobility as well as a basic human right to decent work or source of livelihood, the two remain separated by the virtue of territorial sovereignty of nation states. To the extent that the right to work or livelihood is recognised, the obligation for the realisation of that right is placed on the state in which the individual resides, and not on other states or the global community. Similarly, so long as capital moves more freely across borders than does labour, vulnerabilities will be created in some countries and demand created in others, thus encouraging illegal migration and the concomitant trafficking.

A gender- and rights-based approach is a vision and practice of development that ensures fundamental human entitlements—social, economic and political—in ways that expand human choices and promote human well-being and empowerment. The claim to human rights has a strong moral force: it imposes the obligation that they be not only recognised but fulfilled.

A gender-based approach is necessarily also a rights-based approach, since gender discrimination is now recognised as a fundamental denial of human rights. Women's human rights must therefore lie at the core of any credible anti-trafficking strategy: for violations of human rights are both a cause and a consequence of trafficking in persons. It is unfortunately true that women remain inequitably situated in relation to men in terms of their gender roles and the impact of gender stereotypes; for women generally have different needs than do men. Therefore a human rights orientation to trafficking must also be responsive to gender differences and disparities when focused on realising human rights equally for women and men, girls and boys.[28]

Rights, to be empowering, must be actively claimed by those who hold them; individual and collective empowerment of women is essential. Empowerment involves both a structural dimension— including policy, legal and institutional elements as well as accountability by states—and an individual dimension designed to equip individuals and groups to claim their rights. Policy, legal and institutional measures are necessary to guarantee the rights and dignity of all human beings and all trafficked persons. States, which are duty-bearers as signatories to international human rights agreements, must be accountable for protecting these rights. And these must be complemented by immigration and anti-trafficking strategies that enable all individuals, including women and young people, to claim their rights effectively. Migrant workers whose immigration status is not officially recognised, the so-called 'illegal' migrants, who are often regarded as criminals, currently alas have no way to claim such rights.

Strategies for prevention of trafficking

International Human Rights Law obliges states to respect, protect, promote and ensure the realisation of human rights according to the principle of non-discrimination. In relation to trafficking, this includes preventing violations through appropriate laws, policies and programmes, investigating violations, taking appropriate action against violators and providing remedies and reparation to those trafficked, regardless of their immigration status. Beyond such immediate actions, national development strategies must address the factors generating both supply and demand.

Economic empowerment for women and girls

Strategies for women's economic empowerment must enhance women's ownership and control over productive resources, access to markets, and movement up the production and market value chain in secure and sustainable ways. They must also ensure gender equality in the family, community and society at large. This involves recognising and valuing women's paid and unpaid work equally with men's at all levels of society; examining the gender impact of macroeconomic policy on women's employment and livelihoods; ensuring women's access to and ownership of economic resources, including land and finance; and providing new and better paid employment and business opportunities for women that are not restricted to sectors traditionally dominated by women's labour.

At a practical level, economic empowerment involves building the capacity of women producers and entrepreneurs in product development, production processes, business and financial development; ensuring access to and use of information and marketing, including the ability to effectively respond to market change; and enabling women to recognise and claim their economic rights, including the right to a sustainable livelihood, access to skills, information and markets in accordance with international human rights instruments and relevant international labour conventions.

Livelihood strategies

There is considerable debate around the question of whether creating livelihood opportunities for women and girls will prevent trafficking and promote the resettlement of returnees.[29] In source areas for women migrants (and thus also areas of high risk for women and girls as regards trafficking) the creation of livelihood opportunities may discourage out-migration and reduce the risk of trafficking. To be effective, however, these opportunities must be competitive in terms of earnings and working conditions with those available in the destination areas accessible to local women. This is especially important in programmes that aim to resettle returnees, particularly those who have worked as prostitutes. Programmes to combat trafficking often limit training for women returnees to their traditional occupations, which are usually unskilled and poorly paid, and thus unlikely to be competitive with those available through migration or trafficking, even taking into account the risks involved.

Job training must also address gender relations, especially the burden of women's unpaid household and caregiving work. The drudgery of unpaid housework, gathering fuel and fetching water, as well as the risks of high maternal and infant mortality, tend to drive young women away, especially from rural areas. The public provision of water, power, transport and health services and the macroeconomic policies that support these are important components of trafficking prevention strategies. So too is the creation of more positive attitudes to women's rights, roles and status that will support girls' rights to education and women's rights to paid employment, as well as reduce the unequal burden of unpaid work by promoting more active roles for men in the household and family.

Job creation and income-generation schemes, however, especially those that depend on special donor or government funding, run the risk of creating new dependencies once the funding runs out and the jobs disappear. Even where the jobs continue, rising expectations and information about competing opportunities elsewhere may still contribute to supply side pressures that promote migration and trafficking.

Beyond this the UN Recommended Guidelines on Human Rights and Human Trafficking state that governments and inter-governmental organisations should ensure that interventions address the factors that increase vulnerability to trafficking, including inequality, poverty and all forms of discrimination. Areas of origin for trafficking are typically among the poorest even in poor countries, with limited markets and low skill levels. Gender-sensitive development strategies are needed that combine sustainable markets, the development of products that are saleable in terms of price and quality and empowerment strategies that enable women to build sustainable and profitable businesses, with the capacity to respond to market change when it happens. Such strategies must be so designed that women's economic empowerment promotes gender equality within their families and communities. Thus for women and girls, prevention involves not only providing a viable economic alternative to opportunities elsewhere, but also promoting individual and collective empowerment that will enable them to address the underlying causes of their marginalisation.

Safe migration and citizenship rights for women and adolescent girls

While national development strategies that provide sustainable livelihoods and expand choices for women might limit migration and reduce vulnerability to trafficking, gender-sensitive and rights-based efforts to make migration safe are also needed. These include ensuring that trafficked persons have the right to seek and enjoy asylum from persecution in accord with international refugee law, reviewing and harmonising immigration laws and policies in accord with international human standards, and promoting bilateral and multilateral agreements that protect migrant workers, especially women.

An important step in this respect is the adoption of mechanisms for legal migration between and among states. In Asia Pacific, for example, such mechanisms have been adopted between Thailand and its neighbours; between Malaysia and its neighbours, particularly Indonesia and Bangladesh; between Indonesia and the Middle East and between the Philippines and the Middle East, as well as other countries. Missing in these agreements, however, is a human rights framework that recognises the rights of illegal migrants. Women and girls dominate in many of these migrant labour flows, going into domestic service, low-paid sweatshop industries, street begging and commercial sex work. As a result, many suffer serious violations of their human rights, including illegal deprivation of their travel documents, physical confinement, domestic violence and sexual abuse, and thus continue to be trafficked even by officially registered labour migration agents. Others suffer similar abuses at the hands of their employers, largely because their status as legal migrant workers is dependent on their contract with the specific employer who must pay their registration. It is important to recognise that migrant workers who are doing the work demanded by the economy in the receiving country have a right to the same protections against discrimination and abuse enjoyed by citizens and documented workers in that country. Global recognition of this principle is a critical step in breaking the vicious link between migration and trafficking.

A comprehensive approach also requires a consideration of the impact of macroeconomic policies in both source and destination countries on the supply and demand conditions for migrant and trafficked labour. Policies that promote monetary and fiscal stability over employment security, reduce public expenditure and privatise social services and resources exacerbate existing vulnerabilities in developing countries and have created new vulnerabilities in both developing and transition economies that facilitate trafficking. In particular, gender blind macroeconomic policies that fail to account for their differential impact on women and men contribute directly to trafficking in women and girls.

Transforming gender-biased attitudes in countries of destination

Efforts to reduce demand have focused primarily on the criminal justice system, and have mainly concentrated on trafficking for sexual exploitation. There have been relatively few efforts to transform gender stereotypes and beliefs about gender roles and responsibilities, or notions about male and female sexuality, that create and reinforce the demand for women in such 'woman-oriented' sectors as domestic work and prostitution. To address demand in these sectors, it is essential to challenge stereotypes of women as dependent and confined to the domestic sphere, and men as active in the public sphere, as well as the constructions of women's sexuality as either passive or dangerous, existing only for marriage and childbearing or the provision of sexual pleasure. Moreover, the distorted values that permit and even encourage the commodification of human beings must be replaced by a full understanding and respect for the human rights and dignity of all people, immigrants and citizens, women and men.

Integrating human rights and development strategies

The UN Recommended Guidelines on Human Rights and Human Trafficking call for national plans of action to combat trafficking in persons. To be effective, these need to be integrated into national development policies which must consider the potential impact on human trafficking, particularly in women and girls. While the multi-sectoral strategies for combating HIV/AIDS adopted by several countries in the region provide a good model, the problem of trafficking is more challenging. The social and economic costs of HIV/AIDS are now recognised in high incidence countries, impelling governments to address it in the most effective way. The difficulty with this approach to trafficking is that while recipient countries see the growth of trafficking, especially in women and girls, as a danger, the countries of origin often do not. While recipient countries could do much to reduce the demand for trafficked labour, including reducing the demand for prostitution, the main pressure for prevention tends to fall on source countries. Thus, it will be difficult to persuade departments such as highways and transportation, commerce and industry or even macroeconomic policy-makers in developing countries to consider the impact of their policies on human trafficking.

However, that is exactly what is needed: macroeconomic policies and especially development programmes in poor areas and marginal populations need to be assessed in terms of their potential impact on trafficking. Is demand being created for unskilled and cheap labour likely to generate a demand for trafficked labour and sex workers from poor or marginal populations (especially those lacking citizenship rights)? Are programmes likely to facilitate the entry of traffickers to new areas and vulnerable populations not yet familiar with the risks? Will they promote economic security for women and girls? Could awareness of gender issues and the value of women's work reduce the pressure communities and families often place on young women to migrate illegally or to turn to prostitution?

One way to encourage this approach would be to link the

issues of trafficking and HIV/AIDS more directly than is done now. While the link is clearly strong and implicitly recognised, neither governments nor trafficking or HIV/AIDS programmes currently give it much practical consideration. The issue of trafficking might be more successfully addressed through national development policies in countries that have adopted a national multi-sectoral HIV/AIDS strategy if trafficking is integrated into the AIDS strategy. This also might encourage a regional approach in countries with high incidence of HIV infection, such as those in sub-Saharan Africa. HIV/AIDS is identified as one of the factors fuelling the increase in trafficking in the region, primarily because the large—and growing—number of AIDS orphans tend to be particularly vulnerable to trafficking, while trafficking in turn increases the likelihood of HIV infection.[30]

Globalisation, macroeconomic and trade policies

Ultimately, strategies to prevent trafficking must address the macroeconomic policies in both developed and developing countries that generate the push and pull factors in labour migration and thus, where that movement is illegal, directly promote trafficking. Governments in both sending and receiving countries that seek to combat trafficking must consider the possibility that, in a globalised world, their own policies contribute directly to the phenomenon they seek to eliminate. The current contradictions in trade policy are a case in point. Economically-marginalised people, particularly women, in developing countries are unable to realise their human right to a decent livelihood in their own country partly due to global inequities in trade. On the one hand, the economic liberalisation promoted by industrialised countries exposes them to competition from imports in local markets. On the other, their own products continue to face trade barriers in the markets of those same industrialised economies. The result is strong pressures in those poor countries to migrate to the industrialised economies in search of the means for livelihood, often becoming victims of trafficking in the process. Simultaneously, deregulation and competition push firms in industrialised economies to search for cheap (often trafficked) labour in labour-intensive and protected sectors such as agriculture and the textile industry, thereby providing a labour market for the same victims of trafficking that their governments are trying to combat. By encouraging women's entry into the paid labour force while simultaneously cutting the social services needed to support women's household and caregiving roles, these economies also create the demand for cheap domestic workers.

However, several demographic and economic changes may eventually encourage a move towards reducing such global inequities. Lower fertility rates, some now persistently below replacement level, combined with the resulting rapid population ageing may oblige industrialised countries to look more favourably on labour migration. Even apart from the direct impact on national labour markets, the prospect of growing proportions of the elderly and very high dependency ratios puts national pension and social security schemes at risk.

There are signs that the preoccupation with economic growth to the virtual exclusion of social impact is under review in some countries, and especially following the financial crises in Asia and Latin America. There is some indication that developing countries which embraced market liberalisation and structural adjustment policies as the road to economic growth—often at the insistence of international financial institutions—are finding that economic growth itself is endangered by the negative social and political impact of those policies.[31] Civil society movements, most notably those struggling for a more equitable form of global trade, are forcing a reconsideration of the balance between social and economic objectives.[32]

Ultimately the problems created by global phenomena such as migration and trafficking require global solutions. In an age that has been marked by a huge upsurge of rhetoric about human rights and women's human rights, such global solutions must include full awareness of, and accountability for, the persistence of and need to combat, gender inequality and discrimination everywhere.

Notes

[1] Durga Ghimire. Presentation to a consultative meeting on Anti-trafficking programmes in South Asia, in Dale Huntington, 'Anti-Trafficking Programs in South Asia: Appropriate Activities, Indicators and Evaluation Methodologies: Summary Report of a Technical Consultative Meeting,' Population Council, New Delhi, March 2002.

[2] Suzanne Williams and Rachel Masika, in *Gender, Trafficking and Slavery*, Oxford, Oxfam 2002; According to one report, it grew almost 50 per cent from 1995 to 2000; see *Financial Times*, 19 March 2001.

[3] Communique on 'Combating Transnational Organised Crime', G-8 Ministerial Conference, Moscow, 19–20 October 1999.

[4] As such it is distinct from human smuggling, which involves would-be migrants who turn to illegal channels to pursue their objectives. The United Nations Protocol on Trafficking in Persons, adopted in November 2000, defines trafficking as: 'the recruitment, transportation, transfer, harbouring or receipt of persons, by means of the threat or use of force or other forms of coercion, of abduction, of fraud, or deception, of the abuse of power or of a position of vulnerability or of the giving or receiving of payments or benefits to achieve the consent of a person having control over another person, for the purpose of exploitation. Exploitation shall include, at a minimum, the exploitation of the prostitution of others or other forms of sexual exploitation, forced labour or services, slavery or practices similar to slavery, servitude or the removal of organs.' This protocol currently has 117 signatories. See 'Recommended Principles and Guidelines on Human Rights and Human Trafficking', Report of the United Nations High Commissioner for Human Rights to the Economic and Social Council E/2002/68/Add.1, 20 May 2002. See also, United Nations, *Women, Peace and Security*. New York, 2002, p. 17.

[5] Cited in US Department of State, 'Victims of Trafficking and Violence Protection Act 2000: Trafficking in Persons Report', Washington, DC, 2005, p. 7.

[6] Ibid., p. 6.

[7] Population movements takes many different forms that can range across temporary and seasonal population movements, voluntary short-term labour migration, voluntary permanent migration that may be arranged independently or facilitated by agents; and various forms of forced movement, including slavery, forced migration and exile, and trafficking in persons.

[8] Human Security Commission, *Human Security Now: Protecting and Empowering People*. New York, 2003, p. 41.

[9] Castles, S. and M. Miller, (1998), *The Age of Migration: International Population Movements in the Modern World*, New York, Guildford Press; R. Cohen,

(1987), *The New Helots: Migrants in the International Division of Labour*, Aldershot, Gower.

[10] Human Security Commission, p. 42.

[11] Therese Blanchet, 'Beyond Boundaries. A Critical Look at Women Labour Migration and the Trafficking Within,' USAID, April 2002.

[12] It should be noted that this shift might be somewhat overestimated. Studies in South Asia have shown that movements of men are assumed to be migration, while movements of women and girls are assumed to involve trafficking. In reality, many men and boys are trafficked, and while women migrant workers are at greater risk, not all women migrants are trafficked. Lorraine Corner, 'A Gender Perspective to Combat Trafficking: An integrated approach to livelihood options for women and girls,' paper presented to UNIFEM seminar on Promoting Gender Equality to Combat Trafficking in Women and Children, Bangkok, 2002.

[13] In 2001, 44 per cent of developed countries and 39 per cent of developing countries had restrictive immigration policies. 'International Migration Report 2002', UN Population Division, New York, 2002.

[14] Cited in US Department of State, 'Trafficking in Human Persons Report, 2004'. See also Asian Development Bank, 'Combating Trafficking of Women and Children in South Asia: Summary Regional Synthesis Paper,' May 2002.

[15] Truong, T.D. (2003a) 'The Human Rights Question in the Global Sex Trade' in K. Arts and P. Mihyo (eds.) *Responding to the Human Rights Deficit: Essays in Honour of Bas de Gaay Fortman*, The Hague, Kluwer Law International; Truong, T.D. (2003b) 'Human Trafficking and Organized Crime' in E.C. Viano, J. Magallanes and L. Bridel (eds.) *Transnational Organized Crime: Myth, Power and Profit*, Durham NC, Carolina Academic Press.

[16] Peter Stalker, 'Workers Without Frontiers'. ILO, Geneva 2000, pp. ix–x.

[17] US Department of State, 'Trafficking in Human Persons Report, 2005', p. 18.

[18] See Patrick A. Taran, and Gloria Moreno-Fontes, 'Getting at the Roots. Stopping Exploitation of Migrant Workers by Organised Crime,' paper presented at international symposium on the UN Convention Against Transnational Organised Crime: Requirements for Effective Implementation, Turin, Italy, 22–23 February 2002, ILO.

[19] United Nations Development Fund for Women (UNIFEM), *Progress of the World's Women 2002, vol. 1: Women, War and Peace*. New York, 2002; United Nations, Division for the Advancement of Women, *Women, Peace and Security*, October 2002.

[20] Report of the UN High Commissioner for Refugees, Geneva, 2002 (E/2002/14).

[21] Report of the Special Rapporteur on violence against women, its causes and consequences (E/CN.4/2001/73; see also United Nations, *Women, Peace and Security*, New York, 2002.

[22] United Nations, *Women, Peace and Security*, p. 29. See also UNIFEM, *Women, War and Peace*, p. 13.

[23] See for example, UNAIDS, UNFPA, UNIFEM, *Women and HIV/AIDS: Confronting the Crisis*, New York, 2004; Vital Voices, Trafficking Alert, Washington, DC, June 2004.

[24] UNIFEM, *Women, War and Peace*, p. 16.

[25] See Coalition Against Trafficking in Women, http://www.catwinternational.org; US Department of States, 'Trafficking in Human Persons Report', 2005, p. 20.

[26] Jean D'Cunha, 'Gender Equality, Human Rights and Trafficking: A Framework for Analysis and Action,' UNIFEM seminar on Promoting Gender Equality to Combat Trafficking in Women and Children, Bangkok, October 2002, p. 8; Corner, 'A Gender Perspective to Combat Trafficking', p. 15. Beginning in the 1990s, women from post-communist countries have been joining the supply of docile brides, competing with Asian women who predominated in the 1980s; Truong, T.D. and Del Rosario, V. (1994), 'Captive Outsiders: Trafficked Women in the Sex Industry and Mail-Order-Brides in the European Union' in J. Wiersma (ed.) *Insiders and Outsiders: On the Making of Europe II*, Pharos, Kampen.

[27] 'Rights—South Asia: Slavery Still a Thriving Trade,' IPS, 29 December 1997.

[28] For a fuller outline, see D'Cunha, 'Gender Equality, Human Rights and Trafficking.'

[29] See Corner, 'A Gender Perspective to Combat Trafficking'.

[30] See for example 'Human Trafficking, Especially of Women and Children in Mozambique: Root Causes and Policy Recommendations', Policy Paper Poverty Series, UNESCO, November 2005, pp. 7–8.

[31] See UNDP, *Making Global Trade Work for People*, New York, 2003, ch. 1.

[32] See UNIFEM, *Progress of the World's Women 2000*, New York, 2000, ch. 6.

6

The Politics and Culture of Care
Some Issues in the Netherlands

CARLA RISSEEUW*

Introduction

Within Europe, there is a contradiction between the progressive image of the Netherlands and its local practice. The country has been portrayed as an overly generous wealthy welfare state with progressive forms of citizenship, evidenced by legislative acts concerning a number of areas such as euthanasia, gay marriages and drug use. Politically, the relatively active civil society, the long history of party-coalitions and tradition of a so-called tripartite ruling have formed an image of tolerance and mutual respect.[1] A close examination of these progressive legislations reveals a nuanced interpretation of the notion of 'citizenship' with practical consequences on gender and race relations. Whereas legislation concerning gay marriage and euthanasia bases itself on the notion of rights and duties between the individual citizen and the state, the notions of rights and duties in the domain of care are displaced from this relationship and sited in 'citizen-to-citizen' relations.

* A longer version of this article was earlier published in the *Journal for Gender Studies*, Ochanumizu University, Tokyo and I thank the editors for allowing the publication of this updated and shortened version. I also want to thank Thanh-Dam Truong, Joyce Outshoorn and Marlein van Raalte for their in-depth comments and support.

Although North European welfare states have been undergoing similar demographic and economic changes[2] that led to reforms and care policies have acquired features of 'citizen-to-citizen' relations, the Dutch experience shows that issues of care have less political visibility and the nuclear family is particularly emphasised. For instance in Scandinavian countries, public debates on private and unpaid caretaking activities have led to gender-neutral forms of public and private care provision. By contrast, in the Netherlands the emerging care demands are taking place in a cultural setting which 'traditionally' has not taken into account either the high numbers of women public and private caretakers as an issue of concern in respect of gender equality policy (also known as *emancipatie politiek*) or the fact that quotidian care needs differs along people's life cycles. In spite of a relatively active civil society, a care policy could seldom enter the public agenda.

The implication of this silence on care is a serious contradiction between different goals of Dutch gender equality policy (in the labour market and at home). Furthermore, the family and traditional gender notions also find their place in migration policy, and can at times affect the citizenship of migrant women in comparison to their male counterparts. This chapter seeks to explain why despite the existence of different feminist political groups (female and male) and semi-political bodies which have actively lobbied within civil society and political parties for progressive citizenship, care issues have not gain a comparable level of public legitimacy as achieved in several other European countries.[3] Yet, roughly in the same time frame, lobby groups for other so-called controversial issues as 'euthanasia' and 'gay-marriage' have achieved success.

Culture and welfare: the Netherlands within Europe

Despite a large population of Jews and Muslims, social historians have argued that 'Christian Humanism' has deeply influenced the shaping of the welfare project within the European states, in which many of the key figures (male) are said to have been of the Catholic faith. (Hornsby-Smith 1999; Papini 1997; van Kersbergen

1995). In the Netherlands the Catholic population was estimated to be just over 50 per cent during much of history and van Kersbergen (1995: 184) argues that:

> the notion of solidarity as harmony is an intrinsic component of the Christian democratic tradition and it alternately paraphrased as 'integration, compromise, accommodation and pluralism'.

The Catholic tradition was further marked by a strong element of charity and social service (Coman 1977: 47–59; Whyte 1981; van Kersbergen 1995: 146) and held explicit ideas on the dignity of an individual being firmly linked to 'labour', for which 'one' had to earn 'a just wage to maintain a family'. These premises were coupled with views on the 'proper' role of women as mothers. Parental rights in the education of children were conceived as paramount, over those of the state. These values can be traced in much of the history of Dutch politics and debate.

By contrast the Protestant faith is historically credited for promoting issues of secularisation and individualisation and for laying the base of what is now termed an un-gendered notion of citizenship (van Kersbergen 1995: 194–5; Hornsby-Smith 1999: 176). These two faiths have led to markedly differing 'family policies'. Broadly speaking, Catholic traditions are said to have relatively extensive policies of family support, while Protestant or mixed (Protestant and Catholic) states have less explicit family policies. In the Catholic case family allowances tend to be conceived as part of the wage package, while in Protestant states one finds more individual taxation and the most extensive childcare provisions within Europe.

Next to the dominant religious factor, the Socialists and also the Liberals added to what became known as the phenomenon of 'Pillarisation', which characterised Dutch society and politics. In the first half of the 20th century exponents of these articulate ideological divisions or pillars of Protestants, Catholics, Socialists and Liberals had their own forms of organisation, including specific religion-based schools, organisations etc. Therefore several scholars have argued that during this period the specific character of the

Dutch state was built on ideology rather than on nationalism (Cox 1993).

Within this setting Cox points to the specific culture of political decision-making, characterised by the often unseen political ideological struggles within a consensus world of many diverse Dutch corporatist bodies involved in advising, implementing, and supervising welfare programmes (1993: 29, 45)—a way of governing which often excluded public accountability (*binnenkamers-politiek*).

Over time the culture of accommodation of political interests led to the well-known Roman-Red coalition governments, rather than a political culture of articulated party opposition. Slowly the Socialists consolidated their influence on Dutch politics. Their most famous political leader, Willem Drees (in power from 1948 to 1956), managed to pass the law on a universal old age pension, herewith firmly extracting universal citizen-rights from charity and welfare alone. It is relevant to realise that historically religious forces in the Netherlands were not focused on the creation of a welfare state. They gave preference to the welfare needs of citizens being supplied by non-state organisations (Cox 1993: 206).

Within the often unseen (by the public) power struggle between religious and socialist elements in government, the Dutch welfare state emerged later than in surrounding countries, and became full blown in the 1960s when Pillarisation began to fade (SCP 2000: Introduction).

All over western Europe, including the Netherlands, this period was marked by many forms of protest and challenge. Religions lost a substantial part of their support, while new political insights were translated into new political parties, new social movements and changing cultural lifestyles, especially of the young, leading to substantial generational conflict.

Nevertheless the culture of consensus remained part of Dutch politics, which continues to be ruled by coalitions. Nor have the four former ideological pillars disappeared, although the religious groupings merged and other parties gained prominence. Since 1902 the Dutch political scene only witnessed two governments

(1994–98; 1998–2002) in which the Christians were forced into opposition. It is during these two governmental periods that, hesitatingly, legislation based solely on citizenship, rather than on 'a citizenship seen through the gendered matrix of the nuclear family,' was proposed and at times passed. During the second period legislation was passed on 'euthanasia' and 'gay-marriage'. However, it was also the period in which the first legislation was passed on what was, till then, unknown in the Netherlands: 'care-leave'. It involved the right of a citizen to take periodic leave from work in order to look after someone very ill or dying. Here however, citizenship was not the final criterion, but remained seen through a perspective of the nuclear family.

Due to this Pillarised nature of the society and politics the Netherlands has generally been viewed as a hybrid welfare state, falling between the social democratic and corporate types (SCP 2000: 46). In the early 1990s the Dutch system combined universal target group provisions (particularly the social insurance schemes), generous conditions and high funding costs of the social democratic model with the low incentive to work, low female job-market participation and protection of achieved standards of living of the corporatist mode. The strong internal religious, societal and political divisions which ruled through negotiation and coalition provided a certain inward looking element in Dutch society, which at first glance could remain unnoticed.

The following sections will look into how this chequered political background and the format of political consensus, shaped the policies on the care of elders and the emergence of the concept of 'care-leave'.

The shift from public senior residencies to home care services in the Netherlands

In the 1950s and 60s, the government aimed for a citizen-centred care policy on society's seniors, devoid of family as a direct source of care. Many institutional homes were built during this period as well as in the 1970s, reflecting the usual divisions of society in various religious and income groupings. By the end of the 1960s voices went up in protest that the cost of providing an independent serviced home would be too high in the long run. As in other western European countries the government policy slowly changed from one claiming top priority for joint senior residences, to one which prioritised elders to remain independent in their own homes. Entry criteria based on failing health and lack of family support emerged. By this time the high pressure on post-War housing targets was also much reduced.

The difference to this overall European development in the Netherlands was two-fold. One was the initial straight out policy involving the right for all to enter an old-age home. Second, once policy shifted to home care services instead of joint homes, the accompanying financial scope was not expanded. Denmark for instance, did shift its total financial budget for residential institutions to home care (Hansen 1992), and with Sweden and Denmark spent the highest percentage of the GNP on home care in Europe (Rostgaard and Fridberg 1998). Other countries tried hard to cut down on home care budgets, although they were not always successful. During the 1980s home care budgets rose in nearly all European countries (England, France and Germany), but in the Netherlands, they were reduced several times (Kremer 2000: 38; Tester 1996; Goewie and Keune 1996).

Next to a decreasing budget, one sees the growing emphasis on mobilising family care. By 1994, the government policy was explicit on the involving of 'the family' in care (Tweede Kamer der Staten Generaal: 1994–95). Most of the care needed was to be supplied by the 'direct surroundings of the patient', later known by the term *Mantelzorg* (Kremer 2000: 43). Only when this help was inadequate could professional help be claimed. This shift of policy moved the Dutch State firmly away from the initial social-democratic orientation to a more corporate model of welfare. In 1994, private home care undertook four times as much care as the government home care services did. Further commercial care services were developed at a high speed. In 1997 the commercial care services encompassed 33 per cent of all care given to those over 60 years of age. In Great Britain, a country classified as a

129

liberal state, comparable figures during this period amount to 21 per cent (Walker and Maltby 1997).

This rapid switch in care policy from a social democratic to a corporate welfare state, while also developing a strong liberal/commercial component, make the Netherlands earn its classification of 'a hybrid welfare state'. As a Dutch feminist put it: Home care was not to be a citizenship-right in the Netherlands (Knijn 1999).

One consequence of this political shift has been a reduction in quality of care services (home care, hospitals and GP facilities), which continues to receive much public criticism.[4] On the whole it seems that the full contradiction between the past shift in policy towards involving 'a gendered notion of family' in care services, especially in home caretaking, and a labour policy of promoting women to participate in the labour market, does not seem to have been met with serious analysis. The specific Dutch policy trajectory in this respect becomes more apparent when compared to that of other European Welfare States (SCP 2000: Introduction 1–61). While in the Netherlands 44 per cent of home care is primarily undertaken by 'family', in Denmark 44 per cent of it is primarily undertaken by home care services (OECD 1994; Kremer 2000: 45). In Holland 75 per cent of private home carers are (older), relatively lowly educated women. (Dykstra 1997, cited in Kremer ibid: 21). Sweden follows a comparable development to Denmark. Family is only involved at their own will, while the partner is tapped by government services. These two countries have the most well developed citizen right to care in Europe. (Rostgaard and Fridberg 1998, cited in Kremer 2000: 46). England, a liberal welfare state, followed another trajectory. Here several grass root women's organisations supporting home carers and the right to financial support, resulted in the provision of tax cuts for home carers and forms of financial compensation.

The development of the provision of care-leave

Next to the right to receive care, is the citizen's right to provide care for others.

This new provision of care-leave was passed after extensive debate during the cabinet period of 1998–2002. At the time there was only a 1998 legislation on the possibility of interrupting one's employment track, for a period of six months for care or education.

This leave was obtained, once the employer's consent was acquired and a jobless candidate temporarily replaced the leave-taker. The latter received a small financial compensation (no salary). If leave was required to take care of a terminally ill person, the replacement requirement was dropped (*Wet op de Loopbaanonderbreking*).

This law partly copied a comparable Belgium law of 1985 with the same name, but which held no specific leave conditions. Employees had the right to five periods of six months leave maximum, while one period could be extended to a year. The Belgium law further dropped the condition of the employer's approval, provided not more than one per cent of employees took leave simultaneously. In the case of required home care, the right of the employee was non-negotiable.

In comparison to this Belgium law, the Dutch version did not meet with much success. In 1999 for example 205 people in the Netherlands took such leave. By contrast, in Belgium approximately 50,000 people yearly take this leave (Kremer 2000: 80). In both cases the majority of leave-takers are women. This is due to the low financial compensation involved and the fact that women are second earners in most homes. Germany and the Scandinavian countries both have more elaborate provisions (Kremer 2000; SCP 2000: 1–61). The Netherlands is literally surrounded by countries that have developed leave and care-leave facilities to a varying but greater extent.

The Care-Leave Act explicitly addressed the right to care and followed the above-described law. Certain progress is noted, such as a 70 per cent refund of the salary, which is a major shift, aimed at attracting men as well as women. This leave, however, can be taken only for ten days and requires the employer's permission, although the latter needs to specify objections. Any loss of premium security payments during this period is shared by the employer and the state. But certain problems remain. For one, a period of ten days is often too short. Further the law stipulates that leave can only be taken for illness of family members with whom one shares a house at the moment of requesting leave. This usually means the partner and living-in children. It excludes parents or children living elsewhere or neighbours, friends, non-married partners. Here one sees the notion of nuclear family clashing with the right of citizenship.

As an alternative strategy the law could, for instance, not have brought in the criterion of 'family' at all and proposed the option for each citizen to register two or three other citizens for whom care-leave would be taken, should the need arise. Administratively this would be simpler than the current policy, which requires inspection of actual numbers of household members.

Nevertheless, it is from an economic angle that the stipulation of 'household' over 'nuclear family' makes sense in this context. As Dutch households currently consist of only one-third of nuclear families, one-third of partners and one-third of single people, the condition of 'shared household' substantially curbs potential costs. Demographers expect families to grow even smaller in the future. One could call this narrow focus aimed at budget saving politically shortsighted, in relation to the high pressure on care services and the predicted future of rising numbers of single residencies. Allowing citizens to take care of each other is often cheaper than institutional facilities. One can conclude that the Dutch care-policy has regularly blurred the lines of 'family' and 'citizenship', adding 'household' to the stir, when attempting to curb the costs of state care.

In spite of globalisation and change, gender biases are also noted in the Dutch case. Both national and European sources confirm the same picture. While it has become commonplace to speak of two income earners per family and statistics show rapid increases in numbers of working women, these figures are deceptive as even a low number of working hours, as low as one hour per week, is counted as paid employment. Women's working hours are few and 'by far the shortest in Europe' (SCP 2000: 220; CBS report 2002; OECD 2002). Recently the Dutch Central Bureau of Statistics (CBS 2002) characterised the country as having a 'breadwinner plus' model, as 85.5 per cent of the families running on more than one income, in practice relied on the income of the male partner, which the OECD confirmed (2002).

Further from a comparative perspective, the country has a relatively underdeveloped system of crèches and after-school arrangements, leaving Holland far behind France, Belgium and Scandinavia (SCP 2000: 61, 224). This curbs the possibilities of women seeking work. Further and maybe of even more importance are the taxation policies and subsidies which privilege the (male) breadwinner in the Netherlands, and are estimated to involve more than 8.6 milliard Euro per year (Bruijn and Verhaar 1999, cited in Kremer, ibid: 21). Until very recently taxation measures made it extremely uneconomical for wives of employed husbands to seek work. In comparison: in Denmark 76 per cent of women undertake paid work, while in the Netherlands and Austria, this figure is 65 per cent, mostly part-time and in the lowest paid jobs (OECD 2002). The OECD explains the relatively low percentage of parents making use of childcare facilities in Holland (20 per cent), as not only due to inadequate facilities, but also to a cultural outlook which centralises nuclear family life and exclusive motherhood, and decreases her individual financial security. According to research, Dutch men's contribution to household tasks is shifting very slowly and forms a marked contrast to the more equal degree of task sharing between spouses in Sweden (SCP 2000: 61). In this context the Dutch national social and cultural planning body points to one of the consequences of merging of political and cultural factors. Combining career and family poses specific difficulties in Holland, resulting in young Dutch women having the highest age of nearly 32 years at the birth of their first child worldwide (SCP 2000: 60–61).

So in spite of globalisation, and (in particular) the formation of the European Union, the traditional, nuclear family form of the male breadwinner and the motherly wife is still a reality under a thin varnish of change and is reflected in policy-thinking in more than one way. It has no doubt contributed to the perceived lack of urgency in developing a practice of a gender-neutral and non-familial based citizenship, in spite of the notion of citizenship being an old and well-defended one in the Netherlands.

Gender and family in the Netherlands: a historical perspective

This section will discuss some cultural and historical factors which have influenced the cultural meaning of gender and family in the Netherlands. Viewed within Europe, the current picture seems to reflect the past. The Netherlands was historically marked by a relatively low female involvement in paid work. Between 1900 and 1940, the percentage of working (un-)married women was 20–25 per cent of the total population, compared to 30 per cent in England and 35–40 per cent in France (Tilly and Scott 1978: 70; De Regt 1984). From 1870 to the Second World War, the birthrate had a slower rate of decline than neighbouring countries, and divorce figures also consistently scored lower than surrounding countries (de Regt 1993b: 222).

Historians gave several reasons for this specific gendered demographic development: the relatively high wages paid to men in the first half of the 20th century and the strong presence of the so-called 'homely ideology', stressing the female task of creating a 'homely and nurturing environment'. Further, 'Pillarisation' facilitated religious influence on gender and family norms. The country not having been involved in the First World War meant that family life was exposed to less change than neighbouring countries. Dutch women, for instance, did not undertake employment and factory work after their husbands went to war.

It was in the first half of the 20th century, that the Netherlands was marked by the formation of the so-called bourgeois, nuclear family form[5] (*gezin*).

Social and especially family historians like Ali de Regt (1993a) have described the emergence of the bourgeois Christian morality with its notion of decency (*fatsoen*): the strict separate responsibilities of the breadwinner and his housewife (with a relatively strong sense of motherhood), which slowly developed into a cultural pattern of a homely, privatised family life, in connection to a tradition of religious associations and involvement in the neighbourhood 'to keep up its standards' (de Regt 1993b: 222). De Regt describes the newly emerging society at the end of the 19th century as 'A Moral Nation', in which Pillarisation played an important role. Working class families were influenced to incorporate the bourgeois, middle class moral, implying a certain change in lifestyle involving shifts in housing, privacy, dealing with the body as well as an exclusive linking of sexuality to procreation. Sexuality outside marriage was severely condemned. Further the so-called Morality Laws were passed in 1911, which can be seen as the culmination of the Christian morality offensive. With these laws, brothels became prohibited as Christian men should be able to 'control' themselves, followed by punishments for abortions, contraception and homosexuality for men and women. Sevenhuijsen (1987) provided an insightful study on the 1870–1900 debate on fatherhood responsibilities beyond marriage. At the time the strict Christian convictions provided the feminist movement with the momentum to hold men responsible for their non-legitimate offspring. This movement was not fully successful, but the public positions taken by leading male contributors provide a fascinating insight into this historical period's 'habitus' of a non-disputed male superiority, which to its surprise had to articulate its justification. The political arena of the early 20th century was coloured by this religious offensive, including a greater state involvement in family affairs.

Mainly after the 1950s, but slower than in neighbouring countries, social change emerged in the Netherlands. As a large overarching theme this change involved the demand for a greater social space and liberty for citizens to shape personal lives and relationships. This implied a renegotiation of 'family morality', in which marriage was gradually reshaped and the undisputed male headship of marriage was countered (but not overtaken) by a notion of partnership.

It was only after World War II, in the financially wealthy period of the 1960s, that this process culminated in a period of geographical job mobility and major sociocultural change, including the so-called 'Sexual Revolution', followed by the feminist struggle for abortion rights and birth control methods (Outshoorn 1980) and the Gay Movement.

These cultural changes did not imply equality between the sexes. For instance it was only in 1957 that women were accorded legal and independent property rights within marriage (van den Bergh 1999). Only since 1985 has Dutch citizenship become independent of a woman's marriage, a right long held by their male counterparts (Everard and Aerts 2002: 225). Finally the extensive financial support to the (male) breadwinner within the Dutch wage-earning and taxation system is the clearest and—until very recently—completely undisputed heritage of this specific sociocultural construct.

On the surface this seems to contrast with the Dutch long history of relatively egalitarian citizenship. But on closer scrutiny women, as well as strangers have held conditional entry during this same history of egalitarianism.

Citizenship in the Netherlands

This section goes into the historical development of citizenship and its accessibility to women and also outsiders. Western European welfare states all incorporate a historical developed notion of citizenship. In the Netherlands, the notion of citizenship is traced to the early Middle Ages, where it signified membership of an organised political community of a town, not a (rural) landlord (Kloek and Tilmans 2002: 2). Many of these early citizens were businessmen, who succeeded in making their living outside the rural realm of an aristocracy and its hierarchical labour relations. Historian Plei (2002)[6] describes the typical businessman of this early time as a clever adventurer of a 'lower' social background, who through the successful claiming of his strict individual autonomy shaped the society of his time. While citizenship initially referred only to a town-membership with rights and duties, in the later 17th century citizenship came to imply membership to a political community of a city, republic or monarchy. During this process certain citizens gained more control over town regulations than others, leading to a practice of inequality emerging and a growing prominence of established families with the larger business firms, who to a large extent controlled the towns. By then, 'citizenship' had acquired a legal status, which contrasted to the position of 'strangers': newcomers to town without citizenship.

How did one acquire citizenship? Men inherited it from their fathers; women obtained it through marriage to a citizen (and could lose it because of divorce or widowhood) and thirdly, it could be purchased. Citizenship could also be lost through 'unworthy behaviour'.

This start and growth of the concept of citizenship shaped the later 19th century form of national citizenship. The latter emerged out of a relatively egalitarian political tradition and an increasing prominence of morality on how the citizen should behave. It was further characterised by a tradition of conflict solving between citizens through negotiation and (legal) arbitration, rather than through the military conquest of aristocratic leaders. This relatively inclusive form of moral citizenship prevailed over hierarchy, military power or economic means. In this specific history violent shifts of power were absent and contributed to a form of manhood not characterised by militarism.

Historically, it was only during the 1960s—marked as it was by cultural change and lessening of religious influence—that for the first time 'citizenship' (*burgerschap*) acquired a mainstream negative evaluation on its projected bourgeois qualities of 'reasonableness', sedateness and lack of initiative and/or courage (*burgerlijkheid*).

But, however egalitarian in its source, Dutch citizenship from the start included forms of exclusion towards women and those who were termed 'strangers'. After substantial (feminist) struggle, Dutch women finally achieved the right to vote in 1919, which also involved a step forward in realising their full citizenship. Before this date, the women's right to citizenship had remained ambiguous and prone to shifting interpretations (Everard and Aerts 2002).[7] The upcoming of religious and socialist organisations of the 19th century likewise emphasised women's role of motherhood and homemaking (ibid: 212).

In relation to the issue of 'strangers', Jewish and also Catholic newcomers to town were provided registration rather than citizenship. Acquiring the latter usually involved high costs, excluded ruling powers, and was non-transferable to offspring (ibid: 183).

In view of the current controversial issues of immigration and a multicultural society in the Netherlands, this start of the relation between citizenship and outsiders is worth mentioning. A well-known Somali-born political party member, Ayaan Hirshi Ali, was one of the first to succeed in bringing a political urgency to the existing unequal citizenship between migrant husbands and wives. If divorced within three years of arrival, the husband has the right to stay, while the wife has to return to her 'home country'. From the same set of unquestioned assumptions no policy was developed to support migrant women's entry in the job market nor to educational facilities. Domestic violence remained a secluded family affair. (Only in 2003 a parliamentary proposal was made to enforce change in this context). Here the traditional Dutch values on the centrality of family and the gendered male prominence, left migrant women in a marked unequal position vis-à-vis their men as well as access to Dutch citizenship. The dominant political view was one of respecting 'culture', 'religion' and 'family', resonating earlier formed traditional values and quite successfully blurring the fact that rights to citizenship remained secondary to migrant women. In this way the gender-neutral concept of citizenship surfaced its resilient gendered and family-based practice once again.

Care policy, citizenship and the continuity of the notion of nuclear family

In recent years, the concept of 'care' as a theoretical concept has gained the attention of feminist authors. Western feminists have criticised the implications of Euro-American (state) ideologies which viewed 'care' as a private, gendered and above all an apolitical issue, undervalued next to the over-evaluation of public accomplishment and autonomy combined with a far right image of care receivers as helpless and pitiful.

For example the work of Joan Tronto (1993) offered a first definition and discussion of 'care'.[8] In the Netherlands, Selma Sevenhuijsen (1998) has developed the issue, while the American economist Nancy Folbre (2001) strived to 'globalise' the political component of care: If capitalism is considered global, what global social obligations are to accompany it? The yearly Human Development Report (UNDP 1999) has recently also for the first time taken the concept of 'care' on board in an attempt to integrate it within its development goals.

All these authors/publications point to forms of systematic misrecognition operating in the field of 'care'. Usually the powerful do not participate in actual caregiving tasks, while their tapping of care services remains simple to realise. Tronto termed this a form of 'privileged irresponsibility', which can take the form of 'sincere' ignorance (Tronto 1993: 120–2). Wealthy, privileged sections of societies and, often but not only, men are privileged in this case.

The Dutch welfare state developed substantial forms of security for citizens, based on its relatively egalitarian notion of citizenship. Currently several forms of universal benefits and allowances stand as proof of this inclusive heritage. But during periods of (perceived) economic downturn, historical and cultural gendered notions of family have provided the accepted morality from which to legitimate deviations from this egalitarian perspective on citizenship. For instance as most social benefits are built up through paid employment, one finds the (traditionally male) breadwinner gaining access to extensive financial privileges and security.

Further as was discussed, since the 1980s state care services relatively smoothly shifted their orientation from citizen-support to forms of conditional citizen-support—in absence of family only. Government policy thus successfully curbed state costs in public care systems, while stimulating commercial and/or unpaid family care. In practice 75 per cent of this family care is provided by older, lower educated women. It is relevant to realise that women as home carers are not targeted on the basis of their sex, but as (unemployed) family members.

Simultaneously however in an era of globalisation and change, the Dutch government emphasises the need for increased female paid labour participation. Policy reports and research regularly emphasise the (coming) care gap, which will especially affect the lower income sections of society (Oldersma and Outshoorn forthcoming; Timmermans 2004). Timmermans predicts the care gap for elders to be at its peak from 2020 onwards, which is currently met with a lack of government planning, while no bilateral agreements are foreseen to facilitate the entry of international migrant care workers, as one finds in South European countries.

As has been described the social fabric of Dutch society changed enormously in the 20th century, especially after the 1960s. During Pillarisation and the Christian moral offensive of the end of the 19th century, the 'nuclear family' gained central importance. During the economic expansion of the 1960s there was a culmination of the contrary swing. It aimed at a private domain from the state in family and in 'private relationships', which could exclude marriage and official family altogether. Sexual liberation became paramount, probably understandable, after the former era of tight Puritanism. Marriage also changed: the undisputed male head of family in practice shifted to a negotiated headship. Further alternatives to the traditional marriage were formed in the so-called 'couples living together' and 'couples living apart together'. Next the gay rights activists started their assertion, creating yet another form of 'partnership'—later marriage, in the new age. Divorce and serial monogamy became more acceptable. The period between 1960–1990 therefore experienced a remarkable shift of households: the 'modern nuclear family' which had formed a three-fourth majority of households up to the 1950s, shrank to one-third of all households by 1988 (Zwaan 1993: 258, table 417). In this process of change, the ideological concept of 'nuclear family' (*gezin*) itself initially became viewed as a relic from the narrow-minded, petit bourgeois past—without relevance to the modern era (v.d. Brink 1997).

Several decades later, from 1995 onwards however, due to growing atheism, drug problems and crime among youth, the issue of family returned on the political agenda and societal debate (v.d. Brink 1997). Some promoted a return to traditional family values, which was firmly contested by others. Within this debate the concept of family proved a powerful metaphor, which due to its cultural strength was prone to be used ahistorically. Authors often acclaimed the (nuclear) family to be the deeply natural form of living together, unchanged since the Stone Age. Support for this view was even found in the animal world. Its specific, resilient end-19th and early-20th century sociocultural construct of nuclear family was often overlooked. A fairly monocultural society tended to facilitate such a perception. Thus some time after the 1960s momentum of change, the 'natural' family was (again) seen as nuclear, monogamous and lifelong, with economically dependent wives primarily concerned with motherhood and care, and men primarily interacting with men in the public world, while offering protection to their dependent wife and children at home. Little or no recollection was made to the pre-bourgeois and pre-industrial era of agriculture and shared work activities of husbands and wives or to more extended family forms, as were customary in non-urbanised parts of the country.[9]

During the 1990s increasing work pressures, job mobility and an ageing population, made the issue of care provisions—both public and private—rise rapidly on the political horizon, but this process was not accompanied by political recognition. It is the temporarily outlawed specific, historic form of nuclear family, returned to the debate in the 1990s debate as a 'natural' (and universal) family form, which explains much of the Dutch government's successful appeal to a non-citizenship-based model of family care, which successfully curbed state costs.[10]

Further the lack of perceived urgency in the past and future planning is an example of the earlier mentioned and historically grown systematic misrecognition or 'privileged irresponsibility', as Tronto termed it in relation to care. The extensive feminist analyses of Dutch care policy, however perceptive, on the whole remained without serious response from mainstream politics and policy-making (Outshoorn 2002; Kremer 2000; Knijn 1999).[11]

Research on gender and care in the Netherlands therefore continues to be a relevant issue, manifesting more societal insights than one initially would expect. In relation to gendered care provisions and their planning, government policies have reflected a remarkable tenacity to hold on to a (reinvented) 'tradition' in which women somehow 'take care', without the domain of care requiring much further domestic and/or political reflection. If situated along the Amazon instead of the Rhine, the Dutch would no doubt have been applauded for their ability to retain their way of life and outlook, while surrounded by forces of change.

And maybe indeed this is a central question: How did they do it? In a recent European Value Study (1999–2000) all countries reflected (slightly) differing attitudes between men and women and their priorities to achieve within public life and/or work. In comparison Dutch men indicated a marked higher attraction to public achievement than Dutch women. But overall both sexes in the Netherlands held the lowest score of all European countries studied. Both men and women reported to prioritise their home(ly) life over career as well as a public goal, to a far greater degree than was found in countries such as England, Spain, Portugal, Belgium and the Scandinavian countries (van Luijn and Iedema 2004). It is tempting to see this specific score as a persistent reflection of Dutch sociocultural history as is also expressed in its extensive breadwinner subsidies and articulate views on exclusive and full-time motherhood.

Apart from care receivers/providers and related policy documents, only the policy-maker him/herself seems to have still remained unstudied. Such a research focus seems long overdue, as it could not only provide insights into blind spots in care policy making, but also contribute to an analysis of the sociocultural setting in which such policy seems so effortlessly shaped.

Notes

[1] The government, the employers' and employees' organisational bodies, local organisations and movements, next to a wide political spectrum of political parties (15); and media reflecting the various religious and political groupings.

[2] For example: (1) the rapidly rising numbers of ageing citizens coupled with underdeveloped facilities of public care, and (2) the increasing pressure of paid work for growing numbers of (female) citizens, which reduces the time availability for private caretaking in an environment of under-resourced care services including childcare.

[3] When comparing recent percentages of government funded 'Home Care' to seniors in different European countries, the Dutch score (9.5 per cent) is markedly lower than Denmark (24 per cent) and Sweden (16.6 per cent), (Kremer 2000: 37). Similarly its childcare arrangements still hamper women's ability to join the labour market (Bettio and Plantenga 2004).

[4] The media regularly highlight falling standards within institutional senior care, while in a recent major survey, 90 per cent of the population indicated a fear to land up in them (SCP 2004: 444).

[5] Dutch has a specific concept for the specific nuclear family form of husband, wife and children: *het gezin*. This term is widely used and carries a different meaning from the word *familie*, which involves a larger bilateral sense of kin, in which both sets of parents are included. The latter are not part of the first construct of *gezin*, which contributes to the explanation of the research finding that Holland is marked by relatively strong family norms, while care of one's elders is at the same time conceived of primarily as the state's responsibility (Bettio and Plantenga 2004). In urban Holland it already has been the practice for centuries that elders, widows live alone and separate from their offspring. (Stavenuijter 1996)

[6] Plei, H. 2002. Poorters en Burgers in laatmiddeleeuwse bronnen, in 'Burger, een geschiedenis van het begrip "Burger" in de Nederlanden van de Middeleeuwen tot de 21ste eeuw', by J. Kloek and K. Tilmans, (eds.), Amsterdam, Amsterdam University Press.

[7] Women acquired citizenship through marriage and could lose it after separation or death of their spouse. Single women were accorded temporary citizenship on the basis of their employment. Women with citizenship found their status adjusted to that of their husbands. If widows retained citizenship after the death of their spouse on the basis of shared business, they could lose it at remarriage. Only during two short historical periods was equal citizenship for the sexes articulated with a certain degree of success. The first period was influenced by the French Revolution in 1798, and the second period by the socialist movement of the late 19th century. For further analysis see: Everard and Aerts, 2002.

8 'We suggest caring to be viewed as a special activity that includes everything that we do to maintain, continue and repair our "world" so that we can live in it as well as possible. That world includes our bodies, our selves and our environment, all of which we seek to interweave in a complex, life-sustaining web.' (Tronto 1993: 103).

9 In relation to care this nuclear family form excludes the day-to-day care for one's elders, who in their turn lived in their own nuclear family unit. Therefore in spite of close-knit family life, the care of elders tends to be perceived as mainly an issue of state concern. This in contrast with the close-knit southern European family forms. (Bettio and Plantenga 2004)

10 Further the political choice of leaving arrangements of childcare and care-leave to negotiations between employer and employee, coupled with the slow speed of dismantling the breadwinner advantages, culminate in a successful strategy of weighing the new issues down, instead of pushing them forward with forceful state legislation.

11 New legislation on (care-) leave was passed in 2005. But progress should not be overestimated. Ambiguity remains in relation to how care for one's elder kin will be facilitated. Furthermore in order to curb future financial flows, in 2004 the major pension funds have halved the pension entitlement to the remaining partner after death of the main breadwinner (Nieuw Rotterdamse Courant, 25 September 2004). This new arrangement initially only required the main breadwinner's signature as proof that the couple was informed. It was only after public debate, mainly provoked by public opinion through the media, that eventually this arrangement was altered to require the signature of both partners to ensure the partner's awareness of this significant shift. Without this measure, widows without independently built up pensions—currently still the majority—would be the unwitting victims of such policy. The initial policy shift cannot be fully grasped without an understanding of the historical context of the sociocultural gendered meaning of the Dutch nuclear family and its breadwinner.

References

Bettio, F. and J. Plantenga. 2004. 'Comparing Care Regimes in Europe'. *Feminist Economics*. March 10.1. pp. 85–113.

Brink, van der, Gabriel. 1997. *'Hoge Eisen, Ware Liefde, de opkomst van een nieuw gezinsideaal in Nederland'*. Utrecht: NIZW.

Bruijn, J. and O. Verhaar. 1999. *Waar blijven de financiën voor een nieuwe zorginfrastructuur? Jaarboek Emancipatie, Wie zorgt in de 21ste eeuw?* Den Haag: Elsevier.

Centraal Bureau voor de Statistiek. 2002. *Yearly Report 2002*. The Hague: CBS.

Coman, P. 1977. *Catholics and the Welfare State*. London: Longman.

Cox, Robert. 1993. *The Development of the Dutch Welfare State, From Worker's*

Insurance to Universal Entitlement. Pittsburgh/London: University of Pittsburgh Press.

Dykstra, P. 1997. *Employment and Caring.* Working Paper 1997/7. Den Haag: NIDI.

Everard, Myriam and Mieke De Burgeres Aerts. 2002. 'Geschiedenis van een politiek begrip' in *The Invisible Heart, Economics and Family Values.* eds. Joost Kloek and Nancy Folbre. New York: New York Press.

Folbre, Nancy. 2001. *The Invisible Heart, Economics and Family Values.* New York: New York Press.

Goewie, R. and C. Keune. 1996. *Naar een algemeen aanvaarde standaard. Opvattingen en normen over de inzet van gezinsverzorging.* Utrecht: Verwey-Jonker Instituut.

Hansen, F.K. 1992. *Social Services in Denmark: Consolidated Report 1990–1992.* Kopenhagen: Casa.

Hornsby-Smith, Michael. 1999. 'The Catholic Church and Social Policy in Europe' in *Welfare and Culture in Europe: Towards a New Paradigm in Social Policy.* eds. P. Chamberlayne, A. Cooper, R. Freeman and M. Rustin. London/Philadelphia: Jessica Kingsley Publishers.

Kloek, Joost and Karin Tilmans. 2002. *Burger, een geschiedenis van het begrip 'burger' in de Nederlanden van de Middeleeuwen tot de 21ste eeuw.* Amsterdam: Amsterdam University Press.

Knijn, Trudie. 1999. Strijdende zorglogica's in de kinderopvang en de thuiszorg in *Geregelde gevoelens, Collective Arrangementen en de intieme leefwereld.* C. Brinkgreve and van P. Lieshout. Elsevier/De Tijdstroom: Maarsen.

Kremer, Monique. 2000. *Geven en Claimen, Burgerschap en informele zorg in Europees perspectief.* Utrecht: NIZW.

OECD. 1994. 'Caring for frail elderly people.' *New Directions in Care.* 14. Paris: OECD.

———. 2002. *Babies and Bosses.* Paris: OECD.

Oldersma, J. and J. Outshoorn. forthcoming. *The home care gap: neoliberalism, feminism and the state in the Netherlands.*

Outshoorn, Joyce. 1980. *De Politieke Strijd Rondom de Abortuswetgeving in Nederland 1969-1989.* Amsterdam: Vuga.

———. 2002. 'Gendering the "Graying of Society": a discourse analysis of the care gap'. *Public Administration Review.* March/April. vol. 62. no. 2. pp. 185–95.

Papini, R. 1997. *The Christian Democrat International.* London: Rowman and Littlefield.

Regt, de Ali. 1984: 'Arbeiders, burgers en boeren; gezinsleven in de negentiende eeuw' in *Family, Huwelijk en Gezin.* ed. T. Zwaan. Meppel: Boom. pp. 193–218.

———. 1993a. *Geld en Gezin, Financiële en Emotionele relaties tussen Gezinsleden.* Amsterdam: Boom.

———. 1993b. Het Ontstaan van het 'moderne gezin' 1900–1950. In *Familie, Huwelijk en Gezin.* ed. T. Zwaan Amsterdam/Heerlen: Boom/Open Universiteit. pp. 219–239.

Rostgaard, T. and T. Fridberg. 1998. *Caring for Children and Older People: A Comparison of European Policies and Practices.* Kopenhagen: The Danish National Institute of Social Research.

Sevenhuijsen, Selma. 1987. *De order van het Vaderschap, Politieke Debatten over ongehuwd moederschap, afstamming en het huwelijk in Nederland, 1870–1900.* Amsterdam: IISG.

———. 1998. *Citizenship and the Ethics of Care: Feminist Considerations on Justice, Morality and Politics.* London/New York: Routledge.

Social and Cultural Planning Bureau (SCP). 2000. *The Netherlands in a European Perspective.* Social and Cultural Report 2000. The Hague: Social and Cultural Planning Bureau.

———. 2004. In the Zicht van de Toekomst. Social and Cultural Report 2004. The Hague: Social and Cultural Planning Bureau.

Stavenuiter, M. 1996. 'Last years of life: changes in the living and working arrangements of elderly people in Amsterdam in the second half of the nineteenth century'. *Continuity and Change.* 11.2. pp. 217–242.

Tester, S. 1996. *Community Care for Older People; A Comparative Perspective.* London/ Basingstoke: Macmillan.

Tilly, Louise and Joan Scott. 1978. *Women, Work and the Family.* Rhinehart and Winston. New York: Holt.

Timmermans J. and I. Woittiez. 2004. *Verpleging en verzorging verklaard.* SCP.

Tronto, Joan. 1993. *Moral Boundaries, A Political Argument for an Ethic of Care.* London: Routledge.

Tweede Kamer der Staten Generaal: 1994–1995. 'Gezond en Wel in het kader van het volksgezondheidsbeleid 1995–1998' in Tweede Kamer, vergaderjaar 1994–1995.

UNDP. 1999. *Human Development Report.* UN Development Programme.

van den Berg, G. 1999. Gehuwde vrouwen en (on) vermogen in *Honderd jaar vrouwen recht in Nederland.* R. Holtmaat. Nemesis. Tijdschrift voor Vrouwen en Recht. Tjeenk. Willink. Deventer.

van Kersbergen, Kees. 1995. *Social Capitalism: A Study of Christian Democracy and the Welfare State.* London: Routledge.

van Luijn, H. and J. Iedema. 2004. *Willen Nederlandse vrouwen wel carrière maken?* in Hollandse Taferelen. SCP. pp. 82–87.

Walker, A. and T. Maltby. 1997. *Ageing Europe.* Buckingham/Philadelphia: Open University Press.

Whyte, J.H. 1981. *Catholics in Western Democracies: A Study of Political Behaviour.* Dublin: Gill and Macmillan.

Zwaan, T. 1993. 'De verbroken viereenheid: een interpretatie van recente transities' in *Familie, Huwelijk en Gezin.* ed. T. Zwaan. Amsterdam/Heerlen: Boom/ Open Universiteit.

7

The Globalisation of Domestic Care Services

RACHEL KURIAN

The tension between practices of domestic services as labour of 'love' inside the home and women's employment as paid domestic servants or private care workers constitutes an important link between the private domain of care and the public sphere of business transaction. In recent decades, business transaction involving female private care workers have assumed cross-border dimensions with significant implications for the workers and their families. Married and unmarried migrant women workers have moved from lesser developed countries such as the Philippines, Mexico, Sir Lanka, Ecuador, Peru and other Latin American countries to provide domestic care services to the United States, the European Community, the Middle East, Hong Kong and Canada. Studies have highlighted the transfer of care from the global South to the global North through the employment of 'nannies' (Parrenas 2001) as well as issues of rights and citizenship of these workers (Sarvasy and Longo 2004). The concept of the 'global care chain' has been usefully applied in these cases to analyse the globalisation of domestic care services and it has been conceptually developed to include different types of care work provided by migrants (Yeates 2004).

The purpose of this chapter is to present a political economy and historical framework to analyse the relations of power, privilege and deprivation at macro, meso and micro levels and their synergetic impact on globalisation of domestic care services. The analysis is guided by a feminist perspective identifying the main ways in which women have been affected in this process. It argues that the global migration of domestic workers is linked to historically specific changes which have come about by policies and changes at the macro, meso and micro levels of the economy and which are linked together to create the conditions and contexts for the globalisation of domestic care services. At the macro level are the economic reforms in the 1990s that have promoted the globalisation of care services. At the meso and micro levels the concept of the global care chain highlights the biases that exist with regard to gender, class and ethnicity/race and which have, in turn influenced the distribution of power and resources at these levels. Linking these different levels of analysis provides an integrated perspective of the globalisation of domestic care services including understanding why such a large number of women are involved in export-oriented provision of private care worldwide as well as the characteristics of gender inequality and power at nodal point (migration decision-making, recruitment process, transfer from home to workplace, control over work conditions at the workplace). The role of au pairs as domestic care providers in the Netherlands is used to illustrate some of these issues.

The macro-meso-micro nexus in the globalisation of domestic care services

The literature on globalisation and women's employment has shown that since the late 1970s, there has been a market preference for women in certain industries and services, most notably those associated with labour-intensive work and involved in export of goods and services. However, this so-called feminisation of the labour force has been closely linked to the neo-liberal policies which have emphasised labour market deregulation and flexibility, and promoted the race to the bottom with regard to wages and working conditions in the context of global competition (Standing 1999). The migration of women migrants from the South to the

North for the provision of domestic care services is a particularly stark example of how these advantages and disadvantages have been articulated in the global labour market.

Care work in addition has posed problems of economics stemming largely from its linguistic ambiguity, the universality of caring and the consequent undervaluation of care as well as the different intensities of care work (Daly 2001: 15–16). That the 'care economy' is vital for the functioning of the market economy and that it has an interdependent relationship between the market and the state has been highlighted in several studies (Elson 1995; Elson and Catagay 2000; van Staveren 2001). While women have historically been involved in the provision of care both locally and through migration, these aspects take on new dimensions in the context of the global restructuring in the last three decades. Studies have shown that female migration has increased during this period with typical forms of marginalisation associated with care services (such as low or no economic value attached to them) being exacerbated by other forms of discrimination, based on gender, class, ethnic and race divisions.[1]

The state has played a key role in promoting the migration of workers for the provision of domestic services, largely through economic and migration policies in the context of economic restructuring, and the retention of gendered disadvantages in its policy towards care work. The state in Western Europe is also involved in the reconfiguration and reconsideration of the balance between public and private responsibility for care, and with the exception of Sweden and Denmark, has tended to adopt policies which move away from the egalitarian tendencies of the 1970s to pressurising one parent (usually the mother) to provide the care work within the family for at least part of the time (Williams 2003). Bringing in women migrants to deal with shortfalls and costs of the institutions of care are important under these circumstances, and are reminiscent of the migrations of the 1950s and 1960s in Europe when labour shortages were met by the import of workers for the various needs of the welfare states. The main difference is the significance of female migration for work.

As noted by Williams, 'The new pattern of migrant labour re-inscribes the old "master/servant" relations with post-colonial gendered inequalities'.

The care chain is a useful concept to analyse the power relations that are associated (and sometimes reinforced) in the provision of domestic care that exist at the meso and micro levels. The concept of the 'global care chain' (Hochschild 2000: 13) referring to the 'series of personal links between people across the globe based on the paid or unpaid work of caring' has been usefully employed to understand the transactions, interactions and exchanges that are involved when domestic care services are provided mainly for women in industrialised countries by women from the lesser developed countries. Parrenas (2001) has shown that a global care chain is typically characterised by the mother usually looking after the children and family of a 'nanny' who is migrating to work in a richer region or country and her older daughter staying at home to look after the needs of her siblings and other members of her family. At the other end of the chain the migrating 'nanny' cares for the children of the relatively well off family usually, but not always, in the more industrialised countries. In respect to the United States (where her study is based) she argues that many American working parents are able to do so because of the migrant child care providers.

In her article 'Ketens van zorg: het nieuwe dienstmeisje in the mondiale migratie' Helma Lutz discusses the phenomenon of the 'nieuwe dienstmeisjes' who come to the western industrialised countries in Europe for work. She shows that, in contrast to their historical counterparts, current day 'dienstmeisjes' are relatively well educated, and capable of undertaking the necessary tasks of care in a household. She attributes the increasing numbers of foreign 'dienstmeisjes' to the continued responsibility of reproductive and household chores by women in industrialised countries. As the latter increasingly take up paid professional work, there is pressure to hire other women to take over some of the household chores. Her focus is on the lives of the 'dienstmeisjes' in the Netherlands and Germany, and she highlights some of their vulnerabilities and problems (including physical and sexual intimidation and harassment).

These different studies on the care chain have been important in drawing attention to the global trade in domestic care services as a relatively unacknowledged process within gender and migration studies. They also underlie the need to discard the public/private divide and for work to be viewed as a continuum between these two spheres. In nearly all cases, the global care chain provides the tools for analysing the relations of power and privilege at the meso and micro levels as the departure of women from their homes involves a gap in the care provision in their own families which has to be taken over by another person—usually another woman/girl. The transactions involved in the recruitment procedure as well as in the different nodes of the chain (including the household in the North) are similarly reflective of differences with regard to power and resources and returns. At the same time, there is little attention to the macroeconomic polices and structural changes in the industrialised and developing countries that directly paved the way for this form of female migration.

Linking the macro, meso and micro different levels of analysis indicates that the globalisation of domestic care services is the outcome of a series of complementary pressures and opportunities which have their own contradictions and challenges. Differences in power and resources are important in determining the negotiating positions and outcomes of the different persons and groups in the global care chain. And these have in turn been influenced by macroeconomic policies and reforms that have tended to reinforce class and gender differences both with and between the North and the South.

Industrialised countries, feminisation of labour markets and vulnerability of care: the pull factor

The last two decades have witnessed the acceleration of economic globalisation with the implementation of market oriented reforms in the industrialised economies and developing countries. The monetarist or neo-classical framework, dominating economic policy in the last 20 years, meant that the governments were required to enforce strict monetary and fiscal policies, with public enterprises and other agencies having to tighten their budgets. Under these circumstances, many sectors, notably those involved in health, educational and welfare services—some key areas of care— experienced considerable financial strains to meet the demands placed on them. The situation was exacerbated by the increasing proportion of the elderly in the population—a group that required increasing care.

The countries of the European Union, under pressure to meet the convergence and participation criteria for the European Union (initiated subsequent to the Maastricht Treaty in 1991) undertook measures that often led to increasing costs of care to consumers or even the lack of care with damaging effects. As noted by Folbre (2001: xv).

> ... the increased cost of care has several negative effects. First, it means that more people, especially children, the elderly, and other dependants, cannot always afford the care they need. Second, increased pressure to cut costs leads to reductions in the quality of care, a process already evident in many schools hospitals, and nursing homes.

Daly (2001: 49–50) in her analysis of care policies in Western Europe observed that costs are an important consideration in care policies which in turn have resulted in this care being provided increasingly within homes.

> In developed welfare states, care policies (for either the provider or recipient) may have the intent of reducing the costs of care services to the public budget. It is conventional wisdom that institution care is more costly to the public purse than care in the community. The moves toward paying for care at home, which as we have seen have recently been prevalent in Western Europe, are likely to be motivated as much by expenditure considerations as by the quality of care.

At the same time, these policies were taking place in a context where an increasing number of women were taking up full-time and part-time work in the industrialised countries. In the European

Union for example, women account for the entire growth of the labour force since 1975 with an activity rate in 1995–96 of nearly 70 per cent and their employment increasing steadily from 45,951,000 in 1975 to 68,964,000 in 2001. According to Beneria (2003: 81) it was the 'crisis of care' in the high-income countries together with the high labour market participation of women that was at the 'root' of the international migration of domestic care workers.

In spite of increased labour force participation, women continue to do the main work in the household, much of which is unpaid and often even unrecognised as work. The total number of unpaid hours of work is 1 to 1.5 times higher that the total number of paid hours of work, with the women's share of this being considerably higher than of men (Bruyn-Hundt 1996: 193). A time-use study in industrialised countries estimated that slightly less than half the total work time was spent on paid SNA (System of National Accounts) activities while slightly more than half was spent on unpaid non-SNA activities. Here too women were concentrated with two-thirds of their work in unpaid non-SNA activities, the reverse being the case for men (HDR 1995: 93).

Under these circumstances, there was increased demand for cheap and effective domestic care provided by women. There were two advantages of using migrant women workers from developing countries: first, that the middle classes could benefit from these services which were cheaper than those available in the local market; second, that the industrialised countries could benefit from the human resources and economic contributions of those women who were released from domestic chores. Thus, as noted by Williams (2003: 10) the movement of person power across continents takes care of the problems of both social expenditure *and* the disruption of normative family practices in the West.

Poverty and vulnerability in developing countries: the push factor

The implementation of market oriented reforms in the industrialised and developing countries—mainly through the stabilisation and structural adjustment programmes supported by the International Monetary Fund and the World Bank have tended to negatively affect poor women. The literature and different case studies on these reforms have shown that (a) there are increasing numbers of women seeking income-generating work mainly to maintain the family economy, (b) there are increased numbers of women who are unemployed, (c) the working conditions of these women have deteriorated, and (d) they are joining the informal sector in greater numbers. On the whole, many women have become poor, and the poor women have become poorer (Sparr 1994; UNRISD 2005).

At the same time, evidence suggests that women's unpaid work increases. While they have traditionally been largely responsible for the domestic chores in the household, the reforms placed additional pressure on them in terms of energy, time and other resources. For example, privatisation has often led to unemployment, leaving the household to somehow cope with this loss of income. In addition, there have been increased costs of public sector services such as health care, education and other social services through the implementation of cost cutting measures such as 'user fees' and an increase in the 'through put' of patients, a situation made worse by the lack of adequate social security for the vast majority of the poor. As women continue to be responsible for the services and production within the household, they have to cope with the additional pressure resulting from these problems.

These processes have also been accompanied by increasing disparities in terms of income at the global and national levels. The *Human Development Report* (2002: 19–20) noted that the current level of inequality worldwide was 'grotesque' and that between 1970 and the 1990s the world was 'more unequal than at any time before 1950' with the world's richest one per cent of people receiving as much income as the poorest 57 per cent. Income inequality has also increased within countries even in some of the OECD (Organisation for Economic Cooperation and Development) countries. In fact, 48 out of 73 countries with data (covering 80 per cent of the world's people) have had increased income inequality over the past 30 years. At the same time, the incomes of the richest one per cent grew by 140 per cent over the period. This has implied extremes in terms of purchasing power, with the majority of the poor facing serious problems of deprivation and poverty with little possibility of falling back on social security provisioning for support.

Migration of women

Under these circumstances of increased poverty as well as lack of adequate sources of employment in developing countries, many women have migrated (temporarily or permanently) to the more industrialised countries for employment. These migrant women have been numerically important in care services, most particularly in domestic work and in health, education and entertainment/sex industries. This migration has resulted in a double disadvantage for developing countries: first, that much needed skills are being siphoned off by the industrialised countries; and second, the training costs for these skills are met by the developing countries.

The data on female international migrants has been a 'largely neglected subject', as noted by the United Nations Secretariat in the proceedings of its expert group on *International Migration Policies and the Status of Female Migrants* (1995: 56). Based on censuses of some 157 countries since 1970 the Population Division of the Department for Economic and Social Information and Policy Analysis concludes that women constitute 48 per cent of the 77 million persons who were enumerated outside their country of birth. However, women outnumbered men in the United States of America, the largest host country, constituting 51 per cent of foreign-born in 2000.

The oil-rich countries had provided a stimulus for the immigration of domestic workers on short-term contracts in the 1970s (particularly from South and South-east Asia). This sort of migration—the globalisation of domestic care—has since accelerated in the 1980s and 1990s with many going to the Asian tigers (Singapore, Taiwan and Hong Kong) and Japan. The most important source countries of female migrants were from Sri Lanka, the Philippines, Thailand, Indonesia and Malaysia.

The Philippines was an important source of immigrants. In 1987, there were 81,000 women domestic workers abroad, 32,000 entertainers and 26,000 nurses. Most of the nurses were working in West Asia, although Hong Kong and Singapore were also important hosts. Most of the Filipino women entertainers went to Japan. Quoting official statistics, it noted that in 1988 alone nearly 50,000 Indonesian women were working abroad constituting 78 per cent of all workers deployed. By the late 1990s there were a million Filipino, 500,000 Indonesian and about 40,000 Thai women working outside their countries (Wille 2001: 9).

While the main host countries have been Hong Kong, Japan, Saudi Arabia, Qatar, Taiwan and the United Arab Emirates, Filipino women were also important migrant workers in the more industrialised countries. Most of the women were employed in domestic service and were thus basically catering to the needs of middle-class families which can afford them, particularly as more and more women from industrialised countries seek work. In many cases these women experience a loss of status in terms of occupation and experience, in fact de-skilling as they undertake work which is below their level of skills (Barsotti and Lecchini 1995).

Some of this migration receives support from the national governments as it eases the local unemployment situation and the country benefits from the foreign exchange that is remitted by these workers. The remittances also sustain their families. The Philippine government has been particularly active on this score. By the 1980s, the government had set up several departments and agencies which documented and monitored the migration process. Acts protecting the rights of these workers were enacted and efforts were made to ensure the safety of the migrants in the host countries. Women migrant workers were given special attention and protection. The demand for domestic care in the industrialised countries also spurred the direction of the migration.

Women in the Asian region have been particularly affected

by the recent economic crisis, which has further stimulated the search for work outside their countries. The existing migrants at the same time became even more vulnerable as they faced the problems of retrenchment and threats of arrest or deportation if they remained in the host country. Migrant women also have few prospects if they should return home.

Power and privilege in the domestic care chain: The meso and micro level forms of control

An important source of privilege and power is the recruiter who plays a role in defining the terms of the labour contract. Government agencies play an important role in the recruitment of migrant labour in the Philippines, Indonesia and Thailand. Private recruitment agencies for foreign companies and individuals also recruit domestic workers. A substantial amount of this migration is done through clandestine operators. Given the degree of poverty among the migrant workers, most of them have to borrow money to pay for the expenses of the recruitment. The recruiter also takes a share of this money for the services provided. Sometimes the workers borrow the money from the recruiter. Thus, their lives begin in debt and in control of the recruiter, a position that has often proved to be exploitative. Some recruiters substitute contracts so that the signed contract is different from the actual contract. There is also misrepresentation of actual terms and conditions of work in the host country. All this means that the domestic workers are not able to redress the circumstances upon arrival due to indebtedness incurred prior to departure. In some cases they are even trafficked into vice activities (Shameen and Brady 1998).

In addition there are other concerns in the global care chain.

- First, as already noted, the domestic work in the different segments is done almost universally by women. This reflects the traditional gender division of labour in society whereby women are largely responsible for the care work in households. This division of labour exists and is supported

157

ideologically in both developing and industrialised countries, as well as by most religions and cultures. Under these circumstances, the feminisation of international migration could potentially contribute to the discriminative labour market policies in the host countries as 'gender-selective migration policies and regulations for admission and entry often reproduce and intensify existing social, economic and cultural inequalities between male and female migrants' (Taran and Geronomi 2003).

- Second, that the work done by women in the household is often not seen as 'work'. Conventionally, 'work' is defined as and limited to economic activity involved in the production of goods and services as defined by the United Nations System of National Accounts (UNSNA). However the definition of 'work' also explicitly excludes unpaid services done in the household. Mainly women do this non-paid labour which is effectively made economically 'invisible' (Mata-Greenwood 1999). This bias against domestic care is reflected in low wages being given to providers of domestic care when these services are provided in the market. Migrant women domestic workers are further disadvantaged in that their pay is even lower than the market value—the main rationale for hiring them and not the local women workers.

- Third, while these migrant domestic workers are paid, they function within the so-called 'private' sphere. The latter is traditionally, and continues to remain a 'personal' realm. Most countries do not have legislation that deals with working conditions of paid domestic care, making these workers very vulnerable to the power of the employer. They are not entitled to the minimum wages, sickness and maternity pay and pension rights of the host country and they are not allowed to join unions. Blackett (2000) who studied the regulations for domestic workers noted the following:

> ... few, if any bridges are built to enable domestic workers to enforce realistically their rights. Their working conditions remain,

158

in essence, unregulated. The problem is frequently compounded for foreign domestic workers who are sometimes not covered by the labour laws that exist in the countries in which they work or are unable to claim those rights if they are illegally working in the country. Indeed, because of the heightened vulnerability engendered by the intricate link between their employment immigration statuses, foreign domestic workers are less likely than most other workers to be willing or able to claim their rights.

- Fourth, and linked to the others, is that domestic care is provided within a relationship of paternalism and subordination. Domestic workers are often seen as part of the family—a belief that could have stemmed from a feudal paternalistic concept that servants were part of the family. Parrenas (2001) shows that the domestic worker is often also an important provider of attention and love within the household. However, such a role does not eliminate that the domestic worker essentially is following the instructions of those in charge of the household, and that her role is one of a subordinate even if she is being paid for her work. Such a relationship can potentially lead to many forms of exploitation, including physical and sexual abuse.
- Fifth, the global care chain has in-built notions of discrimination with regard to sex, race, colour and nationality. While, the two ends of the chain reflect the lowest and highest order in a hierarchy based on income and opportunities, these differences are reinforced through the institutions and ideologies of sexism, racism, colour and nationality prejudices. These are often reinforced through the relative social isolation of women in the host country (Shameen and Brady 1998).

The 'au pair' and the globalisation of domestic care: the Netherlands[2]

The au pair arrangement has been in place since the end of the 19th century, the numbers involved increasing from the end of the Second World War. It was originally practised within Europe primarily to facilitate cultural exchange at low cost and to learn the language of the host country. Many of the European countries abide by the European Agreement on Au Pair Placement (1969) while others have interpreted and modified the rules to their own contexts. The basic arrangement was that an au pair is provided with free board and lodging, is treated as a member of a family, and in return provides some help in the household.

However, this system took on a new dimension in the 1990s as workers from the poorer countries came across as au pairs. Many of them migrated as domestic service providers under the au pair framework. They worked long hours (far more than was anticipated or paid for), often undertaking care work which was not part of the agreement. There have been instances when these workers have also been known to provide sexual services. These concerns have been taken up by local, national and regional groups that have strived to better the situation of these workers. In spite of all these pressures, a substantial amount of change still needs to take place in terms of policy and implementation.

The Netherlands has not signed the European Agreement on Au Pair Placement of 1969, but has modified the regulations to its own context. There are government guidelines regarding the working conditions of the au pair. First, the au pair has to be between 18 and 25 years of age and cannot be expected to do more than eight hours of work per day with a maximum of 30 hours per week. In addition, the au pair is entitled to two free days and two free evenings. The au pair is also given a sum of money (a maximum of 340 euros per month) as pocket money. The tasks that an au pair can officially do includes caring for children (babysitting, preparing meals), as well as some domestic chores (light ironing, cleaning, and light shopping) as long as these fit within the agreed arrangement and hours of work. However, there are specific tasks that are not to be done by au pairs. These include gardening, any farm work or office work or work in any business, cleaning up after the parents, working as a maid or butler, acting as a party host or hostess for the parents, and caring for the children for more than a few hours at a time (Oosterbeek-Latoza 2003).

Between 1990 and 2002 the Netherlands experienced a 30 per cent increase in employment, contributed largely by an increase in women's employment. As in other countries in Europe in the 1990s, this process was taking place in a context where 'care' was a financial strain both in terms of government expenditure as well as availability of services for families. One outcome was the increase in part-time flexible work arrangements with 63 per cent of all working women working part-time (the equivalent figure for men being 17 per cent).

However, there remained the fact that the Dutch political agenda regarding the family had been dominated till the 1990s by a model that embraced traditional family values and the full-time mother's (unpaid) role in the household. While this has marginally changed over the period, the main option for most women wanting paid work was to take up part-time employment. This was partly because the availability and the costs of official childcare facilities are relatively poor as compared to many other European countries. In 1995 only 7.5 per cent of children in the ages 0–4 (pre-schoolers) and only 0.8 per cent of children in ages 4–14 were in childcare. There are long waiting lists for this childcare, estimates ranging from 32,000 full-time places for children of all age groups, with the waiting lists in the 0-4 year category being about 23,000 full-time places with the vast majority resorting to informal and unpaid care.

Under these pressures in the 1990s to find affordable and efficient domestic care services, the au pair arrangement was to assume a different dimension. From an arrangement based on cultural exchange it became increasingly a vehicle for getting support for the middle class in the provision of care within households. Women from South Africa, the Philippines and the countries of Eastern Europe were important as service providers in the globalisation of care. While they came across as au pairs, their reality was that they were domestic workers. They were a vulnerable category, as they were neither students, nor foreign immigrants, and they were mainly in search of income and employment opportunities to ameliorate the problems in their home countries.

There are some important differences if the au pair comes from outside the European Union and the European Economic Area (EEA). In this case, the au pair needs to have a valid passport, no tuberculosis (a test is done in the Netherlands to confirm this), no criminal record (a declaration form needs to be signed for this, the *antecedentenverklaring*), an adequate medical insurance, and an authorisation of temporary stay (*Machtinging tot Voorlopig Verblijf*). The latter is of particular importance as it allows the au pair to stay for a period over three months (Ministerie van Justitie 2001; Staatscourant 2000).

These au pairs are generally recruited through a placement or intermediate agency which takes a fee for its services. There are no legal regulations governing the role of these agencies. Many of the au pairs do not have enough money to pay the placement fee and a sum of money is deducted monthly from the 'pocket money' she receives. In addition, the air fare is also usually paid by the host family, and a certain amount is further deducted from the 'pocket money' to return this payment.

The au pair is viewed by the law to have the status similar to a guest in the family and her stay in the country is dependent on the willingness of the host family to support her. A change in her status implies that she has no rights to stay on in the country. And while it is possible to change the host family, this request would have to be submitted to the Alien Police three months before the expiration of the stay permit. All these factors reflect that there is little space and scope for any form of complaint on the part of the au pair from developing countries even if they were to experience exploitation and abuse. For this group of workers, it was the economic reasons that were paramount in their undertaking the au pair job. Thus, any chances of jeopardising their jobs would be viewed with both hesitation and apprehension as they are likely to be sent home and would be unlikely to find another possibility of earning an income either in the host or home countries.

The vast majority of au pairs are women and the work that they are expected to do is within the family. They are expected to take care of children and help with domestic chores. However, as the au pair has the status of a family member/guest, the law does not acknowledge that there is an employer/employee relationship existing between the au pair and the host family. In principle, this means that the work done within the household does not fall within the laws and regulations of the Netherlands with regards to labour rights and obligations. Thus, there is no obligation to pay a wage to the au pair (the sum she is entitled to is 'pocket money' and not a wage).

As in other countries in Europe, the Philippines has been an important exporter of domestic care to the Netherlands. This was particularly so in the 1990s, the numbers rising over the period with Filipina au pairs constituting about one-third of all au pairs in the country. The Filipina au pairs are recruited via four recruiting agencies in the Netherlands or through direct referrals.

The role of the intermediate agency is also one of power and control. In the late 1990s the au pair had to pay 10,000 pesos (about 700 Dutch guilders) as a placement fee, and an additional 4,400 pesos for travel tax, visa, passport and medical examination. This amount was sometimes increased arbitrarily in the Netherlands. In some cases, placement fees were also higher than had been agreed in the Philippines, and in addition, the 'pocket money' was considerably diminished by the amount that had to be paid to the host family or the intermediate agency for the air fare.

Over this period, many of these au pairs functioned as domestic workers, often providing full-time domestic help for the family. They were clearly seen as 'cheap' labour as hiring babysitters and domestic help for the same number of hours was considerably more expensive. A conservative estimate for babysitting is 2.50 euros per hour, while domestic help is eight euros per hour. The maximum of 340 euros given to the au pair per month is easily covered by the costs entailed in hiring local help to do the work. Clearly, learning about another culture is an important incentive.

However, the overwhelming reason for these women to work as au pairs is the need to earn money and send part of their income to their families. Given the deteriorating economic circumstances in the Philippines their remittances were important in supporting their families.

There were several studies and examples provided by the Stichting Bayanihan, the Centre for Filipina Women that indicate that the au pairs were often brought across on false expectations, did work that was beyond the agreement and the regulations on au pairs. In some cases, they were made to work as full-time domestic workers often looking after children and the household needs from early morning to late at night. Sometimes they were deprived of their right to 'free' days, and had to cater to the needs of the host family. In addition, they found it difficult to adjust to the Dutch culture and language, and given the pressure of their work, often did not learn about the society and the people, going out mainly to the market and the grocery stores. There were also cases when the au pair was treated with disrespect, not allowed to eat with the family, and made to call them 'sir' or 'madam'. In most cases, these women were very hesitant about making a complaint as they feared that they would be deported back to the Philippines (Bouwens 2002).

As discussed previously, these gender biases interface with economic need in the participation of women in the globalisation of domestic care. Among the reasons indicated for wanting a Filipina au pair include that she is 'always available', 'works very hard', 'is simple', 'does not demand', 'loves children', 'cheap', 'reliable', 'sweet/nice' and 'not insolent' (Brabants Dagblad 1996 in Stichting Bayanihan 1997: 4). The stereotyping of women, and particularly women from developing countries, in these categories is indicative of patronage, ethno-stereotyping and even racism.

It would be unfair to categorise all employers as treating these women in a negligent or abusive manner. Many au pairs found their time here an important experience in terms of cultural exchange and earning income to send back to their families. The support groups in the country, such as the Stichting Bayanihan, have also helped to overcome the social isolation experienced in the Netherlands and helped some of them to take up their complaints at legal and governmental levels.

Underlying these issues is the role of the government which continues to maintain restrictive domestic migration policies on the service providers of care, while tacitly allowing and benefiting from this work to be done by au pairs (the service providers) in the 'private sphere'. By doing so, the government has effectively disbarred them from the normal labour rights (including unemployment, pensions, etc.).

Conclusions

Overall, we see that the participation of women in the globalisation of domestic care is, in some ways, the outcome of demand and supply at the international level. However, it involves more than 'rational and free choices' on the part of those involved. The choices and outcomes are often influenced by demands on care in industrialised countries as well as by structural dilemmas of poverty and unemployment in developing countries.

There are some important conclusions that have been established through the analysis. The first is the recognition of domestic care as work with value, a factor which needs to be taken on board in terms of remuneration and policy. The second is that women continue to dominate the care work even if this care has to be bought from outside the country. The third is that globalisation of domestic care does play a role in satisfying the demand for care in the industrialised countries while also providing an opportunity for women from developing countries to move away from areas of depression, discrimination and disadvantage.

At the same time, there are other issues that are more ambiguous. The first is that care (including attention and love) cannot be fully valued in purely monetary terms and women experience certain contradictions by giving up the care for their own families and providing this to another family. Second, the globalisation of domestic care involves a displacement of care from the underprivileged to those who command a higher income and power, with these inequalities often being reinforced by gender and race discrimination. An additional important concern is whether this implies a transfer of oppression from privileged women to under-privileged women. And finally, is the disquiet that increasing inequalities in the world economy might tend to promote lowering of wages for these domestic workers as low-waged economies (and low-waged women within them) compete with one another to provide cheaper domestic labour for the industrialised countries.

Notes

[1] For a good review of the recent research on these issues see the different articles in *Gender and Society*, vol. 17. no. 2, April 2003: Special Issue: Global Perspectives on Gender and Carework.

[2] This section is largely based on discussions undertaken with Filipina au pairs in the Netherlands as well as by reports done by their support group Stichting Bayanihan in Utrecht.

References

Barsotti, Odo and Laura Lecchini. 1995. 'The Experience of Filipino Female Migrants in Italy' in *International Migration Policies and the Status of Female Migrants*. Proceedings of the United Nations Expert Group Meeting on International Migration Policies and the Status of Female Migrants. San Miniato. Italy. 28–31 March 1990. New York: United Nations. pp. 153–163.

Beneria, Lourdes. 2003. *Gender, Development and Globalization: Economics as if All People Mattered*. New York/London: Routledge.

Blackett, A. and C. Sheppard. 2000. 'Collective Bargaining and Equality: Making Connections'. *International Labour Review*. vol. 142. pp. 419–158.

Bouwens, A. 2002. 'Toenemend Misbruik Au-Pairs Onderzocht'. *Univers 16*. Januari.

Bruyn-Hundt, Marga. 1996. 'The Economics of Unpaid Work'. Doctorate Dissertation. The Netherlands: Rijksuniversiteit Limburg at Maastricht.

Daly, Mary. ed. 2001. *Care Work: The Quest for Security*. Geneva: International Labour Organisation.

Elson, D. 1995. 'Gender Awareness in Modelling Structural Adjustment'. *World Development*. vol. 23. no. 11. pp. 1851–1868.

Elson, Diane. ed. 1995. *Male Bias in the Development Process*. 2d ed. Manchester: Manchester University Press.

Elson, D. and N. Catagay. 2000. 'The Social Content of Macroeconomic Policies'. *World Development.* vol. 28. no. 7. pp. 1347–64.

Folbre, N. 2001. *The Invisible Heart: Economics and Family Values.* The New Press.

Hochschild, A.R. 2000. 'Global care chains and emotional surplus values' in *On the Edge: Living with Global Capitalism.* eds. N. Hutton and A. Giddens. London: Jonathan Cape.

Human Rights Watch. 2001. *Hidden in the Home: Abuse of Domestic Workers with Special Visas in the United States.* vol. 13. no. 2 (G).

Lutz, H. 2002. 'At your service madam! The globalisation of domestic service'. *Feminist Review.* vol. 70. no. 1. pp. 89–104.

Mata-Greenwood, A. 1999. 'Gender Issues in Labour Statistics'. *International Labour Review.* vol. 138.

Oosterbeek-Latoza, D. 2003. 'Filipina au pairs in the Netherlands'. Stichting Bayanihan: Centrum voor Filippijnse Vrouwen in Nederland. Maart.

Ministerie van Justitie. 2001. *Immigratie en Naturalisatjedienst.* April.

Parrenas, R.S. 2001. *Servants of Globalization: Women, Migration and Domestic Care.* Stanford University Press.

Sarvasy, W. and P. Longo. 2004. 'The Globalization of Care Kant's World Citizenship and Filipina Migrant Domestic Workers'. *International Journal of Feminist Politics.* vol. 6. no. 3. pp. 392–415.

Shameen, S. and E. Brady. 1998. 'Women in Migration' in *Understanding International Migration—A Source Book.* APIM.

Sparr, Pamela. ed. 1994. *Mortgaging Women's Lives: Feminist Critiques of Structural Adjustment.* London/New Jersey: Zed Books.

Staatscourant. 2000. Tussentijds Bericht Vreemdelingencirculaire. no. 144. Au Pair in Nederland. 28 July.

Standing, G. 1999. *Global Labour Flexibility.* Basingstoke: Palgrave MacMillan.

Stichting Bayanihan. 1997. 'The Filipina Au Pairs in the Netherlands: Their Problems and Some Resolutions to Improve their Situation'. Report on 'Philippine International Migration: Issues and Concerns of Filipino Migrants in the Netherlands' for the workshop by the Federation of Filipino Organisations in the Netherlands. The Hague. 24 November.

Taran, Patrick A. and Eduardo Geronomi. 2003. 'Globalization, Labour and Migration: Protection is Paramount'. International Migration Programme. Geneva: International Labour Office.

UNDP. 1995. *Human Development Report 1995.* New York/Oxford: Oxford University Press.

UNDP. 2002. *Human Development Report 2002.* New York/Oxford: Oxford University Press.

United Nations Research Institute for Social Development. 2005. 'Liberalization, Labour Markets and Women's Gains: A Mixed Picture' in *Gender Equality: Striving for Justice in an Unequal World.* France: UNRISD. pp. 35–47.

United Nations. 1995. *International Migration Policies and the Status of Female Migrants*. Proceedings of the United Nations Expert Group Meeting on International Migration Policies and the Status of Female Migrants. San Miniato. Italy. 28–31 March 1990. New York: United Nations.

van Staveren, I. 2001. *The Values of Economics: an Aristotelian Perspective*. London: Routledge.

Wille, C. 2001. 'Introduction' in *Female Labour Migration in South-east Asia: Change and Continuity*. eds. Supang Chantavanich, Christina Wille, Kannika Angsuthanasombat, Maruja MB Asis, Allan Beesey and Sukamdi. Asian Research Centre for Migration: Institute of Asian Studies. Chulalongkorn University.

Williams, F. 2003. 'Rethinking Care in Social Policy'. Paper presented at the Annual Conference of the Finnish Social Policy Association. Finland: University of Joensuu. 24 October.

Yeates, N. 2004. 'Global Care Chains'. *International Feminist Journal of Politics*. vol. 6. no. 3. September. pp. 369–391.

8

From State Duty to Women's Virtue
Care under Liberalisation in Vietnam

THANH-DAM TRUONG

Introduction

The goals of Vietnam's modernist political efforts since the beginning of the last century have been to build a system of governance that fulfils the ideals of social equality, including gender, ethnicity and religious affinity (Marr 1971; 1987). It is now well established that gender issues are systematically significant to the state as an institution rather than a temporal demand imposed by women's organisations. In the current period of *Doi-Moi*[1] gender policy finds itself being lodged in a zone of tension between economic liberalism and social protectionism. The ongoing reforms have produced heterogeneous patterns of gender inequality that cut through different sites (state, firms, household) and places (rural, urban, and peripheral regions) plus a bifurcated system of social protection, which pose considerable challenges to efforts of nation-building.

This chapter analyses changing gender relations in Vietnam through the lens of a gender contract (the combination of social arrangements that governs gender relations) by contrasting two models of social policy. The 'male-the-breadwinner' gender contract is characteristic of the model based on the notion of a family wage and the view that women's earning is supplementary to male earning. This model compromises a woman's economic position in favour of the needs and interests and authority of the husband as the sole earner and decision-maker for allocation of family resources. A 'working mother' gender contract is characteristic of the model of social policy that is built on the significance of a double-income family. It recognises the significance of women's economic contribution and considers their earnings as equally important to family needs and well-being. It supports women's gender interests in motherhood and childrearing by enlarging the public base for childcare services, and uses an array of other measures to change gender norms and values for greater balance in sharing the burdens in matters of health, education, family and maintenance of community relations.

Due to specific political, social and economic dynamics Vietnam's gender policy tends to lean towards the 'working mother' gender contract. From a cultural standpoint the recognition of women's traditional economic contribution to agriculture, artisan production and commune management over centuries is well recognised in social consciousness (Gourou 1965; Houtart and Lemercinier 1984; Dumont 1995; Mai and Le 1978). Demographic trends during the last two decades also display gender features that require state management attention in the deployment of human resources. Over the last two decades the proportion of the female population has remained slightly higher than the male[2] (General Statistical Office 2000). Yet the ratio of female-headed households since the post-war period has been rising[3] (Centre for Women's Studies 1990; UNDP 2002). Women's contribution to economic production remains nearly equal to men, despite fluctuation[4] (UNESCO 1989; UNDP 2002). The choice of export-oriented industrialisation as a strategic path for the country's integration in the global economy—explicit since 2001—appears to be female-led. Against this backdrop recent rhetoric regarding gender equality policy has been concentrated on the inexorable link between the sustainability of this strategy and the full deployment of the female workforce—at pre- and post-childbearing age—whose well-being must be protected. The challenge is how to respond to the polymorphous nature of gender power with corresponding means to ensure the goals of equality in national development.

The gender contract in Vietnam: the tension between moral and economic incentives

Historians have confirmed that there were periods during which women in Vietnam have enjoyed relative gender equality in the domain of formal politics, the economy and family life (Mai and Le 1978; Ta 1981).[5] Half a century of cultural reforms has produced a modern state permeated by a morality of gender equality sustained by a gender contract by which women's role in public life and in the family is formally recognised as equally significant to men's. The Constitution asserts a commitment by the state to work towards equality of social status between men and women in all spheres of social life. In trying to uphold the view that gender equality is morally worthy, the modern state also must mediate between different interests and consider its realistic capacity to allocate responsibilities which will ensure fairness and efficiency in gender relations. Changing relations within the polity and the economy cause the terms of the gender contract to be modified in response to the specific gender needs and interests of women, men and the state.

In the early period after independence in 1946 the gender contract inscribed within the first Constitution reflected a trade-off between gender-based cultural norms of female domesticity[6] and modern politics of state-building guided by norms of female emancipation (Truong 1997; Tetreault 1990). By removing gender-discriminatory norms the state sought to enhance women's participation in public life, production and nation-state building. Given its reliance on women's efforts, the state gave great attention to social arrangements that alleviate women's burdens when they simultaneously take part in national defence as political actors, producers and care providers. In retrospect, while the gender contract in this period appeared to elevate women's status as full citizens, it has tended to subjugate the gender interests of both women and men to concerns for national security and the

171

construction of state socialism (Belanger and Khuat 2001).[7]

In the late 1970s, in an attempt to shift from the autarchy of central planning to a more liberalised society, clandestine reforms were introduced locally through the introduction of the household contract system. This system allowed rural cooperatives to lease land and equipment to individual households for the production and marketing of produce—after delivering a proportionate share to the state at a fixed price. In several localities the result was a greater incentive for women to withdraw from the poorly paid jobs in childcare centres, crèches and primary schools and devote their energy to household production for higher income, which eventually led to the collapse of the gender-based arrangements particularly in rural areas (Truong 1997). Labour market conditions, combined with the institutional context within which individual women choose how they allocate their labour time, appear to have exercised considerable influence in undermining the subsidised system of care which the women dominated.

The economic efficiency of the household contract system began to gain prominence; and the full liberalisation measures of late 1986 turned to the household economy as a means to de-collectivise malfunctioning cooperatives and to redirect alternative livelihood options for workers affected by state-owned enterprise downsizing. New terms in the gender contract emerged in state discourse on the family, in which women were advised to observe family planning and concentrate on child education in accordance with the wider social and economic goals of the state. Women's cooperation was urged through state glorification of motherhood as their noble and natural role. The Politburo redefined women's gender roles as follows:

> Women are simultaneously workers and producers, mothers, the first teachers of humanity. Women's potential, their working conditions, level of education and cultural awareness, their social and economic status and physical and mental health have deep impacts on the development of the future generation (Vietnam Women Union 1998: 4).

The 'New Culture Family' campaign encouraged men and

women to share decision-making and housework and urged the acceptance of the 'household economy' as suitable to women. However, the Family Law—as it now stands—protects women as wives and mothers, but not as home-workers and producers.[8] Land Law does not discriminate against women. Joint titling is permitted but often not observed, particularly in peripheral regions in the highlands (UNDP 2002).

Under the household system of production, women's economic activities as producers and care providers are articulated within the institutional framework of the family. As a self-regulating institution no longer directed by central allocation after the initial redistribution of resources proportionate to family size and needs, the household economy conflates moral duties based on kinship with the economic logic of a private firm. The economic security of women tends to hinge on their own awareness of contributions and rights and their ability to monitor their activities, as shown in previous practices of cooperatives (Appelton 1983). Alas, current media campaigns on role models directed at women tend to foster the image of the woman as a triangulating entity that mediates between the woman's sense of self, the family and the nation; or a social construct of the 'faithful, heroic and resourceful' female subject, reinforcing the notion of sacrifice as women's virtue (Gammeltoft 2001; Blanc 2001).

In practice the working-mother gender contract relies heavily on women's self-exploitation. With over 90 per cent of total employment absorbed by the household sector, support to women workers in the form of paid childcare services remains limited (VWU 1997).[9] Women are left to bargain for themselves in the sharing of housework and the duties of caring for their children and various members of the extended family. The Living-Standards Survey of 1997–98 shows that girls and women tend to carry a disproportionate load of housework, particularly from childbearing age to retirement as illustrated in Figure 1.

The impact of an unequal share of dutiful work in the family is reflected in the gendered patterns of ownership and operation of Non-farm Household Enterprises. As shown in Figure 2, in

Figure 1
Women's and Men's Average Hours Spent in Housework, 1997–98

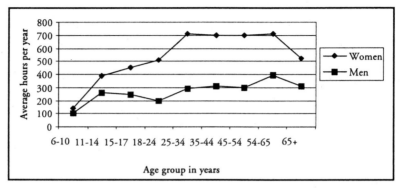

Source: UNDP 2002

both urban and rural areas female-operated enterprises tend to employ fewer wage workers than male-operated enterprises, be more likely to have a fixed location and less likely to function with a business licence. Fixed locations may enable women to combine familial duties with business activities, relying mainly on unpaid family labour. The price of this combination is their invisibility and lack of access to public support in private sector development programmes.

Women's inability to negotiate for a fairer share of domestic burdens often has led to verbal and physical abuse, as revealed through the voices of the women themselves:

> My husband's drinking makes me angry. There are many things put on my shoulders, such as children's study, but he just pay attention to drinking. He brings his friends home and they drink and make my house a mess. (A rural farmer in Ho Chi Minh City, age 39) (Vu 2000: 9)

> In my case, he showed too much filial piety towards his parents and siblings. If I complained about that, it would result in a disagreement between us. So I have to tolerate his behaviour. The wife's tolerance is a necessary condition for a peaceful family life. (Woman in Focus Group, Hue) (Ibid: 12)

Figure 2
Characteristics of Male and Female Operated Non-farm Enterprises
by Location, 1997–1998

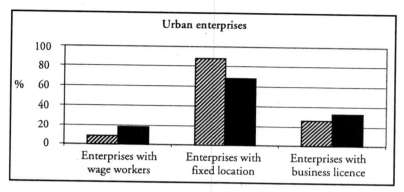

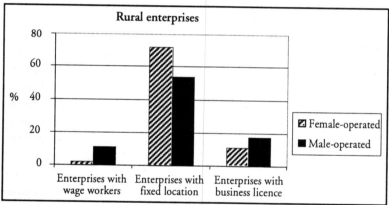

Source: UNDP 2002

Local norms of gender roles continue to defy those inscribed in the Family Law. Advice offered to women suffering from spousal abuse by local reconciliation groups (involving women's organisations as a mediating party) tends to be based on the view that children's interests must be placed above individual interests and therefore women must sacrifice their own interests and well being for the sake of the children (Vu 2000).

In the formal sector, Labour Law introduced in 1994 contains a full chapter on gender-specific labour standards. Rather than pursuing a subsidised approach to the socialisation of childcare the state has adopted instead a new approach based on economic incentives offered to enterprises to remove gender barriers. Article 110 stipulates that firms employing a high number of female workers may benefit from preferential regimes such as tax exemption or deduction and other financial incentives such as favourable access to credit and loans. Compliance with labour standards is found mainly in state-owned enterprises and firms with foreign investment (VWU 1998). Lack of awareness about the law and the impracticality of some of the regulations appear to be key problems.

Findings by the International Development Research Centre and the Research Centre for Female Labour (2002) reveal the low number of firms accredited as employing a high percentage of women workers in the garment and textile sector, despite the fact that 80 per cent of the workforce in this sector is female. Nearly half of those accredited in this sector are state-owned enterprises. From the firms' point of view, the benefits of incentives accorded in gender-specific regulations are outweighed by the costs of disruption of production lines in the event of too many women workers claiming gender-specific benefits (maternity leave and young childcare leave) at the same time. Moreover, women workers in many domestic private enterprises—now constituting a new engine of growth—have no written contract, only a vague verbal contract, and therefore cannot benefit from labour regulations (Pham and Pham 2001). Non-compliance with labour standards makes firms more competitive by lowering labour costs.

According to the national industrial survey of 1999 (GSO 2000b: 61) female labour then constituted 55.1 per cent of total industrial labour. Female labour costs were only 45.2 per cent of the total. The contribution made by firms to the social security of female labour was only 29.7 per cent of the total. More specifically, in the manufacturing sector—comprising state-owned enterprises, foreign direct investment enterprises and domestic private firms—female labour reached 58.3 per cent but their costs were only

45.2 per cent; and the total contribution of firms to their social security was 31.4 per cent of the total. Wages and social security benefits enjoyed by female workers in the manufacturing sector are indeed higher than the average in the industrial sector, but still significantly lower than the level enjoyed by men. Hence, when praising the performance of the private sector, it is important to keep in mind the role of female labour and how gender inequality has served firms' efficiency equations.

In sum, state attempts to balance the tension between liberalisation and social protection have led to the emergence of a new organisational logic of gender relations. In the new logical framework emphasis is placed on firms and families as self-regulating entities who are encouraged to observe gender equality as a morally desirable principle bearing consequences on future generations. But the articulation of gender differences through different institutionalised frameworks of rights and duties at particular sites and places displays tendencies by which the moral power of gender equality is being subjugated to material concerns for efficiency and competitiveness. Signs of resistance against dysfunctional self-regulating frameworks of gender relations may be found in an increasing trend in domestic violence, divorce, avoidance of marriage and single-parent families headed by women. The challenge is how to harmonise the moral and material dimensions of the gender contract to achieve justice and fairness.

Beyond fragments: sisters, what is to be done?

The Vietnamese Women's Union

The Vietnamese Women's Union (VWU) has played a central role in negotiating the terms of the 'working mother' gender contract. Founded in 1930 during the anti-colonial resistance, the organisation has changed its name and structure of operation several times before becoming the actual Vietnam Women's Union in 1976.[10] VWU has inherited a hierarchical structure of administration from state socialism, linking four echelons (central, provincial, district, and communes). Initially the organisation was oriented to the specific goals of national emancipation, operating under the directives of the communist party and later those of the state which provided subsidy for different activities.

With the withdrawal of the state from the social sector the organisation had to choose between two options: to insist on constitutional rules and be marginalised; or to find other means to finance its activities and protect women's interests (Truong 1994). In line with broader administrative reforms, VWU is moving away from a centralised commanding role to one of coordination of activities at different levels of society. It has transformed itself from a closed to an open organisation; and become a service-provider consisting of a coalition of interest groups with local self-regulated women's groups as its clients, the state as the commanding authority in policy choices and funding from the international communities who are backing gender mainstreaming in the country's development programmes.

Activities in the period 1992–2003 show that VWU is gradually shifting its focus beyond the needs of special groups living under problematic conditions. It is moving towards the promotion of alliances between women in all strata, including entrepreneurs, professionals and ethnic minorities; and to a diversified structure of incentives for membership and cooperation. An important feature of these alliances is the formation, through various campaigns, of women's groups in the private sector. One such campaign initiated in 1994, 'Women's Mutual Help in the Household Economy' mobilises women to engage in mutual assistance in cultivation and animal husbandry, in the acquisition of capital for production and in the mutual exchange of free labour days. Cross-class support is also fostered through a yearly campaign on International Women's Day, 8th March, as a 'Day of Savings for Women Living in Poverty', to mobilise successful women entrepreneurs, professionals and civil servants to direct some of their savings to create and sustain a special fund for poor women living without family (Phan 2000).

From major VWU activities over the last 15 years, it is possible to trace the course of a gender-based social policy as follows:

Family Policy	Employment and Labour Policy	Women's Education and Training Policy
Domestic violence	'Working Mother' gender contract	Economic empowerment through the training of women owners of enterprises
Property rights	
Adult literacy	Household enterprise development
Reproductive health	
Nutrition, sanitation and family well-being	Removal of gender barriers to enterprise development (labour, finance, technology, networks of supply and distribution of products)	Education and leadership training
		Training for participation in social activities
Maternity and (young) childcare	
		Special attention to women of ethnic minorities
Special treatment for women of ethnic minorities in distant provinces	Rural home-based day care centres

The formation of sub-groups at different levels—loosely connected with each other under the ideological umbrella of solidarity among women—still maintains a close link between women's gender interests and those of the nation-state, by which culture and tradition remain key constitutive elements of women's identity. Commitment to nation building is now expressed under the rhetoric of modernisation and economic development, in conjunction with national defence. In the words of a woman now retired from the vanguard:

> Sometimes Western sisters don't understand us. For us women's emancipation without national emancipation makes no sense (Mai 1983).

In the words of a VWU staff member:

> Our country can be independent if it is economically strong. If it loses its independence, the household will be destroyed (*nuoc mat nha tan*) (field notes 1994).

The moral power of classical Vietnamese gender ethos, linking women's virtue of self-sacrifice with family stability and the well-being of the community (kin groups, communes, or nation), remains embedded in VWU as an organisation and in society. Commendable as it is, this ethos has placed a considerable burden

179

on working women and on VWU as an organisation during the process of transition and liberalisation. In cooperating with state devolution of its responsibility for the social sector, VWU is finding itself caught in a battle for gender equality on three fronts—women's work and livelihood, family well-being and political representation to prevent further erosion of state accountability.

In the effort to reduce poverty, emphasis has been placed on income-generation credit schemes through the formation of women's savings groups (WSG) using three models of credit (drawn from the South Asian experience).

Model 1 provides access to state banks—the Vietnam Bank for Agriculture and Bank for the Poor—and the National Fund for Poverty Alleviation Programme, through a guarantee fund administered by VWU.

Model 2, *Quy Tinh Thuong* or Affection Fund (QTT) is an adaptation of the Bangladesh Grameen Bank. Capital resources derive from a fund owned by VWU, a loan portfolio from an international Non-governmental Organisation and participants' savings. QTT saving schemes include a component of micro-insurance for education and emergencies.

Model 3 is based on a combination of financial and non-financial intervention—using credit and saving groups as an entry point for other policy objectives such as mother and child health, family planning, water and sanitation, female adult illiteracy eradication, early childhood development, and environmental protection. This model is mainly operational within the context of multilateral and bilateral development cooperation concerned with social development and community and child interests, with women being placed in the position of the main mediator of such interests. Through cooperation between the Ministry of Education and Training and VWU the model combines income-, generation with literacy education and early childhood development. It uses the credit/saving mechanism as an entry point to mobilise women to set up literacy and childcare provision (Albee 1996). By the end of 1999 VWU coverage included six million women, of whom 51 per cent are identified as poor according to locally-based criteria of asset assessment (Phan 2000; Dang 1996).[11]

Despite such an impressive coverage VWU does not command the authority to help women gain more equal access to public funds, and must continue to use the mechanisms of self-supervised short-term loans in small groups that ensure high rates of repayment but place considerable pressure on individual borrowers who cannot afford to lose the trust of the group.[12] The 1997-98 Living-Standards Survey shows that men have more access than women to government banks such as the Agricultural Bank, the Bank for the Poor and the National Fund for Poverty Alleviation. Only 18 per cent of loans obtained by women are from government banks (UNDP 2002: 7). The majority of women still rely on private lenders, or the financial sources of 238 multilateral or bilateral projects run by VWU. These projects involve 1,747 communes and 174,618 households—about one-third of those covered by VWU (Phan 2000).

The involution towards the family carries heavy costs in women's political representation. Women's participation in the National Assembly suffered from a crowding-out syndrome after the war, notably a retreat to the family to ensure its welfare and a yield of political power to men. Their participation began to pick up only after 1997 when economic reforms began to stabilise family livelihoods but seriously undermined women's rights.

Women's representation in the National Assembly is currently high in the Committee for Education, Youth and Children (41.2 per cent) and the Ethnic Council (39.5 per cent). Women's representation in the Committee for Social Affairs is 15.8 per cent; in the Committee for Science and Technology, 10.7 per cent; and in the Committee for Economics and Budget 3.1 per cent (National Assembly Office, 1999).

Insofar as representation in committees of the Communist Party and the government administration is concerned, women appear to play a marginal role. According to NCFAW (2000) the rate of women's representation in the Party's committees is very low, just under 10 per cent at the commune level, a little over 10

Percentage of Females in National Assembly

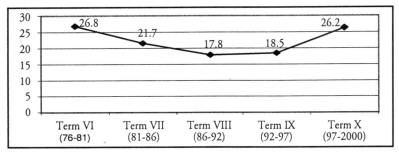

Source: National Assembly Office, 1997 and 1999

per cent at the central level and over 11 per cent at the provincial and district level. Participation in the people's committees, which make decisions and administer government policy from commune to central level, is even weaker—4.54 per cent at commune level, 4.9 per cent at district level and 6.4 per cent at provincial level. By contrast, women's participation in people's councils is significantly much better—22.33 per cent at the provincial level, 20.12 per cent at the district level and 16.56 per cent at the commune level.

The trends in women's political participation show that they have limited power in influencing the vision of the Party and in implementation through executive bodies at all levels. In an economic situation by which the household economy continues to be—and will be for some time to come—the only means of livelihood for many women, without sufficient space for a bottom-up articulation of their quotidian needs and interests, the hard won 'working mother' gender contract may remain a mirage.

Towards a new gender logic of care

In the new era of global integration Vietnam needs to revisit its classical ethos that links the household economy and the family to the nation. A key ideological mechanism is the interchangeable use of the concepts of 'family' and 'household' which conflates emotional relationships with economic relationships. Such

182

conflation hides an ongoing codification of the social domain (family) as economic (household production system)—thus to create self-regulating entities no longer flanked by state support. 'Women's virtue'—when defined as a key feature of the country's cultural identity and a pillar for future generations—serves to cloak the fortification of a masculine political rule. Not only is the return of the 'double-burden' eminent, this return occurs in the household as a gendered terrain of economic, social and emotional power, affecting nearly 90 per cent of the working population. To avoid the negative affects of this trend, the gender logic of care as a virtue must be resurrected. This would require a shift in the line of reasoning from the glorification of women's self-sacrifice (as a virtue and their unique ability to care for others) to another line of reasoning which spreads the notion of care and reciprocity more evenly and fairly between men, women, the state and the market.

One way to initiate this shift would be to appeal to ethical norms of care compatible with local traditions and universal standards of right. Ethical norms of care in the Vietnamese cultural context can be extended beyond care as women's private virtue to cover care as a shared domain, to be maintained by the traditional principle of public virtue, notably *cong-duc*. *Cong-Duc* as a public virtue covers the concern for others, for the commonwealth and common endeavour that may include also the socialisation of markets, or limiting excessive individual profits made at the expense of the collective. The proverb *'an o co duc mac suc ma an'* refers to the principle of *cong-duc* in practice, meaning that: 'observing public virtue in daily practices generates wealth for many generations'.

From the standpoint of childcare, under the United Nations Convention on the Rights of the Child—to which Vietnam is among the first signatories—care can also be seen as a right of the child rather than only as an entitlement of working mothers. In both perspectives—'traditional' virtue and 'modern' universal norms of rights—there is scope for reasoning that care for the next generation in Vietnam should be a common duty of the state and society and not dependent only on women's virtue. From the standpoint of democracy, *cong-duc* as a common concern for others is an explicit expression of the notion of social equality—not uniquely in the sense of redistributive policy but also in the sense of respect for the experiences, viewpoints and needs of others. Concerns for others as a virtue is conditional to the concern for commonwealth and endeavour—or, in modernist terminology, concern for 'development' as a social experience.

The promotion of the household economy has certainly proved to be an efficient means for the state to de-collectivise rural production and to generate self-employment in a period of enterprise 'downsizing'. At one level women's cooperation in the household economy may be seen as individuals' attempts to solve their problems as income earners and care providers, assisted by the efforts of VWU in the different forms. At another level, in the new phase of female-led export industrialisation which is paving the way for the country's integration in the regional and global economy, women's participation in household production and in the domestic private sector can no longer be seen purely as personal choice but as a choice of the state, as an authority; a choice which is also shared by other economic agents. In that regard, the state can neither afford to put further pressure on the household risking an implosion of gender relations, nor ignore women's role in the domestic private sector without the consequent inefficiency in the use of human resources. To maintain its political image as an equaliser and an efficient manager, the state now faces the challenge to foster a social policy no longer based on a dualistic approach to gender, but on a broader notion of gender equality as a public good for all.

Similarly, although VWU through campaigns and action has forged a new role as defender of the social sector, for true success it needs to be free from the cultural image of the 'resourcefulness' of individual women, and from the false notion of female autonomy based on the efficiency of self-regulating women's associations. Claiming their social citizenship rights from the state would help direct necessary resources where needed to foster conditions which enable the 'working mother' gender contract to become activated reality rather than a mirage. Greater balance in the sharing of responsibility for the public good (health, education, community relations) and greater awareness of the significance of a balanced gender division of labour in the household would alleviate both women and men from the tension of combined emotional and economic pressure at the family level.

To summarise: women's specific sociocultural position in Vietnam in the post-war period made it possible for women's organisations to influence state thinking on gender roles in ways honouring equality. The partnership between government and the VWU has sought to reduce male-biased incentives in the labour and credit markets to protect women's employment outside the homes. But it omits the household sector where the majority of women producers are located. Intensification of the process of liberalisation has placed heavy emphasis on women's gender role as mothers; and there has been a subsequent gradual devolution of state responsibilities for women's equal rights onto self-help groups and the family. Thus, although the formulation of the 'working mother' gender contract may be considered as an achievement of the Vietnam Women's Union, state support for crucial gender arrangements that can make this contract actual leaves much room for improvement. The possibility of altering gender norms in political and social institutions remains limited unless VWU can find a new strategy for ethical reasoning on care that brings it beyond a women-centred model to one which emphasises care as a public virtue.

Notes

1 Reforms introduced since 1986 seeking to transform a centrally-planned to a multi-tier market-led economy.

2 50.8 per cent and 49.2 per cent respectively of the 76.3 million total in 2000.

3 From over 18 per cent in 1976 to 26 per cent in 1998.

4 Fluctuating between 53 per cent in 1975 to 51 per cent in 1982 and 48.1 per cent in 2000.

5 Most notable is the Hong-Duc Period ruled by the Le Dynasty (1428–1788) influenced by Buddhist principles. During this period women enjoyed equality in property rights as well as personal rights that protected their

interests as wives, daughters and female citizens. Civil laws also protected women from becoming an object of exchange subject to trafficking and slavery (Ta van Thai 1981).

6 Gender norms introduced under the Nguyen Dynasty (1802–1885) followed orthodox Confucian rules of women's subordination.

7 Matrimonial decision required the approval of the family as well as the workplace administration to ensure loyalty to socialism and to protect state-based entitlements.

8 The law forbids marital violence and divorce initiated by the husband while the wife is pregnant or the infant is under 12 months of age, and recognises housework and childrearing as productive work, which must be viewed as a contribution to family income and common property. Women's economic rights tend to be obliterated by local norms of 'work' and productivity that defy legal definitions.

9 A 1997 survey conducted in three provinces on the effects of social policy on women's well-being reveals that users of childcare services are primarily women workers in the public sector. Women workers in the private sector are more inclined to rely on private means (paid services, grandparents, elder sibling), the overwhelming reason for this being the absence of such services; high fees compared with level of income, distance between home and childcare centre, and the low quality of services.

10 The organisation today has more than 11 million voluntary women members—above 18 years of age—and is the largest mass organisation in the country. Members are predominantly rural women between the age of 30 and 50. A membership fee of 2000 VND (US$ 0.20) is required, but often waived for the poor. It has 4,000 full-time staff including about 300 people (men and women) in its national central office in Hanoi. There are 12,000 grass roots units (women's unions at the commune levels) to implement government policy on women.

11 According to the Office of the Prime Minister, in 2000 the total number of households classified as poor based on international poverty measurement standards was 2.8 million (or 17.2 per cent of the total), of which 2.5 are in the rural areas. Assuming that one woman per poor household had received support, VWU coverage seems to have included the 2.5 per cent of such households in rural areas. Criteria for female poverty assessment—depending on locality—may include: 1) women as 'breadwinners'; 2) thatched roof and earthen dwellings; other assets valued at less than US$ 100; 3) annual food-shortage from three to six months; 4) arable land of less that one *sao* per head; 5) children under 14 with anaemia and other diseases.

12 The repayment rate is highest under model 2 at 99.5 per cent, followed by model 3 at 98 per cent.

References

Albee, A. 1996. *An Evaluation of Credit Mechanisms and Impact for UNICEF-Vietnam and the Vietnam Women's Union*. Project 1: Income Generation and Facts for Life Communications (YF606/f67). Project 2: Income Generation and Literacy Education (YF606/F01).

Appelton, J. 1983. 'Socialist Viet-Nam: Continuity and Change' in *Rural Development and the State: Contradictions and Dilemmas in Developing Countries*. eds. A.M. Lea and D.P. Chaudhuri. London/New York: Methuen.

Belanger, D. and T.H. Khuat. 2001. 'Parents' Involvement in Children's Marriage: Intergenerational relations in the choice of a spouse in Hanoi' in *Vietnamese Society in Transition: The daily politics of reform and change*. ed. J. Kleinen. Amsterdam: Het Spinhuis.

Blanc, M.E. 2001. 'La definition des roles des femmes a travers la presse feminine vietnamienne' in *Vietnamese Society in Transition: The daily politics of reform and change*. ed. J. Kleinen. Amsterdam: Het Spinhuis.

Centre for Women's Studies. 1990. *Selected Indicators on Women in Vietnam*. Hanoi: Statistical Publishing House.

Dang, N.Q. 1996. *Three Credit Models Administered by the Vietnam Women's Union*. Hanoi: Rural Development Service Centre.

Dumont, R. 1995. *La Culture du Riz dans le Delta du Tonkin*. Paris: Maison des Sciences de L'Homme.

Gammeltoft, T. 2001. 'Faithful, Heroic, Resourceful: Changing images of women in Vietnam' in *Vietnamese Society in Transition: The daily politics of reform and change*. ed. J. Kleinen. Amsterdam: Het Spinhuis.

General Statistical Office. 2000. Hanoi.

Gorou P. 1965. *Les Paysans du Delta Tonkinois*. Paris: Ecole Francaise d'Extreme Orient.

Houtart, F. and G. Lemercinier. 1984. *Hai Van: Life in a Vietnamese Commune*. London: Zed Press.

International Development Research Centre and Research Centre for Female Labour. 2002. 'Report on Female Workers of Vietnam's Garment and Textile Industry in the Context of Trade Liberalization'. Hanoi.

Mai, T.T. and T.N.T Le. 1978. *Women in Vietnam*. Hanoi: Foreign Languages Publishing House.

Mai, T.V. 1983. *Vietnam: Un Peuple, Des Voix*. Paris: Pierre Horay.

Marr, D.G. 1971. *Vietnam Anti-Colonialism 1885–1925*. Berkeley: University of California Press.

——. 1981. *Vietnamese Traditions on Trials 1920–1945*. Berkeley: University of California Press.

National Assembly Office. 1997, 1999. cited in Viet Nam Gender Briefing Kit. Canadian International Development Agency 2001.

Pham, T.T.H. and Q.N. Pham. 2001. 'Do Decent Jobs Require Good Policies? Vietnam Country Report'. International Labour Office In Focus Programme. Hanoi: ILO-Vietnam.

Phan, T.T. 2000. *'The Role of Vietnam Women's Union in Creating Economic Opportunities for Women'* (in Vietnamese). Hanoi: VWU Research Department.

Ta, V.T. 1981. 'The Status of Women in Traditional Vietnam: A Comparison of the Code of the Le Dynasty (1428–1788) with the Chinese Code'. *Journal of Asian History.* 15.2. pp. 90–145.

Tetreault, M.A. 1990. 'Women and Revolution in Vietnam' in *Vietnam's Women in Transition.* ed. K. Barry. London: Macmillan Press.

Truong, T.D. 1984. 'Social Consciousness and the Vietnamese Women's Movement in the 20th Century'. A Working Paper. The Hague: Institute of Social Studies.

——. 1994. 'Identification of Areas for Cooperation between the Netherlands Government and the Vietnam Women's Union in the Field of Education and Training'. A Mission Report. The Hague: Institute of Social Studies Advisory Services.

——. 1997. 'Uncertain Horizon: The Women Question in Vietnam Revisited' in *Vietnam—Reform and Transformation.* eds. B. Beckman, E. Hansson and L. Roman. Stockholm: Centre for Pacific Asia Studies.

UNDP. 2002. *Gender Differences in the Transitional Economy of Vietnam.* Hanoi: United Nations Development Programme.

UNESCO. 1989. *The Status of Women in Vietnam.* Bangkok: United Nations Educational, Scientific and Cultural Organisation Regional Office.

Vietnam Human Development Report. 2001. Hanoi: National Political Publishing House.

Vietnam Women's Union. 1997. *An Analysis of the Impact of Social Policy on Women's Living Conditions* (in Vietnamese). Hanoi: Central Office Vietnam Women's Union.

——. 1998. *A Summary of Research Findings on the Implementations of the Labour Codes Concerning the Female Labour Force in Foreign Investment Firms and Domestic Private Firms* (in Vietnamese). Hanoi: Research Department of the Vietnam Women's Union.

Vu, M.L. 2000. *Gender-Based Violence: The Case of Vietnam.* Hanoi: World Bank.

PART III

Human Security

Prospects for Feminist Engagements

9

Globalisation, Social Movements and Feminism
Coming Together at the World Social Forum

VIRGINIA VARGAS

For Julieta Kirkwood, one of the feminist theorists who have contributed the most to a contextualised feminism, the feminist struggle is the 'negation' of factors that alienate women and impede their consolidation as subjects. This struggle is permanently evolving, ensuring that it reflects what is taking place in the 'here and now' and remains linked to the 'global project'. The constant element in the feminist struggle continues to be the active negation of anything that impedes women to develop by permanently affirming the 'right to have rights' (Jelin 2001). The scenarios in which these battles are fought have varied over the decades. In the 1970s and part of the 1980s, the 'here and now' of feminist struggles was aimed at the politicisation of women's struggles in the private sphere (Tamayo 1997), giving a name to what had always remained nameless (violence, sexuality, right to one's own name) and, in the act, broadening and strengthening democracy. This is why 'democracy in the country and at home' was the motto of the Chilean feminists in their struggle against (former dictator General Augusto) Pinochet, which gave a feminist perspective to a global project. In the 1990s, the 'here and now' for many feminists became the urgent need to consolidate what had been given a name through laws and guarantees so that governments were held responsible for women's exclusion, not only at the national level but also globally. In the new millennium, the 'here and now' of many feminist manifestations has taken the form of a struggle for gender and social justice, disputing meanings and orientations with neo-liberal globalisation. And the 'global project' is the dispute over generating alternative contents to this neo-liberal globalisation that can 'govern this globalisation' by challenging its unfair and exclusionary effects with a feminist perspective.

I. Globalisation as the arena of dispute

The process of globalisation is an arena of dispute for social movements with a democratic perspective, with the dispute centring on reclaiming globalisation in all its complexities and dimensions. Doreen Massey (2000: 19) puts it well when she tells us:

> We are faced with a language issue. The word globalization has been 'abducted' to mean just one kind of globalization (neo-liberal and overwhelmingly linked to the economy) ... But 'globalization' really means global inter-connection and it can take on other forms, different meanings and include different kinds of power relations.

As such, some authors prefer to speak about 'processes' of globalisation, alluding to the multiple social dynamics and processes created by the interrelations and interdependent exchanges among social actors at a global level (Mato 2001: 147). The complexities and uneven development of these dimensions have produced new risks, new conflicts and new exclusions, but also have fostered the appearance of new subjectivities, new identities and new social actors who pursue the realisation and enhancement of new rights. Globalisation, considered in all its dimensions, has meant new forms of social organisation [a networked society, according to Castells (1999)], altering the sense of space (for the first time the horizon becomes the whole planet) and time (events happen in real time), making it harder to have a vision of the future and, thus, integrating uncertainty in daily life. These changes have transformed traditional identities, bringing into question old truths and modifying the categories of knowledge.

These are not easy processes because we are not living through an era of intense change but a change of eras.[1] In this change, the crisis of identity is so strong that

'... some discourses change their meaning while others, in different forms and with different goals, challenge the dominant discourses, and new discourses based on old narratives take shape. In sum, the previously existing order is shaken.' (Cairo Carou 2000: 110).

This opens many and unexpected horizons, while at the same time generating new and expanding dynamics of exclusion, especially when (as is happening today) the process of globalisation coincides with the hegemony of the neo-liberal approach, which prioritises market forces and facilitates ungoverned power, without control or regulations, of transnational capital.

These multiple and uncertain processes have generated defensive approaches, more individualism, increased fragmentation, renewed policies for strong identity affirmation, besides various forms of balkanisation and fundamentalism (DAWN 2002; Marchand and Sisson 2000). But they also have fostered broader horizons for transformation of the social movements (the local, the global) and new forms of resistance. By creating new ways to look at reality, this has made previously closed identities more flexible, opening the possibility to expand the contents of citizenship and democracy beyond the notion of nation-state and strengthening new rights and new citizen dynamics at the local and global levels. Globalisation—highly uneven in its scope and impact, which divides at the same time that it integrates—is both a threat and a promise (Waterman 2002).

Because it has been 'abducted', given a hegemonic and partial definition and even seen as some sort of supernatural force that acts independent of human beings (Mato 2001: 147), globalisation is in dispute over its democratic contents, directions and innovations, as well as the need to reclaim its complexities and multiple dimensions. This dispute creates the terrain for new demands and challenges, as well as opening new possibilities for the social movements in general, and Latin American feminisms in particular, to foster new democratic alternatives in the face of this globalisation.

The ambivalent changes

> ... If globalisation is an example of the worst capitalist trends of expansion and domination, we need to know if and why globalisation can also provide opportunities for certain groups of women to leave behind the worst excesses of patriarchal oppression. (Signs 2001)

Feminist analysis of globalisation reveals how economic policies, social movements, the formation of identities and the issues of the subject are generally inseparable from one another (Signs 2001). The uncertainties and multiple meanings of globalisation tend to produce new gender distortions while subverting others, making way for new dynamics of exclusion and inclusion. Rosalba Todaro (2002) analyses that the ongoing economic changes are based on a given gender system, but are the source of tensions that foster changes in its structure, changes that in turn have an impact in the realm of economics. In all structural adjustment processes, women have functioned as a kind of hidden cushion, absorbing the shocks produced by the economic adjustment programmes by intensifying domestic work to compensate for the reduction of social services, as well as bearing the brunt of the privatisation of social security systems due to their reproductive role (social costs of maternity are borne individually, for example). Thus, their position inside the family and the marketplace makes them part of the strategy that deregulates the market. In all the cases, by not taking into account the value of reproductive work,[2] women's workload is substantially increased when the responsibilities for the well-being of citizens are displaced from the public to the private sector.

Previously sustained by a specific paradigm of production and labour relations (based on full-time work in a specific division of labour along sexual lines, among others), this categorisation of gender is eroded by the elimination of the notion of the family income, the lack of work stability for men and the incorporation of women in the workforce (Todaro 2002). The form in which women are incorporated into the workplace through labour flexibility in itself blurs the limits between the public and the private spheres, generating new interrelations among the two.

The uncertainties of globalisation are not only related to the drives and dynamics fostered by the different dimensions in the economic field but also in the political and cultural scenarios, affecting in different ways beliefs and identities. Giddens (1996) alludes to the growing process of de-traditionalisation, which tends to weaken old customs and traditional common practices, among them those related to the relationships between the sexes (toward a flexible sexuality) and univocal family values (which also provoke fundamentalist resistance to defend these values). This does not imply the disappearance of tradition but rather a change in its status, leaving behind the notion of tradition as something that is not questioned and approaching it as something open to interrogation, something about which one can decide. As such, there are considerable changes in reproductive and sexual dimensions and in the institutions that consecrate them. Thus, as Virginia Guzmán (2001) has stated, there has been a weakening of the nuclear family as an institution, a steady acknowledgement of the practices that generate new types of family and a growing trend to separate biological paternity and maternity from social parenting. These changes affect ways to resolve the tension between emancipation and domesticity.

The impact of these economic and cultural changes on women tends to foster an increased capacity for negotiation, since they provide for a greater exposure to notions of autonomy, individuality, freedom and equality, altering their self-perception and condition as subjects of rights, and enabling the proliferation of societal definitions and cultural interpretations about what it would be like to live a 'world as a whole' (Guzmán 2001). Social subjectivities are transformed, and realms for transformation are widened: politics is no longer perceived as existing only in formal spaces, nor is its legitimacy obtained solely through votes or political representation.

It is expanded to forums increasingly more important for citizens of both sexes with daily life on one side and globalised systems on the other (Giddens 1996; Guzmán 2001). This affects notions of citizenship, opening new meanings and multiplying rights that have not been previously considered. National identities are also altered and their centre is removed (de Souza Santos 1994), given that political and territorial borders no longer coincide.

The mutual impact between globalisation and social movements

> The most often touted discourses on ... 'globalization' do not let us see what social actors do, how they perform, and how we can intervene. On the contrary, we need to develop approaches that show us how the processes of globalization come out of policies and practices played by social actors. (Mato 2001: 171)

The impact of globalisation on social movements has been multiple and uncertain. On one side, it has played a role in the fragmentation and particularisation of the struggles. Ongoing economic reforms, as Lechner (1996: 29) has pointed out, not only limit the ability of states to act, but simultaneously foster a vast move toward the 'privatisation of social conducts, generating a "culture of self" reluctant to engage in collective commitments'. It is the same notion put forward by Nancy Fraser (1997: 5) in what she calls the 'post-socialist vision', referring to a cynical state of mind that distrusts the possibility of progressive social change and is reflected in 'the lack of a believable project or emancipation...' and where it would seem that the demands for recognition of the differences have gained considerable importance, while making the demands for social equality irrelevant.

Throughout the 1990s the awareness of rights at a global level slowly expanded thanks to successful global campaigns that positioned new issues (Green Peace and the defence of the environment), new meanings for the classic issues of human rights (Amnesty International), or new meanings of urban mobilisations (people taking to the streets, organising similar mobilisations simultaneously in different countries). United Nations World Conferences have also contributed to this, opening a space to develop critical awareness of what was and was not being addressed in terms of rights on key issues for humanity.

In the past few years, however, there has been a surge of new manifestations with a truly global presence, such as the movements for global justice (also defined as anti-globalisation, or alternative globalisation, or attempts to control the existing globalisation) that had its first dramatic impact in Seattle in 1999 and continues to have a cumulative effect today.[3] These are movements that are expressed as a social and political global force struggling with neo-liberal globalisation in different scenarios and places. Union leaders, ecologists, feminists, old and young fighters for social justice converge in these spaces. The logic of globalisation is thus expressed in the social movements. If national policies are predetermined by guidelines defined at an international level, as Cassen (2001)[4] states, then protests and alternative proposals should also come at this level. 'Anti-globalisation moves forward because it adopts the same logic as the globalisation'. These processes, alternative to the neo-liberal globalisation, have started to converge in different forms in global spaces like the World Social Forum.

Feminisms contribute to this process with multiple experiences and connections, with a rich and long experience of international solidarity, which is demonstrated at the Latin American and Caribbean Feminist Meetings[5] through thematic and identity networks (lesbian groups, Afro-Latin and Caribbean movements) articulated at the regional and global levels. Multiple interactions have also developed through the UN Conferences, especially the 1995 Women's Conference in Beijing, that are constantly widening the network of global connections.

As a result of these alternative global dynamics through which social movements challenge the hegemonic rationale, many authors believe that these movements have the potential for becoming an alternative globalisation based on a model that finds its strength in citizen participation and not the market (Grzybowski 2002). Many authors speak also of the construction of a global civil society

(Held 1995; Waterman 2002; Vargas 1999; Gryzbowski 1995) supported by struggles and resistances, as well as the potential for facing new risks and new rights that arise.

Impact of globalisation in the 'feminist subjects'

In this new context, movements are faced with uncertain trends. Globalisation drives homogenising tendencies, restructuring societies and the forms in which individuals relate to structural and subjective changes (Marchand and Sisson 2000). Fragmentations and re-articulations are generated in a new organisation mode, identified by Castells (1999) as the 'networked society', with ample and cosmopolitan connections. This domain of networks has an

> ... overwhelming multiplicity of possible combinations to exchange tangible and intangible goods ... that flow through a myriad of identifiable nodes and channels that interconnect social groups worldwide. Interactions in the domain of networks comprise all kinds of organisations ... whose interrelations create entangled networks of networks interweaved among themselves, overlapping one onto the other and in constant transformation.

New connections, channels and nodes are thus created, destroying the old ones and experiencing in this process an endless sequence of mutations and evolutions (Sagasti 1998: 21–22).

In this series of connections and interconnections, the existence of social movements is altered and they take on different forms, no longer as unified actors or movements with plural meanings. Instead, they are manifested as a broad, diverse and constantly changing and expanding 'field of actors'. (Jelin 2001). Other authors, such as Sonia Álvarez (in Harcourt and Escobar 2002), reshape the concept of social movements (in reference to feminisms) as a discursive field in expansion, heterogeneous and generating polycentric fields of action that expand on a distinctive set of civil society organisations, building up alternative audiences that reassign and challenge the political and cultural meanings that are dominant in society. These new approaches to the dynamics of movements open the field for endless nuances, trends and spaces through which feminisms move. Forms of resistance vary in this heterogeneous field. Spaces for intervention multiply, connecting and coordinating the collective will of thousands of individuals though electronic exchanges.

In this reality, where diversity and heterogeneity rule, it is not as important or possible to have a defined and agreed upon programme of political, social and economic transformations,[6] but the enunciation and combination of agendas by different collective entities and multiple autonomies interacting from multiple schemes of interpretation. Celiberti (2001) asks, '... What shape should the collective unit take to allow differences to be manifested and respected?' She adds that the forms of organisation that seem too rigid and heavy do not respond to the demand of individuality. New forms of collective action, which are more flexible, lightweight and fleeting, appear to be emerging.

The changes in the directions of feminist struggles at the global level and in their organisational schemes can be analysed from this perspective. While these were never too centralised or hierarchical, the trend toward a looser and more flexible mode begins to stand out and become a common feature of the social movements pursuing an alternative globalisation, stressing the absence of a centralised structure that gives way to flexible articulations and initiatives, which bring together weavings of networks with multiple dynamics. This is not a lack of structure but new forms to articulate connections within and between feminisms.

In this new scenario, the local and the global are not perceived as dichotomies. The global space is such because of the global orientation of the struggles, whose urgency is manifested at the local level but whose resolution can only happen in the global realm that in turn becomes local. Thus, Seattle[7] is a local space, as is Porto Alegre,[8] the Brazilian city where the World Social Forum takes place. The global is, somewhere on the planet, local. Instead of seeing the categories local and global as opposites, Massey (2000) suggests that they be seen as the locations that are related, regardless of distance, and that each becomes a 'knot' in a web of articulations of power. This notion of location expresses very accurately the new dynamics of a networked society.

II. The new dynamics of feminist intervention

Many of the multiple feminist dynamics in Latin America are beginning to look at this new reality. Regional and global networks are analysing and acting upon globalisation. Of all these new dynamics and spaces, I am most interested in analysing feminist advocacy at the World Social Forum (WSF), a plural forum containing proposals for an alternative globalistion where many of the new strategies and concerns of the globalised social movements, like feminism, concur. This is also a complex site in terms of alliances with other movements that do not always acknowledge the position of feminists.

World Social Forum: The place to build alliances and fight against positions of exclusion

The struggle for an alternative globalisation, manifested in many forms in the last decade of the past century comes together in this space. The mottos of the WSF: 'Another world is possible', and 'Say no to a single way of thinking', express the orientation of this new look at globalisation, whose strength lies in the ethical and utopian conviction that democratic and emancipatory forces can build alternative paths.[9] These trends also recognise that there are no recipes or unique actors for this to happen, but a multiplicity of men and women in their role as social actors, contributing their multiple forms of resistance and betting on building democracies with social justice and equality. The 'Charter of Principles' is eloquent with regard to the orientation, interpretation and transformation of the global context.[10] Without a disposition to make decisions, without an inclination to represent anybody, the charter:

> ... rejects the notion of acting as a kind of global vanguard, be it in terms of leadership or as a politically enlightened clique. Its function is to

provide a floor for the discussion to the movement against neo-liberal globalisation'. (Waterman 2002: 4).

Built from new approaches and sensibilities, the WSF also expresses the age-old discrimination and exclusion of women. This is not easy for feminism, as Sonia Correa (2002)[11] has pointed out, because it implies a double strategy: to commit oneself to the collective struggles of the social movements and at the same time to try and transform their approach to feminism, to differences, to gender, to multiple ways of thinking.

Feminisms at the World Social Forum

'Another world is possible', is the motto of the World Social Forum. Looking at it from the perspective of women, the task is much greater than it seems. Without a doubt, we are a troubling spot for the hegemonic way of thinking. But, are we also making ourselves uncomfortable because of our machismo, racism and other forms of intolerance. The motivation behind the WSF is to establish dialogue among diversity. This brings originality and strength to the Forum to build a globalisation of the citizenships of the Planet Earth, but the road is long and full of obstacles. I hope that women force us to be radicals, acting as they have done so far: demanding what is owed to them and making people uncomfortable. (Grzybowsky 2002).

Feminisms bring diversity into this struggle for justice, not only in the lives of women but also in their close relationship with the multicultural and pluri-ethnic characteristics in the region, which are also manifested at the global level. These struggles express two kinds of injustice: socio-economic injustice, rooted in political and economic structures of society and in cultural/symbolic injustice rooted in the social patterns of representation, interpretation and communication. Both types of injustice intersect the lives of women and other racial, ethnic, sexual and geographic dimensions. They are expressed in the uneven distribution of resources and the lack of value assigned to people's lives, and become concrete in the struggle for redistribution and recognition.

Although these struggles have not always been connected, they are intrinsically related,

> ... because the androcentric and sexist norms that become institutionalised in the state and the economy, and the economic disadvantages of women limit their 'voice', preventing their equal participation in cultural creation. (Fraser 1997: 33).

Globalisation of feminisms in the processes of globalisation of the Forum: the Mumbai Forum

The feminisms at the fourth WSF in Mumbai, in January 2004, consolidated what they had been pushing for since the first Forum, and moved forward. The Feminist Dialogue, a meeting held prior to the Forum, brought together 180 feminists from around the world (Asia, the Pacific region, Latin America, Africa, Europe, North America) who had not been involved in a frequent dialogue, let alone in a global feminist dialogue, despite having been connected at different levels. The discussions centred on neo-liberalism, human rights, sexual and reproductive rights, global-local relations and fundamentalisms. It is empowering to see that we are struggling about the same things around the world, and enriching to learn that the common causes of justice and freedom do not necessarily have the same strategies, or the same results. Therefore, we should not expect one single answer or a fixed recipe to deal with the same exclusion and discrimination against women.

The 'dialogue of the differences' between feminists from India and Latin America illustrates this complexity. For many feminists in Latin America, one of the strongest expressions of the struggle to expand women's choices about their lives is the struggle for sexual rights, including abortion. For Indian feminists, however, the struggle for legislation legalising abortion has created other issues given the fact that women tend to abort female embryos. Reproductive rights, also acknowledged by Indian legislation, have not empowered women, but allowed the state to impose ample birth control policies. While this is not an exclusive practice only in India (during the administration of former President Alberto Fujimori in Peru the state's language on women's rights and reproductive rights facilitated forced surgical sterilisation policies aimed at women of childbearing age, mainly poor and of a peasant background), the crudeness with which policies are applied in India is paralysing.

This is probably why many feminists do not see the discourse on rights as the adequate space for the orientation and the transgression of the feminist struggles. This was manifested in one of the documents prepared by the team in charge of the Feminist Dialogues:

> Using a human rights approach to effect cultural transformations to pose a challenge to fundamentalism/s have limited success. This is because the human rights discourse is framed by the existence of the United Nations. This implies that the discourse is grounded in some notion of the nation state as implementer, even as it seeks to move away from it into a collective of nation states ... The human rights discourse would seem to be inadequate because it lacks the vocabulary to unravel collective, social power as it bases itself on the premise of the individual. In defining human rights as accruing to every individual, the human rights discourse puts into shade the multilayered existence of the individual as part of many collectivities. Thus it fails to take cognisance of the multiple, and sometimes contradictory interests that individuals embrace simultaneously as part of these collectivities. Therefore feminist critiques of the family, patriarchy, and state are often used only 'strategically' in the human rights discourse.[12]

It is undoubtedly true that the discourse of the United Nations, which continues to resist democratisation, will continue to revolve around nation states. It is also true that the 'official' discourse is homogenising. At the same time, the United Nations has greatly contributed to positioning these rights universally, and this has been fundamental for these rights to be respected, even if minimally, in countries around the world. World Conferences carried out in the last decade of the 20th century greatly widened the framework of rights. Feminists learned to bargain autonomously in this space opened by the United Nations. The international legislation developed up to now by the United Nations, often pressured for by the social movements, constitutes a fundamental frame of reference even though it is insufficient and needs to be further developed.

However, the relationship between the feminists and the United Nations has been ambivalent and there has been an element of 'contention' about widening the margins of influence and the contents of the legislation related to gender. The expansion of women's human rights has been the focal point of the contention. A widening of human rights to rethink the universality that hides and homogenises differences has been part of the feminist proposals and initiatives. Thus, the equality contained in the discourse on rights cannot be the only principle guiding social emancipation, because it is precisely this equality that has hidden the huge diversities in the faces, sexes, ethnic origins, colours, ages and histories of people's lives. Equality is not the same if it is not based on the acknowledgement of differences. Therefore, we have the right to be equal as well as different. And we have the right to be different when equality obliterates what is characteristic about us, as de Souza Santos (2003: 19) states, hiding and not recognising us.

An effort is underway to reclaim old agendas with new faces and new alliances, which contribute to a greater sense of entitlement to rights. In the case of Latin America, the struggle is increasingly centred on economic and social rights—the most devalued dimension of women's citizenship, and sexual rights—the most controversial and resisted dimension of rights even within the forces of change. The struggle for abortion is part of this process. However, unlike the occurrence in the past, there is an explicit interest in connecting it to wider democratic processes, which is the only way to limit the impact by conservative and fundamentalist forces. While the issue is already being discussed in the legislatures of countries like Uruguay due to pressure from and alliances of the feminist movement, in most other countries the Day of the Unborn is gaining support and becoming official, and even access to information and contraceptive methods are being removed from the public health care system and taken away from women, most of whom are poor. The body is at the centre of the political debate and of discussions on individual freedoms and enhanced democratic frameworks. This is true with respect to feminisms, the movement of sexual orientation in all its variants, and the fight to control AIDS, all of which encounter massive resistance by the hierarchy of all churches and other religious institutions and even democratic governments. The struggle for sexual rights aims at retrieving the body as a political focal point which acts '... as a mediator of the experience of social and cultural relationships ... therefore, the body is not only tied to the private sphere or the individual being, but also linked to the place, to the local level, to the public space' (Harcourt and Escobar 2002). This political body is manifested in all the private and public spaces and interactions. It does not exist as such, however.

This struggle has also been manifested in the global space through the efforts of feminists, especially the campaign by Catholics for Choice, to make the United Nations rescind the Vatican's status as an observer mission of the United Nations. This can also be in seen in the Campaign Against Fundamentalisms, by the Marcosur Feminist Group at the WSF, which attempts to articulate political, economic, cultural and religious issues:

> Religious, economic or cultural fundamentalism always have a political expression that legitimises the mechanisms of violence and constraints exercised by one group over another group, of one person over another person. Essentially exclusive and belligerent, fundamentalism undermines the construction of a project of humanity in which all people have right to have rights. It is fed by a pursuit of a primal, tribal identity that apparently, 'restores' a sense of belonging seen as threatened. But this form of tribal identity which in the name of God or the homeland or the free market, considers those who have and want other ways of living in society as enemies, becomes a true obstacle for the future of human coexistence.[13]

This campaign is now global and visible at the WSF, where the struggle against fundamentalisms is open to all the single ways of thinking, one's own and someone else's.

The Forum is also a place of 'contention' among the

movements, coalitions and networks that take part in the event, preserving identities without bargaining or affirming the difference in connection with the other differences. The dynamics oriented toward a new way of negotiating conflicts and diversities run into dynamics of resistance, both from individuals and groups. The problem is not, however, the existence of tendencies or conflicts—which are the laboratory of democracy—but their simultaneous and conflicting existence, without looking for spaces of 'translation' referred to by de Souza Santos.

These spaces for translation are based on the negation of the existence of a general theory in which diversity is cannibalised by a false universalism or false single strategies, and the affirmation of a theory that connects and 'translates' the life experiences and visions, the partial totalities. It is a '… process which allows mutual intelligibility among experiences of the world, as accessible as possible'. Individual codes, political, symbolical and often contradictory differences, rivalries that produce fragmentation and atomisation, which de Souza Santos (2003: 25) refers to as the dark side of diversity and multiplicity, undoubtedly represent a risk.

> This risk has been assessed by many of the movements but none by itself has the ability to overcome it without a major effort of mutual recognition, dialogue and debate, creating a 'contact zone' in all movements, strategies and practices, in every discourse and piece of knowledge; this contact zone can be porous and therefore permeable to other NGOs and movements. For example, a translation between the concept of human rights and the Hindu and Islamic notions of human dignity; between Western development strategies and Gandhi's *swadeshi;* between Western philosophy and oral sagesse from Africa; between modern democracy and traditional authorities; between indigenous movements and ecologists; between the workers' union movement and feminists. … The future of the counter-hegemonic globalisation depends on it.

Finally, the feminists at the fourth WSF tried to put forward the possibility of this translation. In the India Forum the feminists also launched, as a contribution to the methodology of the Forum, a different way to approach diversity, fostering an ongoing and currently urgent debate. The panel, 'Dialogue among movements', invited feminists, union leaders, and gay, lesbian and transsexual people, to acknowledge their differences and reclaim their similarities. It was an effort to retrieve the plural words represented more and more at the WSF, from the challenge to understand and accept the politics of differences and the notion of multiple and conflicting identities, as well as to build strategies for social justice and equality among inter-movements.

In this way, they were acting upon their political interest to build bridges between the movements, finding common ground in their struggles against globalisation and fundamentalism, and establishing this crossover feminist policy.[14]

It would seem then that the 'here and now' of feminisms in the new millennium consists of reclaiming these plural words, translating them into a political project where diversity is acknowledged and dealt with subjectively, and not simply tolerated. This will allow feminist initiatives to be expressed and enhanced with the lessons learned from the acknowledgements and connections with other democratic struggles, feeding new political cultures that take into account the explosion of new identities and new male and female social actors, and which have justice of redistribution and justice of acknowledgement as the two main axles of its proposal for transformation.

Notes

[1] *Human Development Report*, Chile, 2000.

[2] This is also known as reproductive economy, in charge of the domestic, care and community work carried out in a society, generally by women.

[3] A quick and strong local repression to the mobilisations was set to guard the facilities of the meeting, and armed aggression already left one casualty in Geneva one year later.

[4] Bernard Cassen is president of ATTAC, one of the most active groups around these mobilisations, and director of *Le Monde Diplomatique*.

[5] In 24 years nine Meetings have been organised in various countries of Latin America and the Spanish Caribbean. The tenth was to take place in November 2005, in Brazil, which hosted the third Meeting 20 years ago.

6 Feminists also arrive at this global process differently than they did in the past. That is, they don't come from one single identity or from a hypothetical 'global feminists sisterhood', which derives its present from a context and a political framework to relate to, by alluding to a shared and hegemonic way of being a woman, or to a single position as feminists.

7 Seattle was the first city in which the anti-globalisation movement came out openly and massively in 1999. The mobilisation, including over 50,000 activists from labour unions, environmental and feminist groups, as well as from many other movements, came about the World Trade Organisation Summit, led by the Davos Group. The WTO was a total failure and the anti-globalisation movement continued to grow, holding similar demonstrations through the last five years in the different cities around the world where these meetings have taken place.

8 Porto Alegre is a Brazilian city with a long-standing democratic tradition. This is where the WSF was set to take place, since 2001, in its three first versions, receiving enormous support from the city authorities. The groups organising the WSF were, besides the Brazilian organisations, several groups belonging to the anti-globalisation movement. Later on, many more groups and movements adhered to the initiative. About 13,000 participated in the first Forum, but this number has increased dramatically. The fourth version of the Forum, held in 2004 in India, drew 150,000 people. The WSF in 2005 was held again in Porto Alegre, and after that it will move to other regions of the world again.

9 The dynamism of the Forum is probably its most promising feature. In one year not only did it multiply its participation four-fold (from 13,000 to 60,000 people), but it was also more diverse, opening up in terms of issues covered and discourses, and becoming concerned about its process of democratisation.

10 The Charter of Principles has a plural character and takes no sides. It opposes the armed struggle. The Brazilian Secretariat of the WSF drafted it in June 2001, six months after the first WSF.

11 And we are not alone. The fact that Cándido Grzybowsky, one of the most important visionaries of the WSF and a big supporter of the initiative, had publicly taken a stand on the issue of women's exclusion is in itself an encouraging gesture: 'There is a structural bias that prevents women from taking on a leading role ... It is sad to have to acknowledge that the WSF was still too small in social terms regarding the participation of women' (2002).

12 Concept Note. 'Contested Terrains: Women's Human Rights and the Intersection of Globalisation and Fundamentalism, 2004'.

13 From the 'Political Statement on Fundamentalisms', by the Marcosur Feminist Group.

14 Concept Document of the Panel.

References

Aguiton, Christophe. 2002. *O Mundo nos Pertenece.* Rio de Janeiro: Viramundo.

Álvarez, Sonia. 1998. 'Latin American Feminisms "Go Global": Trend of the 1990s and Challenges for the New Millennium' in *Cultures of Politics, Politics of Cultures: Re-visioning Latin American Social Movements.* eds. Sonia Álvarez, Evelina Dagnino, Arturo Escobar. Boulder: Westview Press.

Cairo Carou, Heriberto. 2000. 'Jano Desorientado. Identidades político-territoriales en América Latina'. *Leviatán.* no. 79. Madrid. pp. 107–119.

Cassen, Bernard. 2001. 'Alarma Neoliberal ante la Oposición Mundial. Ladran, Sancho' in *Le Monde Diplomatique.* España. March.

Castells, Manuel. 1999. 'Los Efectos de la Globalización en América Latina por el Autor de "la Era de la Información."' *Insomnia.* no. 247. June. Uruguay: Separata Cultural.

Celiberti, Lilian. 2001. 'Retos para una Nueva Cultura Política'. *Lola Press.* no. 15. May-October. Uruguay: Lolapress Latinoamérica.

Correa, Sonia, 2002. 'Globalización y Fundamentalismo: Un Paisaje de Género' in *Alternativas de Desarrollo con Mujeres para una Nueva Era.* Porto Alegre, Brasil: Abordando el Foro Social Mundial. Suplemento DAWN.

DAWN Informs. 2002. 'World Social Forum 2002'. Fiji Islands: Development Alternatives for Women in a New Era. March.

De Souza Santos, Boaventura. 1994. *Towards a New Common Sense: Law, Science and Politics in the Paradigmatic Transition.* New York: Routledge.

——. 2003. 'The World Social Forum: Towards a counter-hegemonic globalisation'. Paper presented at the XXIV International Congress of the Latin American Studies Association. Dallas, USA. March.

Feminist Dialogues. 2004. Concept Note. 'Contested Terrains: Women's Human Rights and the Intersection of Globalisation and Fundamentalism'. Mumbai, India.

Fraser, Nancy. 1997. 'Iustitia Interrupta. Reflexiones Críticas desde la Posición "Postsocialist"?' Santa Fe de Bogotá: Siglo del Hombre Editores. Universidad de los Andes, Facultad de Derecho.

Giddens, Anthony. 1996. 'Reflexiones de Anthony Giddens sobre el Proceso de Mundialización' (Extractos de su discurso de apertura en la conferencia de UNRISD sobre Mundialización y Ciudadanía). *Boletín UNRISD Informa.* France. no. 15.

Grzybowski, Cándido. 1995. *Civil Society's Responses to Globalisation.* Rio de Janeiro: Phil Courneyeur.

——. 2002. 'Es Posible un Mundo más Femenino?' in *Foro Social Mundial.* web document. 31 January-5 February.

Guzmán, Virginia. 2001. 'Las Relaciones de Género en un Mundo Global'. Documento elaborado por Virginia Guzmán. Consultora de la Unidad Mujer y Desarrollo-CEPAL.

Harcourt, Wendy and Arturo Escobar. 2002. 'Women and the Politics of Place' in *Development, Place, Politics and Justice: Women Facing Globalization*. *Development*. March. Rome: Society for International Development.

Held, David. 1995. *Democracy and the Global Order. From the Modern State to Cosmopolitan Governance*. London: Polity Press.

Jelin, Elizabeth. 2001. 'Diálogos, Encuentros y Desencuentros: los Movimientos Sociales y el MERCOSUR'. web document.

Lechner, Norbert. 1996. 'La Problemática Invocación de la Sociedad Civil' en *Los Limites de la Sociedad Civil*. Revista *Foro* # 28. Bogotá: Ediciones Foro Nacional por Colombia. pp. 24–33.

Marchand, Marianne H., and Anne Sisson Runyan. 2000. 'Introduction. Feminist Sightings of Global Restructuring: Conceptualizations and Reconceptualizations' in *Gender and Global Restructuring. Sightings, Sites and Resistances*. eds. Marianne Marchand and Anne Sisson Runyan. London/New York: Routledge.

Massey, Doreen. 2000. *The Geography of Power*. London: Red Pepper. July.

Mato, Daniel. 2001. 'Des-fechitizar la "globalización": basta de Reduccionismos, Apologías y Demonizaciones, mostrar la Complejidad y las Prácticas de los Actores', in Estudios Latinoamericanos sobre Cultura y Transformaciones Sociales en Tiempos de Globalización 2. ed. Daniel Mato. Caraças: UNESCO-CLACSO. pp. 147–177.

Sagasti, Francisco R. 1998. 'El Surgimiento y los Desafíos del Orden Global Fracturado'. *Agenda*. Lima, Peru. October.

SIGNS 2001. 'Editorial' in *SIGNS Journal of Women in Culture and Society*. vol. 26. no. 4. summer. Chicago: University of Chicago Press.

Sisson Runyan, Anne and Marchand, Marianne H. 2000. 'Conclusion. Feminist Approaches to Global Restructuring' in *Gender and Global Restructuring. Sightings, Sites and Resistances*. eds. Marianne H. Marchand and Anne Sisson Runyan. London/New York: Routledge.

Tamayo, Giulia, 1997. 'La "Cuestión de la Ciudadanía" y la Experiencia de Paridad'. Centro Flora Tristán. Unpublished document.

Todaro, Rosalba. 2002. 'El Género en la Economía Global'. Paper presented at Panel Regional de Desarrollo, Globalización, Mercados y Derechos. La Perspectiva de las Mujeres. Organizado por Iniciativa Feminista de Cartagena en el Foro Social Mundial. 3 February.

Vargas Valente, Virginia. 1999. 'Ciudadanías Globales y Sociedades'. *Nueva Sociedad*. Caracas. no. 163. September-October.

Waterman, Peter. 2002. 'What is Left Internationally? Reflections on the 2nd World Social Forum in Porto Alegre'. Working Paper Series 362. The Hague: ISS.

10

Measuring Women's Empowerment
Developing a Global Tool

SASKIA E. WIERINGA

Introduction

Gender equality and women's empowerment have become key concepts in the international development discourse. This chapter argues that—being an extremely important step forward at the time—the major index developed by the United Nations Development Programme (UNDP) in the mid 1990s to measure women's empowerment on a global scale, the Gender Empowerment Measure (GEM), has serious flaws. A more in-depth theorisation on concepts of gender, power and women's empowerment that underlies the GEM would lead to a more sensitive instrument. It discusses the measurement of women's empowerment in the African Gender and Development Index (AGDI) which was recently launched and stresses the need to pay particular attention to care, sexuality and women's rights, issues which are not captured in the GEM.

Gender and power—contested concepts

The GEM was constructed to assess the measure of gender inequality on the global scale and to provide a tool to monitor women's empowerment for policy purposes. In the flow of debate that followed its introduction in 1995, the central concepts deployed—gender, power and women's empowerment—have

211

received little attention. Most discussion focused on an assessment of the Gender-related Development Index (GDI) that was introduced at the same time. The strong reliance of the GDI on a country's Gross Domestic Product (GDP) was especially criticised (see e.g. Bardhan and Klasen 1999; Dijkstra 2002). Both the GDI and the GEM have been discussed elsewhere with the arithmetic used in the GDI, the conceptualisation of gender and labour, and the reliance of these instruments on international data sets which may lead to various shortcomings (Charmes and Wieringa 2003). This chapter will focus on power and empowerment.

The GEM is built on three indicators, women's participation in economic, political and professional activities. This means that important aspects of women's lives are not taken into account. The way even these three indicators are defined ignores central aspects within each of them. For instance, political power is measured by the number (as a proportion) of women in parliament. But the concepts of gender and women's empowerment should be used in a more holistic and critical way, incorporating a fuller range of concerns with which women are confronted.

The development of the concept of gender as an analytical tool is one of the greatest gains of women's studies. Seeing the categories of 'women' and 'men' not as biological phenomena (sex)[1] but as cultural constructions (gender) and thus as essentially unstable, has had major theoretical consequences. The concept of gender makes it possible to see how particular discursive practices produce and reproduce both feminities and masculinities in particular patterns. It also allows the understanding of the wide variety of gender patterns, including the grafting of more than one gender upon one particular sex (Blackwood and Wieringa 1999).[2] Neither women nor men are homogeneous social categories; they are divided by class, age, race, ethnicity and sexual preference. These intersectionalities are complex and dynamic.

Gender relations have both social and political dimensions, are embedded in discursive constructions, and operate in four interrelated configurations (Scott 1989). The first is the set of cultural symbols which portray both womanhood and manhood. The prevalence of these symbols and myths is universal, but the symbolic arrangements themselves are culturally specific. The second are the normative concepts that usually operate in binary ways. Scott then notes, thirdly, that struggles over these concepts and symbols are political—clearly seen in periods of social or political upheaval when they can be rewritten. Lastly, gender is an important part of an individual's identity.

Gender regimes, like other binary constructs, typically operate in a combination of three critical dimensions. First, a particular phenomenon, for instance bodily difference in human beings, is ontologically divided in two types, females and males. Second, the variations within the two poles of this binary division are suppressed and homogenised ('all wo/men are the same'). Third, a hierarchy is created, when one pole gets precedence over the other. In this way differences, that may initially not be all that significant, become the basis of power formations. Thus the similarities between women and men as human beings are downplayed, the differences stressed and then hierarchised.

In this chapter, power is understood not only as operating 'from above' but as permeating all discursive formations. In Foucault's work power is perceived as being deployed at all levels of society, from interpersonal relations to the state level (Foucault 1972, 1976, 1980a and b). The intention of power structures is not tied to individuals, as the power games acquire their own logic. The force relations operating at different levels are in eternal conflict. Confrontation and opposition are inherent, and the inevitable effects of the power games.

People are not passive beings, but through exercising agency they have the power to either resist or submit to oppressive relations. This may result in new (either more egalitarian or more oppressive) relations of power, and/or reproduce existing power structures (McNay 2000). The reiteration inherent in any process of reproduction ensures continuity at the same time as it enables transformation (Butler 1993). The distinction between compliance, support, resistance or submission depends on the level of consciousness people have about their lives, their political awareness of gender concerns, the material and symbolic strength of the power relations they are faced with and the interests particular actors (both women and men) have or perceive they have in the current system of power relations. In this respect it is important to realise that silence may constitute a critical dimension of power. That which is not spoken about also cannot be contested. In various countries for instance HIV/AIDS is an area in which publicly a culture of silence reigns related to the taboo of speaking on sexuality. It is more accepted to attribute an AIDS death to a less controversial disease, such as tuberculosis, or to stress the economic connotations the HIV pandemic has, than to talk about the ways the infection gets transmitted sexually (Wieringa 2002, 2003).

Power is the motor that creates, reproduces and sustains but also changes hierarchies. In our assessment of the GEM and the subsequent work on the AGDI the focus is on three ways of looking at power and power relations: a) the mode of operation, b) the conditions and situations in which it appears and c) its mode of visibility.

In the mode of operation of power three aspects can be distinguished: it can be oppressive as in the form of military or patriarchal power; it can be challenging and counter women's oppression and hegemonic masculinity (Connell 1995) in the form of women's and queer movements and organisations worldwide; and it can be a creative force, not only in the sense of arts and culture, but also in the realisation of individual potential. The processes of empowerment of both women and men are related to all three dimensions: exposing the oppressive power of the existing gender relations, critically challenging them and creatively trying to shape different social relations.

In considering the mode of appearance of power we see that power relations are pervasive. They operate not only at the level of state power, but also in intimate relations. They manifest themselves at various levels of human existence both in speech and written texts and also at the level of institutions and in other discursive formations. They can also be seen at work in daily practices.

In looking at its mode of visibility Lukes' (1986) theory on the three dimensions of power is relevant. The first distinguishes those processes that are manifest in open confrontations: the 'power to' effect changes which can be exercised through the use of open force, or conversely through open rebellion against oppression. The second relates to 'power over', by which one group manages to suppress certain conflicts, to prevent their being discussed by not even putting them on the agenda. Usually this kind of power operates within certain biases and assumptions that effectively serve to deny the validity of specific concerns or interests. These latent power imbalances are recognised by women and felt as injustice, but they are powerless to do much about it.

With the third dimension of power, Lukes points to those invisible processes which deny the 'real interests' of certain groups of people which may not even be recognised as such by them. They also occur when certain issues are seen as natural and unchangeable or because they are valued as divinely ordained and beneficial. Bourdieu (1977) calls this the level of the doxa, the 'common sense'. This is the level of the 'natural', that which is generally accepted, that which is never contested, not even experienced as unequal. This level is the most difficult to reach, because it is ingrained so deeply in the psyches of both women and men, often strongly supported by various institutions, such as legal structures, educational and religious institutions and the media. This is where power masquerades not only as silence, and as acquiescence, but even in glorification of suffering. A major difficulty here is to determine what women's 'real interests' are. Wide cultural, political and psychological differences will be noted. For this discussion of women's empowerment at a global scale, perhaps CEDAW, the Convention on the Elimination of Discrimination Against Women, can be assumed to represent women's 'real interests'.

Women's empowerment

To examine the concept of women's empowerment it is important to distinguish its field of operation, its dimensions, its linkages, and its intersections with other fields of power relations, such as those of race/ethnicity and class. To map this field, the Women's Empowerment Matrix (WEM) was constructed (Wieringa 1994, 1997) with the main purpose, as will be explained, to increase the visibility of the fields of operation of gender power.

Women's empowerment can also be seen as a process in which the following elements must be considered: awareness/consciousness, choice/alternatives, resources, voice, agency and participation. This dimension of women's empowerment is linked to enhancing women's ability to make choices over the areas in their lives that matter to them, both the 'strategic life choices' that Kabeer (1999) discusses and choices related to daily life.

The Women's Empowerment Matrix (WEM)

The WEM can be used both to map general gender issues at the national level and to sketch the contours and demonstrate the linkages between gender issues within specific domains, such as education, women's labour or HIV/AIDS. It emphasises the interconnections between the various spheres in which women's (dis)empowerment takes place and is acted out.

The spheres distinguished are: physical, sociocultural, religious, political, legal and economic. The levels range from the personal to the global. The matrix does not indicate possible causal relationships or correlations. It is simply a tool that may help researchers/planners to get an overview of the area in which they are working, and to point to possible linkages with other areas. Thus on one axis the various levels of women's subordination are presented, and on the other axis the various spheres in which women's subordination is acted out. The intersections in the field between these two axes indicate some of the multiple interconnections that are relevant to this topic. There are many ways of filling in the matrix, depending on the purpose for which it is used, awareness-raising, planning, policy analysis etc.

For reasons of space the WEM will not be discussed at length here, except for a few remarks to illustrate its usefulness. If the economic sphere in the WEM is considered, the interconnections

Women's Empowerment Matrix (WEM)

	Physical	*Socio-cultural*	*Religious*	*Political*	*Legal*	*Economic*
Individual						
Household						
Community						
State						
Region						
Global						

between the various levels, from the global to the personal can immediately be recognised. Many development projects that aim to empower women focus on economic issues at the household or community level, such as the provision of micro-credit. However, religious or sociocultural constraints or economic development at the supra-community level can impede the realisation of the full potential of the loan. Similarly, structural adjustment policies, trade liberalisation and other processes of economic restructuring and globalisation have a direct impact on the employability and wage levels of individuals. These are well-known issues and often demonstrated. But more aspects spring to mind if the horizontal linkages are also considered. The link with the legal sphere is the first one encountered: labour laws for instance, and especially their implementation. Further away, in the political sphere, one can think of freedom of organisation and speech. In the sociocultural and religious spheres, the sexual division of labour, and the effects of religions such as Christianity and Islam are important factors. The link between the physical and the economic spheres can be illustrated by issues of sexual harassment at work, control over women's mobility and sexuality that may have an impact on their employability. It is also possible to make care work visible. Under the headings 'household' and 'sociocultural' the various aspects of women's work in relation to the caring of children and the sick can be assumed. Under the headings of 'individual' and 'physical' sexual services are located.

217

The major purpose of the matrix is to make theoreticians and practitioners in the field of women and development aware of the holistic nature of the specific issues they are dealing with. It may help in incorporating critical concerns in areas related to particular policy interventions that otherwise may have escaped attention. The matrix in itself, however, is only useful for qualitative purposes. It can only indicate areas on which quantitative data might be collected but it cannot be used as such for purposes of quantification. Also, it does not in itself provide historical depth, although it might be used to indicate areas where historical research might be enlightening. The matrix should ideally be made three-dimensional, following the model outlined above to capture the full dimensions of the mode of visibility, the manifest, the latent and the doxa-related levels of power.

Women's empowerment as a process

While the Women's Empowerment Matrix calls attention to the interconnections between the various spheres and levels in which women's power is acted out, awareness of these issues does not automatically lead to the process of empowering women. This is not a linear process. Increased visibility of gender inequalities and the disruption of 'common sense' may not directly lead to women's empowerment. The motivation to change existing gender relations, even when they are perceived to be unequal depends on many factors, such as women's subjectivities, their personal histories and the perceived costs and risks of transformation. In line with these complexities of the concepts of gender and power, different aspects of the process of empowerment have different dynamics and operate from the level of women's collective empowerment to women's movement and organisations, to policy interventions.

Awareness and consciousness come first at the manifest level of power relations, where women's subordination is most clearly visible and felt. Yet, whether this awareness of oppression can be translated into agency depends on many factors which range from education to the existence of alternatives, and from political conditions to subjective qualities such as inner strength and self-esteem. In the process of women's empowerment the existence of alternatives is crucial. Women may be aware of the conditions of their oppression, but if they see no viable alternatives, if there are no choices available, they can only turn their anger inwards, into frustration and bitterness, or into (religious) acceptance of suffering. Women's capability to make meaningful decisions over critical areas of their lives depends to a large extent on the existence of alternatives. For women's empowerment to be successful, they must have access to resources. These can be of different kinds, such as a sufficient government budget to implement policies; social resources such as health care, or various forms of training (management, accounting, leadership skills, gender training); and physical resources, such as access to office space and legal instruments, including the potential to make use of them.

An important step is for women to have a voice to discuss their grievances, and to find a legitimate base to resolve such grievances when they enter the public and the political arena. Women's political power spans many more areas than national parliaments, the indicator that the GEM uses. Ideally women should be accepted as full and equal partners at all levels where decisions are made about their lives. We see from the WEM that this effectively means that there are very few corners in social and political life that, do not affect women's existence.

Another important factor in empowerment is when women acquire agency, when they start acting on their own behalf. Agency may imply meaningful and purposeful intervention, the construction of something 'new' which may be at the personal level, when they fight to get an education, to start an enterprise, or to resist contracting a marriage they don't want. Or it may be at the collective level, when women set up their own group, or collective, or carry out some research. But agency may not lead only to such positive outcomes. In situations where women accept the doxa level of gender regimes that construct men as inherently superior, women's agency may be turned against other particular interests of their own, or may negatively affect other women who are in inferior hierarchies of a different order (age, class, ethnicity).

They may for instance accept limitations on their mobility or social contacts in order to be perceived as 'good women', and force others (daughters) to do so likewise. Agency starts with critical reflection and may involve resistance, but also bargaining, manipulation or deception, if overt resistance is perceived to be too dangerous.

In this respect, Kabeer's (1999) discussion on the linkages between resources, agency and achievements in relation to women's empowerment is interesting. She draws among others on Sen's (1985) work on capabilities, the potential that people have for living the lives they want. This implies that women must be able to make choices and thus must have the resources to distinguish between various sets of alternatives. Kabeer focuses on what she defines as 'strategic life choices', related to marriage, children, residence, choice of livelihood and friends. However, when women make 'choices' in these areas, these may not always decrease their marginalisation or subordination, due to particular cultural constraints, in which they have come to accept particular forms of disempowerment as 'natural'. On the other hand it can be very empowering for women to make choices in other areas of life. It depends on the particular gender regime whether the choices they make in everyday life are empowering or whether within a particular sexual division of labour women are only 'allowed' to make choices in those areas and not in others.

Global instruments: the GDI and the GEM

The most widely used global instruments to indicate the gender gap in socio-economic and political development are the GDI, the Gender-related Development Index, and the GEM, the Gender Empowerment Measure. In preparation for the Fourth World Conference on Women, which was held in September 1995 in Beijing, the Human Development Report Office of the UNDP devoted its annual report to women's empowerment. Equality, sustainability and empowerment are the three keywords the UNDP uses to assess development efforts. In its analysis the UNDP demonstrates that human development, if not engendered, is endangered, a conclusion that turned into a powerful slogan. Secondly, the UNDP stresses that women's emancipation, far from being dependent on national income levels, as is often assumed, is actually a political process. These are important conclusions that have had a wide impact. For the first time gender issues were measured on a global scale, and countries were ranked on their treatment of women. Gender planners at all levels and women's NGOs alike have used the GDI and the GEM to argue for certain measures. However, using the above analysis of gender and empowerment, the GEM particularly falls far short of what it promises: it measures women's empowerment only to a very limited extent.

The GDI concentrates on the same variables as the Human Development Index, (HDI), built on the work of Sen (1985) and others (Streeten et al., 1981).[3] The GDI, in focusing on the same indicators as the HDI, life expectancy, educational attainment and adjusted real income, adjusts the HDI for gender inequality. In the ensuing debates several points of critique were raised to the HDI in general, and its dependence on the GDP. A major reason for this close fit is that the HDI itself is strongly positively correlated to GDP per capita (Dijkstra and Hanmer 2000, citing Pyatt 1992) and due to the close relationship between them, the GDI will also show that strong correlation. Dijkstra and Hanmer (2000) computed a scatter plot of GDI against the natural log of real GDP (per capita) for 137 developing countries. Their findings demonstrate that the GDI and GDP are closely correlated. This means that the level of gender (in)equity is substantially 'explained' by the income level of a country (see also Bardhan and Klasen 1999, Dijkstra 2002). The GDI thus measures general welfare rather than gender (in)equality in itself.

GEM, scope and limitations

In 1995 the Human Development Report Office (HDRO) also presented a second index, the Gender Empowerment Measure (GEM), which focuses on three variables that reflect women's participation in society. While the GDI simply is the HDI disaggregated for gender, the GEM is more ambitious, as it aims to measure women's empowerment on a global scale. The indicators on which the GEM is built measure the female share in political power (seats in parliament), or political decision making; managerial positions in the administrative and professional sectors; and income. As with the GDI, the HDR does not measure simple relative shares that would measure inequality, but the population-weighted harmonic means. The income variable is computed in a similar fashion as the GDI with the only difference that unadjusted per capita income is used, as the UNDP views income here as a source of power and does not take its contribution to basic development into account. Dijkstra (2002) computed that the income component of the GEM is even more influenced by absolute levels of income than is the case with the GDI. This means, for instance, that rich countries, such as the Netherlands, will always be ranked much higher than poor countries such as Bhutan, although Bhutan may feel it has reached a high level of gender equality (Wieringa 1997). What is lacking is an instrument that measures the gender gap.

Another reliability problem is that political power is measured by women's share of parliamentary seats. There are various points of concern here. First, parliaments are not always the locus of power in a country. A military dictatorship, with a parliament that can only accept decisions taken by the country's ruling generals, is not a powerful body. In those cases change may come from below, as happened in Indonesia in 1998, when its President, General Suharto, was forced to resign. Women's political participation was better measured at that time by the strength of the women's movement, and by the share of women in the leadership of the student demonstrations than by the number of women in the powerless and corrupt parliament. Many forms of power, both formal and informal, exist outside of parliament. Second, (high) numbers of women in parliament may not always indicate women's power, even when parliaments may have more power than in the case mentioned above. Sometimes the use of a quota system, as in the former socialist countries, can hide underlying power inequalities (Wieringa 1997). Women's power base did not decrease dramatically, for instance, after the fall of the Berlin Wall when women's share in parliamentary seats dropped sharply in various former socialist countries. Rather the number of seats women previously occupied masked the extent of women's subordination, which only became more visible in the period of transition. In general, a quota for women can only be critical in their political empowerment if the quota system is embedded in a feminist consciousness raising campaign which sensitises both the society as a whole and the women parliamentarians to gender issues (Lycklama, Vargas and Wieringa 1998).

Thus, apart from the reliance on the income indicator, the major problem of the GEM lies in its validity as a measure of empowerment. On what understanding of gender power is the GEM built? How is empowerment conceptualised? If the GEM is mapped out on the Women's Empowerment Matrix the gaps become immediately clear. The GEM, which deals with the same concept as the WEM, only covers a part of the whole map. Its field of operation is quite limited. Clearly the two instruments are devised for different uses; the matrix does not allow for the quantification of the interconnections it demonstrates and cannot be used for the global scale at which the GEM operates.

Yet a comparison is interesting, as it reveals two important issues. First, the GEM is not concerned with issues related to the body and sexuality, the trafficking of women and children, sexual violence against women and harmful practices, such as female genital mutilation. Neither is the GEM concerned with religious, cultural or legal issues. Ethics, women's rights and care are ignored. The lack of consideration for the human rights dimension is striking, as other UN bodies, such as United Nations Development Fund for Women (UNIFEM), do pay attention to this issue (UNIFEM 1998). The GEM is not concerned with the violation of women's rights and does not measure, for instance, whether the UN Convention on the Elimination of All Forms of Discrimination Against Women (CEDAW) is ratified without reservations or adhered to. Inequalities in marriage relations such as polygyny, men's unilateral right to divorce, inheritance rules or age at marriage are sidestepped. This is covered in the WEM boxes under the headings of 'legal' combined with 'global', 'state', 'household' and 'individual'. CEDAW also stipulates that countries must 'modify the social and cultural patterns of conduct of men and women, with a view to achieving the elimination of prejudices and customary and other practices which are based on the inferiority or the superiority of either of the sexes or on stereotyped roles for men and women' (art. 5a). CEDAW here touches on the latent and invisible power dimensions discussed above. The 1995 *Human Development Report* does list the countries that had ratified the CEDAW at the time, but the GEM itself does not include it (UNDP 1995: 43).

With such few dimensions the GEM is a very limited instrument of measuring women's empowerment. If we consider the various modes of gender power discussed the following issues can be noted. The operation of power, with its emphasis on formal forms of power (economic and political power, access to higher echelon jobs) ignores the challenging and creative ways in which power also operates, such as the informal power of women's groups, changes in the sexual division of labour, growing self-esteem. Second, the GEM demonstrates the appearance of gender power only at the level of very few institutions, such as parliaments and leaves out many institutions such as the law, education, religious structures and civil society. No attention is paid to issues of ideology and daily practices. Third, as far as visibility is concerned, only the manifest level of power relations is taken into account.

Another limitation of the GEM is in its inability to capture empowerment as a process. Since 1995, when it was introduced, the values of many countries hardly changed because of the dominance of the income variable. Variance in the other variables seems hardly to have resulted in any marked rise or drop in the ranking system. This means the GEM is not a very sensitive instrument to measure government performance on gender policies.

It is also important to note the limited database on which the GEM is built. As is the case with the GDI, the GEM is built on international data bases.' Elsewhere we have discussed in more detail the limitations of these international data sets (Charmes and Wieringa 2003). This limitation is responsible for the low number of countries for which the GEM can be computed. Almost all countries in the low development segment and half of the countries in the medium development segment fall outside of its scope. Yet the data on which the GEM is built are generally available at the national level.[4]

Towards a new measure of women's empowerment

Is it possible to go beyond the GEM? To devise a global instrument to measure women's empowerment that does justice to more dimensions of the WEM and that captures the various modes of gender power in a more inclusive way, for instance including issues of care and sexuality? This was the challenge I was faced with in 2002 when I was asked by the Economic Commission for Africa to design the African Gender and Development Index (AGDI). This index is constructed on the following principles:

1. The AGDI is divided into two parts. The Gender Status Index (GSI) measures the purely quantitative aspects of gender power; the African Women's Progress Scoreboard (AWPS) captures the more qualitative aspects. The quantitative part incorporates all the critique we had on the GDI (Charmes and Wieringa 2003) and some issues discussed above in relation to the GEM, such as the limited conceptualisation of power. The issue of care work is included in the incorporation of time use surveys, and if these are not available, in the use of a proxy in the form of various forms of informal labour.

2. The quantitative measurement of power in the GSI is built on the following variables: share of women in parliaments, as cabinet ministers, as higher courts judges, as members of local councils, in the higher positions in civil services and at senior positions in political parties, trade unions, employers' associations and professional syndicates. Two other variables

are the share of women as heads or managers of NGOs and as heads of community-based associations or unions.

3. The qualitative scorecard consists of two axes. The horizontal axis of performance indicators capture the process of empowerment at the national level. They deal with the range of steps to be taken before a Convention such as the CEDAW, or issues agreed upon in the Beijing Platform for Action, 1995, is fully implemented. The various aspects of the process of empowerment discussed above are incorporated in indicators of government performance at the national level, from awareness (information campaign), to alternatives (the measures themselves), to resources (budget, trained gender staff), to voice (various platforms where women may speak out).

4. The index should be made user-friendly. As much as possible both Women's Bureaux or Ministries and women's NGOs should be able to construct and use it, for their own countries. In that way the AGDI itself will be a tool for awareness raising. Thus a simple computing mechanism for the GSI is used, and similarly a simple scoring mechanism for the AWPS.

5. The index should be as inclusive as possible in its field of operation of the issues indicated in the WEM. Particular subjective issues are difficult to measure at the national and global scale at which the index operates, such as self-esteem. But it is possible to include issues related to sexuality, such as HIV/AIDS (measured both quantitatively and qualitatively), violence against women, sexual harassment, harmful social practices and trafficking. Implementation of the CEDAW (and its Optional Protocol) is a basic element of the scorecard. Other international conventions or consensus documents that feature prominently in the AWPS are the various ILO conventions that deal with women's issues, and the documents adopted at the 1994 International Conference on Population and Development in Cairo, and the 1995 Fourth Women's World Conference in Beijing.

6. The index should, as much as possible, not only measure

the manifest, but also the latent aspects of gender power. Every country report that accompanies the computation of the index should point to such latent aspects of women's oppression. It is hoped that these reports will contribute to a process of awareness-raising and by paying attention to the doxic levels of women's subordination also bring up certain invisible aspects of it. This process of awareness-raising is stimulated through the institution of national advisory panels (NAPs) that have to validate the national reports. The NAPs consist of representatives of government and civil society, as well as the researchers themselves.

7. The index should be made culturally sensitive. As it has been constructed now it includes specific features that are of importance to Africa. Without changing the number of variables particular indicators can be changed to accommodate salient interests of other regions in the world.

8. Certain conditions were set for the collection of data. First, it was decided that the index should use national data which can be harmonised wherever necessary at the national level. Second, the index should only measure the gender gap, not the GDP. The Human Poverty Index or the Human Development Index can measure poverty and well-being respectively. The Gini coefficient is very useful to indicate inequalities in income distribution in a country.

9. The index should pay particular attention to the power of institutions. Several indicators deal with aspects related to gender mainstreaming within institutions.

10. As much as possible the index should incorporate the major international and regional documents that deal with gender issues. These include not only CEDAW and Beijing 1995's Platform of Action, but also the Women's Protocol of the African Charter of Human and People's Rights, the African Charter on the Right of the Child and the Programme of Action of the 1994 International Conference on Population and Development in 1994.

The African Women's Progress Scoreboard

		Ratification	Reporting	Law	Policy commitment	Development of a plan	Targets	Institutional mechanism	Budget	Human resources	Research	Involvement of civil society	Information & dissemination	Monitoring & evaluation	Total	%
Women's rights	CEDAW — Ratification without reservation															
	Optional protocol															
	Art 2															
	Art 16															
	African Charter of Human and People's Rights—															
	Women's Rights Protocol—harmful practices															
	Beijing Platform of Action															
	Violence against Women — Domestic violence															
	Rape															
	Sexual harassment															
	Traffic in women															
	African Charter on the Rights of the Child (art XXVII)															
Social	Health — STIs															
	ICPD — HIV/AIDS															
	POA — Maternal mortality															
	Plus Five — Contraception															

	2001 Abuja Declaration on HIV/AIDS and Women															
Economic	Education	Policy on girl school dropouts														
		Education on human/women's rights														
	ILO	Convention 100														
		Convention 111														
		Convention 183														
		Policy on HIV/AIDS														
		Engendering NPRS														
		Access to agricultural extension services														
		Access to technology														
		Equal access to land														
Political		UN 1325 conflict resolution														
		Beijing PFA effective and accessible national machinery														
		Support for women's quota and affirmative action														
	Policies	Decision making positions within parliament/ministries														
		Gender mainstreaming in all departments														
	Total score															

Source: Economic Commission for Africa, 2004, The African Gender and Development Index. p. 30

Process

After the AGDI was designed and the GSI and AWPS constructed a process of validation followed. A regional advisory panel was formed that consisted of high level politicians, bureaucrats and researchers. The AGDI was then tested in 12 African countries. In this trial process it became clear that national data were available on most of the variables of the AGDI. Thus data have become available in a comprehensive way that so far had been scattered in various government offices. In some cases new data had to be collected. Where data could not be found the research team made suggestions on how the data collection process in their countries could be improved. On the basis of the trial reports the regional advisory panel met again and the AGDI was validated (Economic Commission for Africa 2004). It was officially launched on 12 October 2004, in a plenary session of the African Union. The Economic Commission for Africa will now coordinate the utilisation of the AGDI for all 52 countries of the African Union. The results of the 12 trials will be published in the African Women's Report for 2006. The AWPS is given on pages 228, 229.

Conclusion

The GDI and the GEM are valuable instruments in the field of gender policy. They made it possible to compare countries globally in relation to gender issues. Their introduction opened an interesting field of debates. But they do have certain limitations. The challenge in constructing the AGDI was to design a tool that would have a higher level of validity and reliability than these indices. Neither the GDI nor the GEM measures gender inequality as such. Therefore another measure is needed that does not rely on the GDP per capita and only indicates the gender gap and women's subordination. This measure should also cover many more aspects of gender relations and gender power than the ones captured by the GDI and the GEM. These aspects were taken into account for the construction of the African index.

There are many critical issues related to women's

empowerment that escape quantification in the conventional sense. These includes topics such as the implementation of the CEDAW and other international documents, such as those drawn up after the major world conferences held in the mid-1990s, the International Conference on Population and Development in 1994 and the Fourth International Women's Conference, held in Beijing 1995. It is however possible to indicate a country's adherence to these documents in a qualitative way. Other issues that have usually escaped quantification such as care and sexuality, violence against women, and the eradication of harmful practices can be dealt with in a way that is much more sensitive to the various elements related to women's empowerment discussed above. A scorecard such as the AWPS can serve that purpose. Performance indicators can be used to measure the effectiveness of policy interventions. At the same time care should be taken to make this instrument useful for NGOs and national machineries that are entrusted with drafting and implementing gender policies. In designing the AGDI these have been taken into account.

The AGDI is an innovative tool. It will be further developed in the coming few years, as the data both from the trial countries and from subsequent sets of countries will become available. The AGDI is not only an interesting academic exercise, it has the potential to become a powerful political tool. The first indications are that it will be used in the Peer Review Mechanism of the countries that adhere to NEPAD, the New Partnership for African Development, launched in Abuja, Nigeria in 2001. During the launch on October 2004 the South African Minister of Social Affairs, Mr Pahad, called for African states to ratify the Women's Rights Protocol to the African Charter of Human and People's Rights. Many governments have been slow to ratify this Protocol, as it deals with the controversial topic of traditional harmful practices. The AGDI is a new instrument that can be developed further. Its methodology can be adapted to various other situations, both at regional and national levels.

Notes

[1] The way the concept of 'sex' is discursively constructed is analysed for instance by Butler (1993).

[2] This illustrates why the use of the concept of 'gender-disaggregated' data is misplaced. What is usually collected is data by sex, male or female.

[3] Since 1990 the HDR (*Human Development Report*) has contained the Human Development Index (HDI). The HDR is based on a concept of human development that takes enhancing human well-being, not the growth of national income as its end goal. To achieve well-being, people's choices must be enlarged, by the formation of what Sen calls human capabilities (improved health, knowledge and skills). People must have the (economic) opportunities to make use of these capabilities and they must be empowered to have a voice in the major decisions that shape their lives. The HDI measures the average achievement of a country in what it calls 'basic human capabilities'. It indicates whether people lead a long and healthy life (longevity), are educated and knowledgeable and enjoy a decent standard of living. Thus defined, development was no longer measured in economic terms only, by the usual indicator of growth and wealth, the GDP per capita. The introduction of the HDI had an enormous impact on development thinking. From the mid-1990s onwards various developing and transition countries published their own development reports, in which this thinking was carried further. After 1995 many reports included gender concerns.

[4] This is demonstrated by the field trials of several African countries in which the AGDI is being tested.

References

Bardhan, Kalpana and Stephan Klasen. 1999. 'UNDP's Gender-Related Indices: A Critical Review'. *World Development.* vol. 27. no.6. pp. 985–1010.

Blackwood, E. and Saskia E. Wieringa. 1999. *Female Desires; Women's Same Sex Practices in Cross Cultural Perspective.* New York: Columbia University Press.

Bourdieu, Pierre. 1977. *Outline of a Theory of Practice.* Cambridge: Cambridge University Press.

Butler, Judith. 1993. *Bodies that Matter; on the discursive limits of 'sex'.* New York: Routledge.

Charmes, Jacques and S.E. Wieringa. 2003. Measuring Women's Empowerment: an Assessment of the Gender-related Development Index and the Gender Empowerment Measure. *Journal of Human Development.* vol. 4. no. 3. November. pp. 419–437.

Connell, R.W. 1995. *Masculinities: Knowledge, Power and Social Change.* Berkeley/ Los Angeles: University of California Press.

Dijkstra, Geske A. 2002. 'Revisiting UNDP's GDI and GEM: Towards an Alternative'. *Social Indicators Research.* 57. pp. 301–338.

Dijkstra, Geske A. and Lucia Hanmer. 2000. 'Measuring Socio-Economic Gender Inequality, Towards an Alternative to the UNDP Gender-Related Development Index'. *Feminist Economics*. vol. 6. no. 2.

Economic Commission for Africa. 2004. The African Gender and Development Index. Addis Ababa: UNECA Publications.

Foucault, Michel. 1972. *The Archaeology of Knowledge*. New York: Pantheon.

——. 1976. *Power/Knowledge*. New York: Pantheon.

——. 1980a. *The History of Sexuality*. vol. I: An Introduction. New York: Vintage Books.

——. 1980b. *Power/Knowledge: Selected Interviews and Other Writings, 1972–1977*. New York: Pantheon.

Kabeer, Naila. 1999. *The Conditions and Consequences of Choice: Reflections on the Measurement of Women's Empowerment*. Discussion Paper 108. Geneva: UNRISD. p. 58.

Lycklama à Nijeholt, Geertje, Virginia Vargas and Saskia E. Wieringa. eds. 1998. *Women's Movements and Public Policy in Europe, Latin America and the Caribbean*. New York/London: Garland.

Lukes, S. ed. 1986. *Power, Readings in Social and Political Theory*. Oxford: Basil Blackwell.

McNay, Lois. 2000. *Gender and Agency; Reconfiguring the Subject in Feminism and Social Theory*. Cambridge: Polity Press.

Scott, Joan W. 1989. 'Gender: A Useful Category of Historical Analysis' in *Coming to Terms; Feminism, Theory, Politics*. ed. Elizabeth Weed. New York: Routledge.

Sen, Amartya. 1985. *Commodities and Capabilities, Lectures in Economics Theory Policy*. New York: Oxford University Press.

Streeten, Paul, Shahid J. Burki, Mahbub ul Haq, Norman Hicks, and Frances Stewart.1981. *First Things First: Meeting Basic Human Needs in the Developing Countries*. New York: University Press.

UNDP. 1995. *Human Development Report*. New York: UNDP.

UNIFEM. 1998. *Bringing Equality Home; Implementing the Convention on the Elimination of All Forms of Discrimination Against Women (CEDAW)*. New York: UNIFEM.

Wieringa, Saskia E. 1994. 'Women's Interests and Empowerment: Gender Planning Reconsidered'. *Development and Change*. vol. 25. no. 4. October. pp. 829-849.

——. ed. 1997. *Workshop on GDI/GEM Indicators*. The Hague: ISS.

——. 2002. 'Gender, Tradition Sexual Diversity and AIDS in Postcolonial Southern Africa: Some Suggestions for Research' in *Challenges for Anthropology in the 'African Renaissance' A Southern African Contribution*. eds. Debie LeBeau and Robert J. Gordon. Windhoek: University of Namibia Press.

——. 2003. *Women's Rights, Sexual Health and HIV/AIDS; a Training Manual*. Jakarta: Koalisi Perempuan Indonesia.

11

Eroding Citizenship
Gender, Labour and Liberalisation in India

AMRITA CHHACHHI

Introduction

> Economic security promotes happiness, and is beneficial for growth and social stability. (ILO 2004)

It is a sign of our times that international organisations such as the United Nations Commission on Human Security and now the International Labour Organisation (ILO) are articulating broader, all-encompassing notions of development as freedom which places the multidimensionality of a person's capabilities and the pursuit of 'happiness' as central (Commission on Human Security 2003; ILO 2004). It is not accidental that the (re-)emergence of normative frameworks for distributive justice occurs at this conjuncture. The increasing financial instability inherent in the world economy, the convergence of short-term structural adjustment programmes with long-term macroeconomic polices with new forms of economic governance are locking governments into a neo-liberal disciplinary framework of accumulation with little room for manoeuvre to deal with the globalisation of the 'crisis of reproduction' (Bakker and Gill 2003; Young 2003). In the context of crumbling social protection systems and increasing job insecurity, the key issue today globally is the undermining and ensuing fragility of the conditions that ensure the reproduction of labour power i.e. human life itself. This chapter draws on a gendered political economy and social citizenship framework, integrating issues of redistribution and recognition (Fraser 1997), to highlight the implications of contemporary processes of globalisation and liberalisation for women workers. It recasts the discussion on gender, labour and globalisation from the employment versus exploitation thesis which dominated earlier assessments of the implications of women's work in globalised production (Elson and Pearson 1981; Pearson 1998; Lim 1990), and shows that given the limited nature of state provision of citizenship-based entitlements in India, and the secondary status accorded to women in most community personal laws regulating the private domain, regular employment remains an important route for women to access independent rights to social citizenship entitlements. These provide the enabling conditions for individual and collective agency at the workplace and within the household, thereby creating the basis for democratic citizenship.

Contemporary processes of globalisation are leading to an erosion of such enabling conditions for the assertions of 'citizenship in practice' and a new model of 'market oriented citizenship' is being ushered. There has been a increase in women's overall share in paid employment and a 'feminisation' of working conditions in that most current employment is irregular and insecure sharing the characteristics of 'women's work' in the informal economy. The 'global feminisation' thesis has been challenged and qualified by feminists who argue that the increase is due partly to better recording of women's work and partly to a demand from export-oriented, labour-intensive sectors (Elson 1996; Pearson 1998; Razavi 1999) where the process of feminisation has not necessarily been sustainable in the long run or irreversible.[1] The ILO report on global employment trends notes that the increase in unemployment globally (from 20 million in 2001 to 180 million in 2002) was most severe among women who were mainly in sectors directly vulnerable to economic shocks (ILO 2003: 13).

Concomitantly policies to deal with human insecurity and informalisation of the labour market propose trade-offs between citizenship-based and employment-based entitlements. For instance the *Human Security Now* report (Commision on Human Security 2003) recognises the devastating effects of recurrent financial crises since the 1980s and the increasing informalisation of labour and lists four priorities for policy action to promote economic security: encouraging growth that reaches the extreme poor; supporting sustainable livelihoods and decent work; preventing and containing the effects of economic crises and natural disasters; providing social protection for all situations. It endorses the ILO goal to promote 'opportunities for women and men to obtain decent and productive work, in conditions of freedom, equity, security and human dignity' which should apply to 'all workers', irrespective of their sectors and whether they are waged or unwaged, home workers, or regulated, unregulated or self-regulated.

However, despite an inclusive notion of decent work, the more concrete suggestions for social protection mentioned in this report sidestep around corporate and state strategies which have led to labour market flexibility and 'indecent' work and instead make recommendations for retraining, micro-enterprises, and access to micro-credit to encourage self-employment, with state provision of a social minimum for those in chronic poverty or situations of sudden vulnerability. Implicit in this approach is the offsetting of job insecurity and vulnerability by a minimal, contingent state-based provision of social assistance.

There is a danger that such proposals can lead to a trade-off between employment security and social security, result in a process of levelling down and reduction in the possibilities for the enhancement of human capabilities. This limits the possibilities for distributive justice as well as the assertion of democratic citizenship through collective organisation. Engendering human security requires both employment security and citizenship-based entitlements, to achieve gender equality and social transformation.

Despite substantial documentation on the processes and impact of globalisation on labour the analysis has tended to be fragmented. Studies on poverty and economic restructuring have taken the household as a unit and focused on livelihood strategies without entering the 'abode of production'. Studies on labour have had a singular focus on the workplace and ignored the 'abode of reproduction'. This has led to fragmentation in policy formulations with a continued separation of economic and social policies despite criticism by feminist economists of such a compartmentalisation. Challenging the narrow understanding of the 'social' as referring only to the social effects of macroeconomic adjustment policies, feminists (Elson and Cagatay 2000) have shown how these policies in fact have a social content and the gender bias of macroeconomic models is evident in the disregard of three crucial areas: the implications of gendered labour markets; unpaid reproductive work; and power asymmetries in intra-household relations based on the neo-classical assumption of the household as a unity and a site of common interests. The conceptual silence on the contribution made by the care economy (such as cooking, cleaning, childcare, looking after the elderly and other family members), is also a strategic silence. Acknowledgement would imply recognition that economic restructuring has hidden costs and usually implies the transfer of costs to the unpaid care economy based on the implicit assumption of the 'infinite elasticity of women's labour time'—an assumption that underpins the financial risk-taking characteristic of contemporary restructuring (Elson 2002; Bakker 1994; Staveren 2002).

Numerous studies have illustrated that economic restructuring has direct implications on the distribution and intensity of women's labour time between market and non-market activities, and has increased aspects of unpaid reproductive work, which falls disproportionately on women and is vital for social reproduction and human security (Floro 1995). This 'reproductive tax' directly affects women's well-being, agency and the development of the next generation. The inter-linkage between paid and unpaid work is therefore crucial for the reformulation of macro-socioeconomic policies and the full acknowledgement of citizenship entitlements which can substantially ensure human security.

Such a reframing is required also of the two dominant normative frameworks in development institutions today (United Nations Development Programme and the International Labour Organisation in particular) based on the work of Amartya Sen and Guy Standing which inform policy perspectives (Sen 1999; Standing 1999). Both have conceptual roots in Aristotle, Marx and Rawls, though their emphasis on development as freedom and distributive justice may differ. Both approaches re-establish the principle of universalism in citizenship-based entitlements, and recognise agency as well as the role of the state as a major actor in social provisioning. Sen's entitlement approach which underlies the *Human Security Report*, emphasises not only state-based entitlements and individual endowments, but also public action. Guy Standing extends this to social justice in the labour market in the era of global flexibility. These principles have been incorporated to a large extent in the ILO concept of 'Decent Work' (Standing 1999; ILO 2001).

However, neither Sen nor Standing opposes liberalisation/globalisation per se, arguing instead for the process to be supplemented with regulatory controls over the market. Sen maintains a 'tactical silence' on issues of international and national power blocs as well as on the nature of the state which could prevent the realisation of development as freedom (Patnaik 1998). Gasper (2002) points out ambiguities in Sen's conception of capability and agency. Though both thinkers do address issues of gender inequality and have recently taken on board some feminist concerns (Sen et al. 2003; Standing 2003) they do not incorporate feminist concepts fully into their analyses, particularly the complex power dynamics, linkages and mutually constituting spheres of paid work-care work, production-reproduction, workplace and household (Chhachhi 2004; Robeyns 2001). The concept of 'Decent Work' is limited being enterprise based, ignoring the linkages with the care economy.

This chapter explores the interconnections between these two domains and elaborates the concept of 'citizenship in practice'[2] as a bridging link to understand the processes, consequences and strategic and policy alternatives to contemporary trends of global restructuring and flexible employment. Social and economic citizenship rights develop 'through a process of struggle' (Cook 2000) and the exercise of individual and collective agency at the workplace and the assertions of autonomy within the household and community.[3] These struggles occur in and through different collectivities reflecting the multilayered construction of citizenship particularly in developing countries (Yuval-Davis 1999). This is illustrated through a case study of women workers from the electronics industry in India over the last decade,[4] a period when there was a major policy shift and a process initiated to dismantle the structures of state intervention and openly embrace liberalisation and integration into the world economy. This micro-level analysis of gendered labour regimes, domestic regimes and instances of 'citizenship in practice', brings in women workers' experiences and voices and relates them to the ongoing broader debates on distributive justice and citizenship entitlements.

The Indian context

In India, as in most developing countries, the near absence of citizenship-based entitlements to social protection has meant an extreme dependence on selling one's labour power as the only means for survival and security.[5] Although the Indian Constitution professes a commitment to a welfare state, and there are constitutional provisions for the right to work and education, support for old age, sickness and disability and social assistance for disadvantaged groups these are rarely implemented. Overall there has been a focus on 'promotive' forms of social security through anti-poverty and targeted development schemes, employment guarantee programmes and food security through a public distribution system rather than strengthening protective measures (Harriss-White and Subramanian 1999; Ahmad et al. 1999; Dreze and Sen 1991). These limited measures have been patchily implemented, and employment in the organised sector regulated by labour legislation remains the main basis for social citizenship entitlements such as pensions, health insurance, etc.

(Gore, Figueiredo and Rodgers 1995; Appasamy et al. 1996).

After independence, India's industrialisation strategy resulted in a three-tiered structure: the public sector controlling the 'commanding heights of the economy'; the private corporate sector operating as monopolies in certain fields; and a mass of small-scale enterprises. Till today industrial output relies on the coexistence of different structures of production, industrial organisation and concomitantly different types of employment ranging from household and cottage industries to large modern factories, consisting of multilayered categories of capital and labour (Kannan and Rutten 2003).

Despite idealising and striving towards Fordism,[6] cheap unprotected labour remained contiguous to a Fordist core which was restricted primarily to the public sector and the large-scale private sector where unionisation was strong. Similar to the experience in other countries the dominant basis of entitlements has been employment in the organised manufacturing sector which has essentially been male, reinforcing 'male industrial citizenship'. In the first phase of Indian industrialisation though women formed a critical segment of the industrial labour force, they were relatively excluded from modern production. In the early 1920s they were around 20–25 per cent of the labour force in textile mills and 35–40 per cent in the coal mines and plantations (Nair 1996; Sen 2003). The progressive decline of women in all these industries, started from the 1930s and the extension of labour regulations and the emergence of an organised sector ran in tandem with the masculinisation of industrial employment. The explicit and implicit assumptions about gender relations and the family in labour regulations forged a male-breadwinner gender contract which underpinned the subsequent marginalisation of women confirming Guy Standing's assessment of the 20th century as 'the century of the labouring man' (Standing 2003).

It is worth noting that in 1938 the subcommittee of the National Planning Commission formed by the Congress party on 'Women's Role in the Planned Economy' articulated a universal breadwinner model: it recognised domestic labour and argued for recognition of women's labour as a separate unit of production, for property rights and the need for them to develop as individuals. However these formulations disappeared from state discourse after independence (Chaudhuri 1996) and the non-recognition of women's entitlement to employment remains an important factor which affects the implementation of labour rights for women.

Labour regulations in the post-independence period in fact have reinforced the segmentation of labour. The inclusions and exclusions parallel the organised/unorganised sector division which is also a gender division. It is estimated that in the early 1990s only 10 per cent of workers (out of a labour force of 375 million) were covered by social security schemes in the organised sector (Harriss-White and Gooptu 2000; Ginneken 1998). The Second National Commission on Labour notes that only about seven to eight per cent of the workforce in the organised sector is protected (Government of India 2003: 26). The bulk of women's employment (96 per cent) is concentrated in the unorganised sector. Unlike welfare regimes in the North or erstwhile socialist countries where the 'reproductive bargain' between the state and corporate sector provided for a range of non-wage benefits and other measures of social protection, access to such entitlements were limited to a very small section of Indian women workers.

The segmentation of the labour market persists, though in theory the Trade Unions Act (1926), and the Minimum Wages Act (1948) apply to informal labour and new laws to extend this protection were passed in the 1970s such as the Contract Labour Regulation and Abolition Act (1971). These laws were difficult to implement and had many loopholes. Already in 1982 the Industrial Disputes Act was amended to allow employers flexibility in retrenching workers. The initiation of economic reforms in 1991 led to a major shift in state discourse from a surface commitment to social protection to explicit talk of 'rigidities' in the Indian labour market and the need for flexibility through labour market reforms. Although overall drastic changes have not yet been made in labour laws—though they have been recommended by the Second National Commission on Labour 2002—in many

241

industries there has been implicit deregulation since the 1980s onwards. Existing legal regulations have been made less effective or have been bypassed.

Labour regimes in the electronics industry in Delhi

The electronics industry in Delhi represents a good example to assess these changes since it spans a wide range of enterprises in the unorganised and organised sectors, includes enterprises from a pre-liberalisation policy regime as well as those established in the post-liberalisation period and employs women in large numbers. Unlike this industry in South-east Asia, which grew as a direct result of the relocation and shift towards offshore manufacturing by US and Japanese companies, India's electronic industry, although linked to global commodity chains, grew within the framework of state intervention and import substitution. The growth, structure and development of this industry reflects three different policy regimes: self-reliance with regulation (1960–1980); self-reliance and partial liberalisation (1980–1990); and liberalisation and globalisation (1991 onwards). From the 1980s there was a process of 'creeping liberalisation' leading to changes in the structure of the industry. By the 1990s with the entry of multinational giants, electronics production in India was subject to the forces of global competition through a variety of indirect and direct subcontracting relations and systems of governance but it is primarily oriented towards the local market.

This case study on television manufacturing is interesting as it departs from the overwhelming focus on and contemporary debates about women's employment in export-oriented manufacturing (Razavi and Pearson 2004). In addition it analyses gendered labour regimes as 'negotiated orders that emerge through the interplay of state intervention via labour regulations and industrial policy, the social organisation of the labour market, market competition, managerial strategies of labour control and workers' responses' (Chhachhi 2004). This enables capturing the multidimensionality of conditions of employment rather than a simple focus on the presence or absence of labour regulations.

Such a perspective identifies the degree of workers' dependence on the enterprise or the state for social protection and examines the enabling and constraining conditions for asserting entitlements.

In the television industry in Delhi it is possible to distinguish four coexistent gendered labour regimes today (differentiated on the basis of domestic or foreign capital, age of enterprise and labour process) which reveals variations in recruitment strategies, gendered forms of labour control, construction of gendered work identities, and resistance and struggle over employment-based entitlements. The liberalisation of the Indian economy particularly in the electronics sector has affected its workers in different ways.

The pre-liberalisation era

Highlighting the inclusion/exclusion dynamic inherent in labour regulations and the multi-structural character of Indian manufacturing there were two characteristic labour regimes of this period in the industry. The first was a classical example of the unorganised sector consisting of tiny enterprises employing less than 10 workers with minimal labour regulation. Manufacturing television components such as printed circuit boards, they were the lowest link in a subcontracting chain extending down from large electronics enterprises. A company's survival depended on extreme flexibility and was contingent on a quick shift in product items. The overall nature of this regime was characterised by market despotism as suspicion and fear, internally and externally, dominated interactions and relationships. Owners were in constant fear of raids from tax departments and government inspectors. Internally, this was reflected in the recruitment and control over workers who were employed only on the basis of personal recommendations with very few women—the ratio of women to men rarely exceeding 1:3. The women came primarily from Delhi-based poor households and typified the 'distress entry' worker i.e. they were main earners, a large proportion were divorced or deserted, and had minimal education. Coming from extremely vulnerable households, with no other support systems, they were completely dependent on wage work. There was therefore an in-built element of labour control given their socio-economic backgrounds.

Work discipline was directly supervised by the owner, relations were personalised, and management control ranged from moderate to extreme despotism. There was flexibility in the sexual division of labour which was a simple, manual assembly of components with no clear wage discrimination between men and women. Given this, what reason did owners have to employ women at all? The main reason for the presence of women was a conscious strategy to control men workers because of their 'calming influence', their 'natural' docility and most importantly, their 'trustworthiness' rather than the standard assumption of 'nimble fingers'. Aware of their limited options, owners constantly used the term *bechari* (poor thing) and implied they were doing them a favour by employing them. Women workers colluded in and were themselves controlled through this mutual construction of victimhood and vulnerability.

Given the inapplicability of most labour regulations, workers did not have formal contracts and none of them were permanent, although many had worked for over 10 years in the same enterprise. The only benefit was the minimum stipulated yearly bonus of 8.33 per cent. Women complained most about wage cuts due to leave, delayed payment of wages and the bad conditions of the toilets—they never went to the toilet at all during their working hours. Socialised into bodily self-regulation, with restrictions on associating with strange men, plus domestic responsibilities which limited their time and mobility in public spaces, these women were constituted as an ideal docile and reliable workforce.

Although all the workers were equally vulnerable men, at least intermittently, challenged this and looked for other options. Women, however, were tied into total dependence and colluded with the construction of themselves as *becharis*.[7] Rather than confront the owner on wage cuts, they often used their victim status as widows, main earners or mothers with small children, to get leave and exemption from too large deductions. Financial assistance locked the workers and owners further into a relationship of loyalty and trust which however, was not totally hegemonic. In spite of stressing that they had no choice but to accept the low wages, bad working conditions and the despotic disciplinary regime, even to be grateful for them, a number of women also expressed their frustration and awareness of exploitation, but were trapped by the absence of labour regulations and difficulties of unionisation.

The second type of labour regime based on a different stage of the labour process and a different structure of the workforce was characteristic of enterprises established in the mid-1960s, all indigenously owned with some technical collaboration agreements with foreign companies. These small and medium scale companies employed between 100–200 workers and all statutory labour regulations were applicable. A crucial mediating factor was the unionisation of workers since the 1980s which freed them from absolute dependence. Both job security and housing security were significant in changing the despotic nature of the regime to one of moderate control that resulted in a social compact between labour and capital illustrative of the pre-liberalisation era.

The workers came from different segments of the labour market: hinterland migrants, Delhi-based industrial worker households, middle/lower-middle class and poor households. Recruited mainly through informal channels, their educational background ranged from functional literacy to graduates, with some who also had technical diplomas.

The semi-automatic labour process and distinct gender division of labour was subject to classic Taylorist principles of control and discipline.[8] There were wide variations in wages across, as well as within, particular occupations with a clear gendered job hierarchy. There were very few women assistant technicians or junior engineers, and none in the senior categories such as engineer, technician and foreman. Overtime, which was often compulsory, led to further gender differentials in take home pay. Non-wage benefits varied across the factories, except for the provision of Provident Fund and Employees State Insurance Scheme (ESI) benefits (which included maternity benefits) for all workers. Some

245

factories also provided conveyance allowance, washing allowance, and uniforms but none had a creche or subsidised canteen.

Labour control combined hierarchical and technical methods. Line speeds pushed production quotas up constantly and piece-rate wage systems were introduced. The imposition of daily discipline was both crude and gendered. During periods of pressured production, women were not allowed to go to the toilet. If they did, the foreman would stand outside 'making eyes', described by them as *badtamizi* and *nazar theek nahi* (lewd behaviour). The foreman's behaviour often extended to actual physical harassment and assault. A common general punishment for defying the foreman, or for any act of 'indiscipline', consisted of sending workers out to sit at the gate in the blazing summer sun until they apologised and begged to be allowed to return to work. Punishment was more often given for links with the union rather than production issues. Women or men who spoke up were sent off to sit in the men's section or vice versa. This form of humiliation used gendered cultural attributes making women feel insecure and stigmatised amongst strange men, and the men 'unmanly' if they were sent to sit among the women.

Control and discipline needed to be asserted and reasserted almost on a daily basis since all the workers were aware of and used their legal entitlements. Women for instance would take leave immediately if they were sick or wanted to avoid a conflict or had domestic pressures. One of the first issues that J. Dey, a woman union leader, fought for was a stop to the 'memos' that were handed to women workers if they came even five minutes late to work. In this environment women were able to assert their woman worker identity as reflected in their demands and their use of legal entitlements. They were conscious and proud of their skills, asked for further training and higher designations and initiated actions for leave due to household responsibilities.

Worker resistance, in spite of the swift and severe forms of punishment, came from three crucial factors: long labour histories in the same company; a union which would defend them; and security of housing. The mere existence of labour legislation and mediating institutions of the state in regulating industrial relations was not enough. Labour rights were not just given by the management—they were demanded and struggled for by the workers. The process of unionisation led to a more moderate despotic regime and simultaneously made workers aware of their rights. Subsidised housing provided by the state also involved a process of struggle and gave the workers an important fallback position, illustrating the significance of the linkage between citizenship-based and employment-based entitlements (see Chhachhi 2004 for details).

This small but significant generation of women workers is being eliminated. Enterprises of this era have closed down, retrenching all workers and relocating to low-wage, non-unionised industrial areas in neighbouring states.

The post-liberalisation period

A different picture emerges in the third type of enterprises that were established or expanded in the era of liberalisation with closer ties with multinational capital where the labour process and the labour market were more significant factors. There was a far more conscious managerial strategy to recruit a particular kind of mixed workforce. Differences of region and class played an important role through the recruitment of single women migrants from Kerala in South India and young unmarried women from Delhi and neighbouring areas. There was also a more specific demand for young unmarried men and women with secondary school education.

These enterprises approximate most closely to the stereotype that emerged from the early literature on women workers in world market factories. Characterised by a more automated production process, clear job designations and an occupational hierarchy in each production line and department, the sexual division of labour was sharpest at the two ends of the production process: only women did insertion of components and only men did servicing of the final product. All of them had permanent job status and written contracts though within a gendered job hierarchy that was reflected in the higher maximum wage available for men.

247

Labour control in these 'new' enterprises was based on a more sophisticated combination of technological/bureaucratic controls, gender and ethnic divisions, and institutional structures and ideologies outside the factory—crucially, the family and the neighbourhood. Continuous process production required an evolved system of work discipline and a formalised procedure of reward and punishment was instituted. Gender and ethnic differences in the workforce were consciously used to create divisions and the tension was expressed in the shifting meanings of masculinity and femininity. As men tried to carve out and preserve an 'essentially masculine, heavy machine' area of work, management stressed women's natural qualities and women workers asserted simultaneously their special dexterity as well as capability to handle all jobs. Ethnic differences between the Delhi-based North Indians and the Kerala migrants were accentuated and played out around perceptions of productivity and capacity to work. The managerial construction of the migrant women workers as more 'productive, clever and educated' functioned as a mechanism of pace setting and regulating productivity. The North Indian women saw the migrants as 'clever, liars and promiscuous' and just as men were threatened with replacement by women, they felt threatened by the migrants. In the subtle power play by management, the North Indian women were threatened but also treated paternalistically as daughters/insiders and migrant women were held up as models but still treated as 'outsiders'. Here extra-factory institutional structures and ideologies played a role: the migrants lived in rented rooms and as single young women were constantly subjected to high levels of harassment by landlords and local goons. Residential space contained a constant threat of violence, and the factory provided safety and security. The lack of neighbourhood and housing security played a key role in their acquiescent attitude and non-involvement in collective action.

Until 1995, the situation in these factories was one of a complex form of despotism and conflict directed laterally rather than vertically, presenting a typical picture of hegemonic despotism. However, this was ruptured by an outbreak of spontaneous militancy. From a first assertion against a supervisor's harassment and struggle to abolish the 'toilet register' which were demands to be treated with dignity and respect, young women workers moved on to challenge the management's attempts to abolish job designations and bypass payment of statutory minimum wages. They formed a union and carried their struggle into the public space of the labour office and courtrooms. As factory daughters turned disobedient, management tried to reimpose control through appealing to parental authority, the ideology of the factory as a family, and direct threat and coercion.

Contrary to the paradigmatic image of the 'docile third world woman worker', these women did not succumb to these pressures.[9] Once this ideological hegemony was ruptured they challenged and confronted managerial control, organised and engaged in a classical industrial dispute. A broader awareness of workers' rights and organisational strategies developed as the dynamics of organising collectively led to a 'leap in consciousness' from which there was no turning back and they were transformed from dutiful daughters to 'disobedient daughters' and then into industrial worker citizens.

The fourth type of enterprises, symptomatic of the liberalisation process, were large units with foreign collaboration, established from 1993 onwards, and located in low-wage industrial estates and export processing zones. The production process was modern and highly automated with a rigid gender division of labour and a gendered hierarchy of control and supervision. A polarisation was created between employees from middle class families with technical degrees who were granted all statutory rights and given further training; and the mass of production workers who were maintained as a non-permanent 'apprentice' workforce and denied job security. Voice representation in particular was crushed through gendered methods of labour control.

Managers gave the classic reasons of 'nimble fingers' and docility for employing girls but an additional criterion was that these girls were 'freshers' which implied not just that they were unmarried and straight out of school, but also that their minds

249

were fresh for indoctrination. Training involved a transfer of key 'home practices' associated with the general features of Total Quality Management emphasised by all Japanese companies introducing a new work ethic and corporate culture. The gendered nature of labour control lay in the reconstitution of high school girls and electronic engineering graduates into 'industrial housekeepers' committed to the company ideology through inculcation of the five principles of Japanese housekeeping—the 5Ss, based on five Japanese ideograms whose meaning starts with 'S': *Seiri* (Sorting), *Seiton* (Systematising), *Seisou* (Sweeping), *Seiketsu* (Sanitising) and *Shitsuke* (Self-disciplining). This carefully planned training started with the recitation of the morning prayer and continued through the day. Boards with the 5Ss were placed strategically all around, daily discipline was very strict and workers were dismissed for the smallest errors. They were frisked whenever they left the production hall, departments were kept segregated, transport was provided by the company bus and all contact with other workers was controlled. Based on sophisticated methods of surveillance and labour control, the training in 'industrial housekeeping' combined the skills of domesticity with industrial efficiency to create a new kind of gendered workforce. Till this research ended women in these factories had not challenged management except in one instance over the required uniforms of trousers and shirt which was resisted as being against Indian culture. Despite the controls however, the possibilities for unionisation do exist in these new multinational labour regimes.

Resistance, collective action and the struggle for entitlements

What is interesting about the second and third labour regimes is the involvement of women workers in collective action and the emergence of women union leaders—a phenomenon rarely mentioned in the general representation of working women in India.

Given that over 96 per cent of women work in the unorganised sector, their level of unionisation is extremely low.

While there are difficulties in organising in the informal economy this is not directly due to lack of the legal right to representation. A contributing factor has also been that trade unions have tended to concentrate on large-scale factories. In addition the male biased culture, structure, procedures and violence associated with trade unions prevent women's involvement whose demands are often focused on non-wage benefits and their struggle more non-confrontational (Chhachhi and Pittin 1996).[10] In all four labour regimes women workers resisted managerial controls through individualised actions of 'using managerial logic against them', controlling speed-ups, negotiating leave etc. These forms of resistance were most characteristic of the first and fourth labour regimes where possibilities for collective action were limited, not so much due to absence of legal regulations but due to the composition of the workforce and gendered forms of labour control (personalised in the first case and sophisticated in the second) and worker dependence on the enterprise.

In the second and third regimes there was a shift over time and women workers were able to demand the implementation of employment-based entitlements through 'citizenship in practice', i.e. the collective action by workers to force management to implement statutory labour rights where they were applicable.[11] This process forged a 'woman worker identity' which encapsulated consciousness and solidarity around issues and entitlements related to being workers as well as women. In the course of various struggles the younger women workers challenged gender roles and norms such as the good behaviour required for marriage and the acceptance of male leadership. Interestingly their families supported them in these struggles. In many cases the challenge to managerial authority was paralleled with a demand within the family to reciprocate the financial support that the young women had provided to the family. As a 23-year-old worker stated:

> We have no fear of pressure from the family. I tell my family that all these years I gave my entire salary. Now you better feed and maintain me these few months. They have no choice!

Women union leaders continued to face gendered constraints—freedom from domestic responsibilities, reliance on male support and constant proof of moral respectability were important elements which influenced their involvement. However, the experience of wage work and collective action together led to a transformation in their consciousness individually as well as in the subjectivities of other workers involved.

Even if these struggles could not be sustained in the long run, the learning process itself and the ways it has changed their own self-perception remain significant. As Elson points out, even if workers lose their jobs, they would have acquired something permanent: 'more self confidence, more organisational and advocacy skills, more knowledge of how their society works' (Elson 1996: 50). As the 25-year-old union leader reflected on the struggle after a few months:

> There are many things we have learnt from this experience, especially if one has to organise in a new unit. We should first form a union inside and get it registered. We need to save money from our salaries before we go on a long *dharna* (strike) or when we are thrown out. We could have supported the South Indian girls who are still working inside, though for how long I cannot say. But now one is more prepared for such situations.

These transformations were only one aspect of the changes women workers in unionised enterprises have undergone. A more subtle process of change also occurred within domestic regimes, involving women from both unionised and non-unionised enterprises.

Negotiating autonomy in domestic regimes

While in many cases there was a link between industrial militancy and domestic autonomy, the process of negotiating autonomy varied in different domestic regimes and also in relation to the woman's life cycle status, i.e. whether she was a daughter, mother or wife. Drawing on feminist extensions of A. Sen's 'bargaining model' of the household as a site of cooperative conflict (Sen 1990;

Agarwal 1997) domestic regimes are conceptualised as a 'locus of competing interests, rights, obligations and resources, where household members are often involved in bargaining, negotiation and possibly even conflict. Socially and historically specific views about the rights, responsibilities and needs of particular individuals which draw on normative understandings and practices, linked to accepted power differences and ideologies determine the dynamics of relations within the household' (adapted from Moore 1994: 91).

There were significant differences in the structures and forms of internal patriarchal control, of power and entitlements based on whether the household was complex, nuclear or sub-nuclear. Patriarchal controls were more stringent in general in complex households that had in-laws. Three aspects of the transformational potential of women's waged work were examined: perception of income earning and control over income; marriage choice and exit options; and perceptions of gender roles. *In half the households (50 per cent), the responsibility for household provisioning rests predominantly on women workers.*

Women workers were making substantial contributions to total household income: 46 per cent contributed from 50 to 100 per cent and 38 per cent contributed from 25 to 50 per cent of total household income, with only 17 per cent contributing less than 25 per cent. Despite the substantial and visible nature of women's earnings, the translation of this into 'perception' and further into greater autonomy was not automatic.[12] Gendered cultural norms, rules and practices, conferred different degrees of power and entitlements, with a sharp distinction between the ways in which the income of daughters and wives are perceived. In neither complex nor nuclear households did wives mention direct confrontation and assertions of absolute control over their incomes. Yet in both situations, mainly through covert strategies, wives were able to claim and use parts of their income autonomously. These 'reclaimed wages' provided a sense of self-worth and independence even though the retrieved portion was often disbursed in household expenses. It was only in situations of open marital conflict that wives overtly used their earning capacity to bargain. Independent access to an income did notionally strengthen a woman's fallback position, but this did not necessarily mean that they used the 'exit option' in every case. The social opprobrium attached to divorced women, which limited the possibility of remarriage, plus the continued need for male protection, made 'exit' an option only in extreme cases.

Amongst single women, widows spoke with pride about not being dependent on relatives and the companionship offered at work. Single mothers had to subordinate their needs to accommodate natal family members but had some bargaining power. Older single women who had virtually given up the possibility of marriage since taking on the role of main 'male provider' of the family were able to exercise a great deal of autonomy. They were proud of and respected for taking on the role of fathers.

Daughters' income earning was more complicated—their actual contribution to the household was euphemised as earning for a dowry or just passing time before getting married, leading to a non-recognition/non-perception of these earnings. This lack of overt recognition did not mean that there was no change in their status. They could and did use their 'non-recognised' contribution to household income to bargain and assert choices when it was necessary particularly in decisions about further education, delaying marriage and choosing their own marriage partner without 'verbalising' their contributions.

Gender roles showed rigidity as well as some flexibility. Overall freedom from a specific aspect of reproductive work, childcare, was important for women's entry into waged work, and the primary responsibility for this remained with women through a redistribution of domestic tasks between women in the family. Men's contribution to domestic labour was limited. However, a large section of men did contribute by doing external jobs such as shopping and paying bills (confirming the private/public divide). In some nuclear households, men also cooked, looked after children, and repaired things in the house. While no young man (brother/son) contributed to care work, fathers and husbands in many cases did do so. Despite the small number it is important to note that there was a change in the traditional division of domestic responsibilities. Partly due to work demands such as overtime but also in many cases due to a conscious articulation of sharing household tasks, a process of democratisation was occurring in some households. A similar observation was made in a study of women workers employed in the industrial area of NOIDA near Delhi (Soni-Sinha 2001).

Finally in discussion with young women workers quite radical views on marriage, work and typical gender roles emerged. For instance the polarised ideal qualities of husband and wife symbolised by the legendary Ram and his devoted wife Sita were seen as good and correct, but at the same time almost all the women stated that this ideal was unrealistic and could not be emulated. The strongest statement on this came from one of the young women:

'If today a man is not like Ram, then why should we be like Sita?'

These young women expressed a more pragmatic and less romanticised view of marriage and men, a point noted by Kabeer (2000: 171) in her study of Bangladeshi garment workers. While marriage remained a necessary objective, it was not seen as taking predominance over work and study. As stated in our earlier work, 'In computer terms, marriage and associated domesticity are the "default setting", the norm, the ever-present point at which one arrives, or to which one returns, although other possibilities may (temporarily) intervene' (Chhachhi and Pittin 1996: 110). Despite the 'non-recognition' of daughters' contribution to the family economy, it did strengthen their fallback position and expand the horizon of choices available to them, without an open acknowledgement of the source of that strength. The fact that daughters have taken over the traditional responsibilities of fathers and brothers to provide for their dowries heralds a major shift in the material structure of patriarchal authority, even if at an ideological level there has been no overt, direct challenge to elder male authority.

The complexities of internal power dynamics and cultural

norms within the household make it difficult to identify the transformational potential of waged work. As Kabeer points out, formal control over income was not as important as the expansion of choice and options due to wage work. The resort to covert strategies, particularly by young wives, the 'games' played by wives in nuclear households and the non-recognition of daughters' earnings in this study all confirm Kabeer's major finding that male protection remains socially significant, even though male provisioning has been undermined in many cases. It is important to note that waged work here is regular, visible and undertaken in a collective context—an important qualification to Sen's blanket endorsement of waged work per se and the promotion of any kind of income earning as good for women (Sen 1990).

The younger women workers, in particular are of a new kind. They are aware of rights at their workplace and in relation to the family. Their views on male protection are far more cynical and overt acceptance more pragmatic. They are aware that the getting of a good dowry for a good stable marriage no longer holds. Dowry demands continue and refusal to meet them often leads to murder. Public exposure of this by the women's movement and the media has had an effect and these women express their disillusionment with the idea that marriage means lifetime security. So while the discourse of earning one's dowry may still be used to explain their entry into waged work yet many see employment as a more reliable and long-term basis for security. This perception also gives them an interest in ensuring that they gain independent entitlements via employment.

However, as a result of industrial and economic restructuring in India, two processes are undermining the enabling conditions that facilitated the practice of citizenship: informalisation of labour at the workplace and increasing vulnerability of the household.

Erosion of employment-based entitlements through informalisation of labour

All the four gendered labour regimes analysed earlier are undergoing major restructuring due to market competition in the present phase of liberalisation leading to informalisation and increasing vulnerability of labour. The Vulnerability/Security Index below shows changes in the status of women workers in the total sample between 1993 and 1999. This is a composite of data on work status, nature of contract, legally entitled benefits, minimum wages and trade union organisation. Based on the presence/absence of legally specified entitlements, the index highlights three dimensions of protection and security: employment security, income security and labour representation security. Employment security depends on the job being permanent or temporary and if there is a written or verbal contract. Income security refers to the implementation of minimum wage regulations and legally entitled benefits for health, pension etc. Labour representation security refers to the presence or absence of a trade union.[13] The index resulted in the classification of women workers into three broad categories, which in 1993 were: Unprotected (17 per cent), Marginally Protected (41 per cent) and Protected (42 per cent). In six years, the number of workers who fell into the unprotected and insecure category increased from 17 per cent to 60 per cent (including those who were retrenched) and this shift has been primarily from the protected, secure category.

This major change clearly demonstrates that enterprises in the Delhi electronics industry are resorting to labour market flexibility. Changes due to market competition and restructuring led to: 1) the dismantling of the organised sector and mass retrenchment of workers with long service records. This generation of unionised workers has been eliminated. There has been a reversal of regularisation and implementation of statutory rights and a ban on new recruitment in locally-owned enterprises with closer ties to multinationals and an overall shift from a permanent to non-permanent workforce; 2) a shrinking of the lowest end of the unorganised sector as tiny and small enterprises, which always employed a casual workforce, are faced with extinction due to the flood of cheap electronics imports from China; 3) an increase in income insecurity—in 1994, 42 per cent of the workers interviewed were getting wages below the minimum wage and in 1995 this

Vulnerability/Security Index

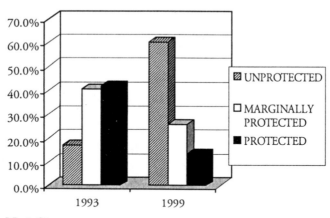

N=162

category increased to 57 per cent; 4) new employment in multinational enterprises is creating a hierarchy between a mass of non-permanent women workers with minimum benefits and a layer of women workers from middle class backgrounds who receive specialised training, full statutory benefits and permanent status; 5) representation insecurity has increased with unions in a defensive position. The increased harassment of militant union leaders, demoralisation, spatial distancing of labour courts from industrial areas and the reduction in the scope and lifting of the mandatory requirement of labour inspection have made unionisation difficult.

These reflect a managerial strategy of 'defensive flexibility'. This is not new—what is new is that this strategy of informalisation is implicitly sanctioned by the state today. In the pre-liberalisation era, similar attempts to 'dis-organise the organised sector' could be and often were successfully challenged and checked. But now, this 'organised informalisation' appears to have state sanction, as the state withdraws its commitment to the provision or implementation of statutory labour regulations.

Erosion of citizenship-based entitlements and increasing vulnerability of the household

The process of undermining the enabling conditions at the workplace has been accompanied by increasing vulnerability at the household level. The phenomenal increase in prices of basic necessities since 1991, have forced workers to make major household budgetary adjustments in levels and quality of consumption, health and education leading to changes in everyday life and tensions in gender relations. The most significant finding on food consumption modifications in the period under review was related to changes in the public distribution system (PDS) from one of universal entitlement to targeted distribution to below poverty level households. While earlier the majority of worker households used the PDS for part of their consumption requirements now there was a large section who only bought from the open market and a significant section that were completely dependent on subsidised food. Changes in consumption took gender-differentiated forms, with further differences between married and unmarried women. The hidden costs were borne primarily by married women workers, particularly mothers in nuclear families, who experienced an increase in care-work labour time and reduction in food intake. There was an increase in the intangible aspects of care-work and an intra-household transfer of costs of reproduction. The increased demands on women's physical labour and emotional labour has led to a tremendous rise in anxiety, tension and insecurity due to greater responsibility for the overall reproduction of the household, and from changes in traditionally defined as well as incipient less traditional gender relations. In 50 per cent of the households surveyed the responsibility for household provisioning rested predominantly on female earners. There is a shift from women making a contribution to household income to women taking on the primary responsibility (due to increasing male unemployment or low male wages and precarious irregular jobs), a transfer of even the few tasks that men undertook in domestic labour (shopping) and the help provided by daughters or domestic servants to mothers having complete responsibility for domestic labour. This has meant an increase in 'time poverty' for these women. The stress and strain of a situation where pre-existing gender roles, rights and responsibilities can no longer be relied upon has in some cases led to an increase in domestic conflict and violence. Clearly, these tensions affect the well-being of members of the household.

There did not appear to be a reduction of food for children, although there was a shift to bad quality and junk food that will have long-term health implications. Despite a rise in costs of schooling, children were not withdrawn, and primary education was prioritised through taking loans and cutting other areas of consumption. Gender differences occurred in higher education as young men undertook vocational training while young women took up jobs. Unlike studies in Latin America and Africa which point to drastic reductions in consumption, the worker households in this study have managed to cope, partly through the 'cushioning' of the effects of price rise through women's labour and ingenuity, and partly through the deployment of labour.

The significance of employment as the basis for livelihood and entitlement clearly emerged through an examination of household assets—apart from a section of workers who had housing security—all other households were primarily dependent on the labour market for survival and security. The consequences are seen clearly through an in-depth case study of workers who had lost their jobs particularly from the second labour regime of the pre-liberalisation era. A large section remained unemployed. Some men managed to enter self-employment, and the rest only got irregular jobs in the unorganised sector. Hinterland male migrant workers from Uttar Pradesh and Bihar did not return to their villages, contrary to earlier patterns. The village did not constitute a refuge; rural links only acted as a short-term buffer. Women's earnings became crucial for the survival of these households. No woman worker could enter into the higher end of work in the unorganised sector, i.e. self-employment. Instead, they were pushed into the lowest paid work as domestic servants or at best, home-based garment workers. Income reduction in the space of two years was drastic. Cuts in household budgets, the changes in everyday life, food reduction, an increase in ill health, and the negative effects on education of children—all had immediate and intergenerational consequences. Gender relations within these households were under great stress. Men hid the fact that women were sustaining the household, and women felt their autonomy was being restricted and there were increased controls on their mobility. There was a loss of dignity and identity as workers slipped from a self-identity of being organised, unionised workers with a highly developed consciousness and pride in their skills and contribution to the industry, to extreme vulnerability, insecurity, and in some cases destitution.

These processes foreground the linkage between changes in the workplace and the household. The undermining of enabling conditions in both locales are reversing the possibility for women to assert 'citizenship in practice' in both arenas. The absence of a strong asset base and strong and extensive citizenship entitlements from the state sector implies that,

> It is over-optimistic to expect the domestic sector to absorb all the risks. When people have to live from hand to mouth, human energies and morale are weakened, 'contingent labour' is conducive to 'contingent households' which fragment and disintegrate with costs for the people from these households and for the wider society. (Elson 2002: 94)

Both men and women workers are paying these costs, but with a greater burden on women who continue to provide a buffer to prevent a descent into more extreme conditions of distress, insecurity and vulnerability—a thin line as the experience of job loss workers illustrates. Apart from the limits to the 'elasticity' of women's labour, noted by feminist economists, the emotional pressures can also reverse the processes which were leading to a democratisation of gender relations. There is increasing discussion of a 'crisis of masculinity' as a key gender marker—a permanent job—is under threat.[14] Some recent studies document a variety of responses to job scarcity and job loss. In some cases the weakening

261

of the basis of male authority led to increased sexual control of wives, violence, multiple partners, instability of the family and an increased risk of HIV/AIDS for women. In others men accepted women's increased autonomy as household providers and even took on domestic labour tasks (Silberschmidt 2001; Chant 2000). Studies of job loss amongst public sector workers in Bangladesh highlighted a distinction between household masculinity which was upheld and public masculinity which was being undermined (Haque and Kusakbe 2005). My study of unionised workers who were retrenched revealed a pattern where men continued to maintain hegemonic masculinity in the public sphere and denied the undermining of male authority within the household. In reaction to the changes and stresses on gender roles a number of men committed suicide, disappeared or were depressed. In contrast all the women, though extremely pressured, continued to juggle limited household resources and searched for means of livelihood saying they were too busy to be depressed (Chhachhi 2004).

Whether this is only a crisis of masculinity or a 'crisis of the working class' (Heartfield 2002) the consequences are detrimental to both men and women, since attempts at reconstituting and re-asserting hegemonic masculinity can take violent forms at an individual level. At a collective level, forces of religious fundamentalisms (Hindutva in India for instance) provide legitimised practices, compensations and constructed collectivities for this reconstitution. The reversal in the process of democratisation at the workplace and within the household therefore has wider and disturbing implications.

Social protection and contending models of citizenship

The processes traced above are similar to the experiences documented globally. What then are the alternatives proposed and how far do they address the interlocking experience of the gendered effects of liberalisation and globalisation and allow for both redistribution and recognition from a feminist perspective? There are four standard alternatives/policy interventions proposed which address different institutional levels:

- Global governance institutions such as the World Trade Organisation to enforce labour standards through linkage with trade agreements or the ILO to enforce decent work;
- National governments to provide basic social security;
- Corporate capital to subscribe to voluntary codes of conduct and adhere to corporate social responsibility;
- Non-state organisations/civil society groups to provide micro-credit and social security.

Some of these relate to job-based entitlements and others to market-based or citizenship-based entitlements—none of them singly address the full consequences of liberalisation.

The labour standards debate has polarised groups in the North and the South and the linkage with trade agreements is seen as a form of protectionism. The alternative, that the ILO ensures labour standards is meaningless since it has no power of sanctions against violations. The discussion in the South has shifted now to a proposal for a universal 'social minimum floor' for all workers provided by the state combined with global redistribution and accelerated economic growth (Kabeer 2004; Singh and Zammit 2000).

Existing state based systems of social protection are limited, costly and subject to leakage as the experience of schemes such as employment guarantee, food for work etc. show in India. Means tested support to vulnerable groups provide only risk compensation, are contingency based, stigmatise groups and do not have a redistributive affect.

An alternative gaining much support today is corporate social responsibility. After exposure by consumer and labour groups some transnational corporations have instituted voluntary codes of conduct including those in subcontracted subsidiaries using informal labour. Organisations such as the Clean Clothes campaign and Women Working Worldwide have had some success in formulating and monitoring these codes particularly in the export garment sector. However, these codes are limited—they apply primarily to export production; they presuppose a consumer movement which is yet to fully develop in countries of the South; their implementation and monitoring remains North dominated with little worker representation; their content vary widely and are limited to selective core ILO conventions, often excluding the freedom of association and right to collective bargaining; and very few include rights to a minimum or living wage (Jenkins et al. 2002). Importantly the shift from statutory regulation to self-regulation exonerates the state from any responsibility towards labour and issues of trade are not included in the framework of corporate social responsibility.

Finally the standard prescription for poverty alleviation and women's empowerment remains micro-credit—now promoted as part of 'social capital' by the World Bank—as the magic bullet to solve all problems. The evidence from case studies, including assessments of the 'best practice' example of Grameen Bank in Bangladesh, shows contradictory results (Mahmud 2003; Kabeer 2001). Most studies reveal that in fact there is limited participation of clients from extremely poor households and the majority cluster just above or just below the poverty line; interest rates are high often touching 30 per cent; targeting is based on income/ consumption definitions of poverty which excludes large numbers of disadvantaged women; the small savings and loans do not allow graduation to higher income activities; and women take on responsibilities for income and savings while men are freed from responsibility for household well-being. Some studies even note an increase in domestic violence and surveillance over women (Schuler, Hashemi and Badal 1998).

Examples of positive outcomes such as programmes initiated by the Self-Employed Women's Association (SEWA) in India remain exceptional since micro-credit is only one component in a broader multipronged programme. While the SEWA model is presented as blueprint for micro-credit what is usually not mentioned is that it is a workers' organisation combining struggle for rights and recognition with development and social security for workers in the informal economy (ILO 2001; Lund and Srinivas 2000). Micro-credit initiatives focus more on economic empowerment and issues of gender subordination often remain secondary based on an implicit or explicit linear logic: credit = poverty alleviation = women's empowerment and a conflation of household well-being with women's well-being. Other multipronged initiatives are under donor pressure to expand micro-credit coverage and become financially self-sustaining, which often jettisons the gender equality objectives. More significantly the emphasis on self-help transfers costs to participants and legitimises non-allocation of state resources for social protection.

All the four main policy interventions and programmes discussed above are minimalist and reductionist, whether in terms of citizenship-based entitlements or work/employment-based entitlements. Despite being couched in the language of 'rights' and 'empowerment' these are not necessarily a challenge to neo-liberalism and do not create the conditions for fully enabling 'citizenship in practice' for women workers in particular. Globalisation has initiated a new individualistic, liberal and market-oriented discourse on women's rights through policy interventions as well as in the broader social context. As Veronica Schild points out, social citizenship is being reconfigured from a 'welfare state conception as resting on a notion of universal rights to basic public goods' to a notion of citizens as 'empowered clients, who as individuals are viewed as capable of enhancing their lives through judicious, responsible choices as consumers of services and other goods' (Schild 2002: 195).[15]

The challenge today is to navigate between contending models of citizenship.[16] 'Industrial citizenship' which provides employment-based entitlements has historically been based on the male breadwinner model. The universal breadwinner model which recognises women's participation (also called the 'adult worker family' in current western welfare state discussions), does challenge this male monopoly but also relies on employment as the primary basis for citizenship entitlements. These models remains androcentric since they valorise paid work and either ignore care work or assume that it can be shifted to the market and/or the state (Fraser 1997: 53).[17] Overall they have positive outcomes

265

for women who are childless or without major domestic responsibilities and their promotion today in the European Union for instance is linked more with the shift from welfare to workfare rather than a concern with gender equality.

The model of 'market citizenship' being promoted in current policies especially for the South is epitomised in the micro-credit approach, but is also implicit in the broader process of commoditisation and privatisation in the areas of insurance, pensions, health, etc. Given that women's identities are usually subsumed within the family and community the process of 'individuation' for women, i.e. developing an individual sense of identity and autonomy is indeed important. However this neo-liberal model fosters a market oriented, atomistic individualist, consumerist sense of self which remains trapped within liberal notions of gender equality.

'Democratic citizenship' is a third emerging model which brings back the focus on rights as well as state responsibility for social provisioning (Pateman 2004). It integrates both employment and citizenship entitlements. Within this the proposal for a universal basic income can address some fundamental aspects of insecurity and also provide the enabling conditions for democratisation at many levels. 'A basic income is an income paid by a political community to all its members on an individual basis, without means test or work requirement' (Van Parijs 2004). What is significant about this proposal is that it is universal, unconditional and can be disbursed by a global, regional, national or local level institution. Conceived as a right of economic citizenship, a universal basic income could lead to elimination of the unemployment and poverty trap; strengthen workers' bargaining position to demand decent work; strengthen women's fallback position within the household and lead to wider redistribution based on principles of moral solidarity and the interdependence of society and the world (Standing 2003; Robeyns 2001a).[18]

This is no utopian idea—in different forms it is already being introduced. In Brazil a number of municipalities have started minimum income programmes with the Bolsa-Escola programmes making this support conditional on school attendance of children and in South Africa today there is an ongoing campaign for a Basic Income Grant (Matisonn and Seekings 2002). In exemplary campaigns social movements in India have struggled for the right to information, the right to work and a universal employment guarantee scheme. Though the latter remains within the framework of work-based entitlements yet it asserts the principle of a right to a citizenship-based entitlement. Despite the truncated forms in which these were finally passed (as the Right to Information Act and Rural Employment Guarantee Act 2005) the principles of democratic citizenship were powerfully articulated in these campaigns. In Venezuela the constitutional recognition of housework in Article 88, as economic activity which produces wealth and well-being, has now been translated into a citizenship entitlement with the president Hugo Chavez granting roughly US$ 200 each per month to 200,000 poor homemakers.

The arguments of lack of resources against such universal citizenship entitlements are spurious. There are concrete proposals such as the global level Tobin tax on international financial flows and the national level 'Maria tax' on exporters reflecting the proportion of women in employment, the revenues of which could be used for supporting social reproduction (Pearson 2004). Redeployment of resources from socially destructive expenditures such as military spending would release substantial resources for socially useful productive activities. Estimates of costs of a universal basic income grant are as low as half to one per cent of GDP. For example Indian military expenditure of Rs 450,000 million (US$ 9783 million) is double the cost of its Employment Guarantee Scheme. What is needed is political will and imagination. A universal basic income is no panacea but this simple but powerful idea is feasible, presenting a coalescing strategy (linking issues of economic justice and gender justice) which could create the enabling conditions for comprehensive and humane security.

Other coalescing strategies which incorporate the linkages

between employment and household, and the intertwining of reproductive and productive roles have been powerfully articulated by women in social movements and workers' organisations in the last few years. For instance labour codes developed by women workers organisations through a participatory process go beyond the minimalist core conventions and emphasise other aspects such as dignity, decent wages, refusal of arbitrary and inhumane treatment, freedom of association and collective bargaining, protection against violence and harassment, care work and recognition and respect for home-based workers, social security, unemployment and sickness benefits, health services and pensions, and issues relating to gendered forms of labour control (e.g. Nicaraguan Ethical Code 1998, in Jenkins et al. 2002). It is indeed time that the world responds to the demand made by indigenous peasant women in the Zapatista movement when in addition to land rights and gender equality they asked for the 'right to rest'.

These demands emerge from women workers' quotidian life experiences and articulate principles[19] which would radically engender frameworks of distributive justice and current policy interventions. Both feminist scholarship and activism already present visions for a new gender order and the possibility for a 'universal care giver model' which challenges gender coding of work and the divisions between the workplace and domestic space. What is needed is incorporation of these voices and political articulation of these demands into truly gendered redistributive policies.

Notes

[1] The erosion in the gender wage gap, skill upgrading, technological change and product diversification have led to a decline in women's employment and in some cases even a substitution by men (Razavi 1999).

[2] Such a perspective shifts the emphasis from citizenship as status to citizenship as process exploring how 'citizenship is lived in practice—in the courts, in the polity, in the household, as well as in the understandings different sectors of the population have of their rights and of the terms of their social participation or exclusion' (Lister 2000; Molyneux 2000: 122).

[3] Negotiating autonomy is used to refer to the processes that allow for an

expansion of choices rather than a set of attributes which can be measured. This allows for a more grounded analysis rather than an open concept of 'female agency' per se and the more ambiguous and loaded concept of empowerment. The concept of empowerment is used today in a loose way ranging from female literacy as women's empowerment and agency to more comprehensive formulations which are then converted into indicators (see Kabeer 2001). The term 'empowerment' is too heavy to describe the non-linear, often reversible, constantly negotiated dynamics of gender relations in the workplace and the household.

4 The main database for this study is research done in 1994–96 of 20 enterprises manufacturing televisions in the industrial areas around Delhi with interviews with women and men workers, employers, managers and trade unionists. A follow up survey of 100 workers' households was conducted in 2000 (see Chhachhi 2004 for more details).

5 Three basic principles of entitlement: need (relief, public assistance), employment (earnings related social insurance) and citizenship (membership of society) have been deployed by welfare states to provide security (Fraser 1997: 50).

6 Fordism was characteristic of post-war western countries and refers to the combination of a mass production paradigm (the assembly line introduced by Henry Ford) with stabilising economic policies, high wages and state subsidies and transfers. Since the 1980s this model has been undermined in the West with rising inflation, unemployment and dismantling of the welfare state.

7 Karen Hossfeld (1990) describes a similar situation in Silicon Valley. Immigrant workers pretended not to understand English or instructions at times, thereby fitting into the ethnic stereotypes created by management. The strategy of 'using their logic against them' was not consciously articulated, but it allowed women some respite from work discipline.

8 The application of principles of scientific management to mass production in manufacturing, developed by Frederick Taylor in 1911 introduced fragmentation, specialisation and control in the labour process characteristic of industrial manufacturing since the 20th century.

9 Studies in South-east Asia have emphasised the congruence between the rural family and the factory through reproduction of pre-industrial authority structures within the factory, as well as continued control and surveillance of 'factory daughters' by the family, community leaders and religious ideology. Protest against this took pre-industrial forms such as spirit possession, personal crisis, and withdrawal (Ong 1987; Wolf 1992). Wolf's study differs showing certain degrees of individual autonomy in relation to the family. In all these studies, however, assertions of female agency do not take direct, confrontational forms in the factory. At the most, real fathers (and mothers)

are challenged on the basis of economic independence, but 'patron-fathers' in the factory are still paid obeisance. This case study in the electronics industry in Delhi gives another picture of factory daughters.

10 Despite being a minority, they have also joined and even initiated the formation of unions. Studies of women workers in the pharmaceutical industry, iron ore mines, tobacco processing and the garment export industry testify to the capacity of women to organise around general as well as women-specific demands. A significant case was the struggle by women pharmaceutical workers against the 'marriage clause' and early retirement age for women (Gothoskar 1992). The capacity of women to organise in alternative structures is seen in SEWA which has played a key role in making informal workers visible, advocating international and national legislation, and forming coalitions with other unorganised sector workers (Jhabvala and Subramanya 2000).

11 It is important not to freeze analysis of women workers situation to one time period—a point forcefully made by Lim (1990).

12 The Engelian assumption that waged work is a sufficient condition for improving women's status has been qualified further with A. Sen's notion of 'perceived income contribution'(Sen 1990).

13 The index is a modification of the labour status approach developed by J. Harris, K.P. Kannan and G. Rodgers (1990). Here the focus is on different dimensions of protection and security, many included in the Decent Work Index developed by the ILO.

14 The generalised crisis of masculinity causing anxiety and moral panic is attributed to a number of factors which are often conflated such as: girls improving educational attainment, feminisation of the labour force, increased violence against women, male concern with body images, female-headed households, new family forms, backlash to feminism etc.

15 Media analysts in India for instance note a shift from general social issues to the resurgence of the 'family' since the 1990s in the content of television serials and advertisements. In advertising, a niche customer—the super homemaker—is being targeted. Women's aspirations for freedom of choice and decision-making (factors identified by qualitative product market research) are promoted by advertisements for ovens, washing machines, and other consumer durables, and are simultaneously translated into product acquisition. As they point out, women's power is converted into 'product power' (Vij 1999).

16 In recent discussions on social policy feminists have reviewed the employment of women workers in export industries in different contexts and raised questions whether paid work can be a route to welfare entitlements for women workers (Razavi and Pearson 2004). A similar concern emerges from debates on global labour standards with Kabeer arguing against the 'social

clause' in international trade agreements and advocating instead 'the principle of a universal social floor, which covers the minimum basic needs of food, health, and shelter' (Kabeer 2004: 29).

[17] An analysis of this model shows wide variations between the United States where there is very little provision for care work and Scandinavian countries where there are services for care of children, the elderly and cash transfers for parental leave (the 'daddy-quota' for men). However these measures did not lead to changes in vertical and horizontal gender segregation in the labour market (Gulliari and Lewis 2005).

[18] Feminist have expressed misgivings about the proposal for universal basic income fearing that it would reinforce the sexual division of labour—an objection raised in earlier years to the wages for housework demand.

[19] The connection between feminist movements and scholarship is evident in the ways in which these demands have been elaborated in theoretical terms by developing evaluative standards to assess policies, demands and strategies in so far as they incorporate the leisure-time equality principle, the equality of respect principle, the anti-marginalisation principle, and the anti-androcentrism principle which together could constitute a basis for gender equality (Fraser 1997: 44–51).

References

Agarwal, B. 1997, '"Bargaining" and Gender Relations: Within and Beyond the Household'. *Feminist Economics*. 3 (1). pp. 1–51.

Ahmad, E., J. Dreze, J. Hills and A. Sen. eds. 1999. *Social Security in Developing Countries*. New Delhi: Oxford University Press.

Appasamy, P., S. Guhan, R. Hema, M. Majumdar and A. Vaidyanathan. 1996. 'Social exclusion from a welfare rights perspective in India'. International Institute for Labour Studies. Research Series 106. Geneva: International Labour Organisation.

Bakker, I. 1994. 'Engendering Macro-Economic Policy Reform in the Era of Global Restructuring and Adjustment' in *The Strategic Silence*. ed. I. Bakker. London: Zed Books. pp. 1–23.

Bakker, I. and S. Gill. eds. 2003. *Power, Production and Social Reproduction*. New York: Palgrave Macmillan.

Chant, S. 2000. 'Men in Crisis? Reflections on Masculinities, Work and Family in North-West Costa Rica'. *The European Journal of Development Research*. 12 (2). pp. 199–218.

Chaudhuri, M. 1996. 'Citizens, Workers and Emblems of Culture: An Analysis of the First Plan Document on Women' in *Social Reform, Sexuality and the State*. ed. P. Uberoi. New Delhi: Sage Publications. pp. 211–235.

Chhachhi, A. (forthcoming). *Eroding Citizenship: Gender and Labour in Contemporary India*. UK: Routledge.

Chhachhi, A. and R. Pittin. eds. 1996. *Confronting State, Capital and Patriarchy: Women Organising in the Process of Industrialisation.* London: Macmillan Press.

Cook, J. 2000. 'Flexible Employment—Implications for a Gendered Political Economy of Citizenship' in *Towards a Gendered Political Economy.* eds. J. Cook, J. Roberts and G. Waylen. London: Macmillan Press. pp. 145–164.

Commission on Human Security (CHS). 2003. *Human Security Now.* New York: United Nations.

Dreze, J. and A. Sen. 1991. 'Public Action for Social Security: Foundations and Strategy' in *Social Security in Developing Countries.* eds. E. Ahmad, J. Dreze, J. Hills and A. Sen. New Delhi: Oxford University Press.

Elson, D. 1996. 'Appraising Recent Developments in the World Market for Nimble Fingers' in *Confronting State, Capital and Patriarchy: Women Organising in the Process of Industrialisation.* eds. A. Chhachhi and R. Pittin. London: Macmillan Press. pp. 35-55.

——. 2002. 'Gender Justice, Human Rights, and Neo-Liberal Economic Policies' in *Gender Justice, Development, and Rights.* eds. M. Molyneux and S. Razavi. Oxford: Oxford University Press. pp. 78–114.

Elson, D. and N. Cagatay. 2000. 'The Social Content of Macroeconomics Policies'. *World Development.* vol. 28. 7 July. pp. 1347–64.

Elson, D. and R. Pearson. 1981. 'The Subordination of Women and the Internationalization of Factory Production' *in Of Marriage and the Market: Women's Subordination in an International Perspective.* eds. K. Young, C. Wolkowitz and R. McCullagh. London: Routledge. pp. 144–66.

Floro, M.S. 1995. 'Economic Restructuring, Gender and the Allocation of Time'. *World Development.* vol. 23. no.11. pp. 1913–29.

Fraser, N. 1997. *Justice Interruptus: Critical Reflections on the 'Post-Socialist' Condition.* London/New York: Routledge.

Gasper, D. 2002. 'Is Sen's Capability Approach an Adequate Basis for Considering Human Development?' *Review of Political Economy.* vol. 14. no. 4. pp. 435–61.

Ginneken, Wouter van. ed. 1998. *Social Security for All Indians.* New Delhi: Oxford University Press.

Government of India (GOI). 2003. 'Report of Second National Commission on Labour'. New Delhi: Ministry of Labour.

Gore, C., J.B. Figueiredo and G. Rodgers. 1995. 'Introduction: Markets, Citizenship and Social Exclusion' in *Social Exclusion: Rhetoric, Reality, Responses: A Contribution to the World Summit for Social Development.* eds. G. Rodgers, C. Gore and J.B. Figueiredo. Geneva: International Institute for Labour Studies. pp. 1–40.

Gothoskar, S. ed. 1992. *Struggles of Women at Work*. New Delhi: Vikas Publishing House Pvt. Ltd.

Gulliari, S. and J. Lewis. 2005. 'The Adult Worker Model Family, Gender Equality and Care'. Social Policy and Development Programme Paper. no. 5. Geneva: United Nations Research Institute for Social Development.

Haque, Md. Mozammel and K. Kusakbe. 2005. 'Retrenched Men Workers in Bangladesh: A Crisis of Masculinities? *Gender, Technology and Development*. vol. 9(2). pp. 185–208.

Harris, J., K.P. Kannan and G. Rodgers. 1990. *Urban Labour Market Structure and Job Access in India: A Study of Coimbatore*. Geneva: International Institute for Labour Studies.

Harriss-White, B. and N. Gooptu. 2000. 'Mapping India's World of Unorganized Labour'. *Socialist Register 2001*. London: The Merlin Press. pp. 89–118.

Harriss-White, B. and S. Subramanian. eds. 1999. *Illfare in India: Essays on India's Social Sector in Honour of S. Guhan*. New Delhi: Sage Publications.

Heartfield, J. 2002. 'There is no Masculinity Crisis'. Genders 35. available at www.genders.org/g35/g35_heartfield.html.

Hossfeld, K. 1990. '"Using their Logic against Them": Contradictions in Sex, Race, and Class in Silicon Valley' in *Women Workers and Global Restructuring*. ed. K. Ward. Cornell International Industrial and Labour Relations Report Series. no. 17. Ithaca: ILR Press. pp. 149–78.

International Labour Organisation. 2001. 'Women Organizing for Social Protection. The Self-Employed Women's Association's Integrated Insurance Scheme, India'. Geneva: Strategies and Tools against Social Exclusion and Poverty/International Labour Organisation (STEP/ILO).

——. 2003. 'Global Employment Trends'. Geneva: ILO.

——. 2004. 'Economic Security for a Better World'. Geneva: ILO.

Jenkins, R., R. Pearson and G. Seyfang. eds. 2002. *Corporate Social Responsibility and Labour Rights: Codes of Conduct in the Global Economy*. London/Sterling, VA: Earthscan Publications Ltd.

Jhabvala, R. and R. Subramanya. eds. 2000. *The Unorganised Sector: Work Security and Social Protection*. New Delhi: Sage Publications.

Kabeer, N. 2000. *The Power to Choose: Bangladeshi Women and Labour Market Decisions in London and Dhaka*. London: Verso.

——. 2001. 'Conflicts over Credit: Re-evaluating the Empowerment Potential of Loans to Women in Rural Bangladesh'. *World Development*. January. 29(1). pp. 63–84.

——. 2004. 'Globalization, Labour Standards, and Women's Rights: Dilemmas of Collective (In)Action in an Interdependent World'. *Feminist Economics*. 10(1). pp.3–35.

Kannan, K.P. and M. Rutten. 2003. 'Labour and Capital in Asia's Transformation:

on Dichotomies, Continuities and Linkages' in *Work and Social Change in Asia: Essays in Honour of Jan Breman.* eds. A. Das and M. van der Linden. New Delhi: Manohar Publishers and Distributors. pp. 111–30.

Lim, L. 1990. 'Women's Work in Export Factories: The Politics of a Cause' in *Persistent Inequalities.* ed. Irene Tinker. Oxford: Oxford University Press.

Lister, R. 2000. 'Inclusion/Exclusion: The Janus Face of Citizenship' in *Towards a Gendered Political Economy.* eds. J. Cook, J. Roberts and G. Waylen. London: Macmillan Press. pp. 98–117.

Lund, F. and S. Srinivas. 2000. 'Learning from Experience: A Gendered Approach to Social Protection for Workers in the Informal Economy'. Geneva: Strategies and Tools against Social Exclusion and Poverty/International Labour Organisation (STEP/ILO), and Women in the Informal Economy: Globalizing and Organizing (WIEGO).

Mahmud, S. 2003. 'Actually how Empowering is Micro-credit?' *Development and Change.* vol. 34. no. 4. pp. 577–605.

Matisonn H. and J. Seekings. 2002. 'Welfare in Wonderland: The Politics of Basic Income Grant in South Africa, 1996–2002'. Paper presented at 9th International Conference on Basic Income. Geneva.

Molyneux, M. 2000. 'Comparative Perspectives on Gender and Citizenship: Latin America and the Former Socialist States' in *Towards a Gendered Political Economy.* eds. J. Cook, J. Roberts and G. Waylen. London: Macmillan Press. pp. 121–144.

Moore, H.L. 1994. *A Passion for Difference.* Cambridge: Polity Press.

Nair, Janaki. 1996. *Women and Law in Colonial India.* New Delhi: Kali for Women.

Ong, A. 1987. *Spirits of Resistance and Capitalist Discipline: Factory Women in Malaysia.* Albany, NY: State University of New York Press.

Pateman, C. 2004. 'Democratizing Citizenship: Some advantages of a basic income'. *Politics and Society.* vol. 32. no.1. March. pp. 89–105.

Patnaik, P. 1998. 'Amartya Sen and the Theory of Public Action'. *Economic and Political Weekly.* vol. 10. no. 4. pp. 2855–58.

Pearson, R. 1998. '"Nimble Fingers" Revisited: Reflections on women and third world industrialization in the late twentieth century' in *Feminist Visions of Development: Gender Analysis and Policy.* eds. C. Jackson and R. Pearson. London/New York: Routledge. pp. 171–88.

——. 2004. 'The Social is Political: Towards the re-Politicisation of Feminist Analysis of the Global Economy'. *International Feminist Journal of Politics.* vol. 6. no. 4.

Razavi, S. 1999. 'Export-Oriented Employment, Poverty and Gender: Contesting Accounts'. *Development and Change.* vol. 30. no. 3. pp. 653–82.

Razavi, S. and R. Pearson. 2004. 'Globalization, Export-oriented Employment and Social Policy: Gendered Connections' in *Globalization, Export-oriented*

Employment and Social Policy: Gendered Connections. eds. S. Razavi, R. Pearson and C. Danloy. Basingstoke, UK: Palgrave Macmillan.

Robeyns, I. 2001. 'Sen's Capability Approach and Feminist Theory'. Paper presented at the Conference on Sen's Capability Approach. Cambridge University: St Edmund's College.

——. 2001a. 'An Income of one's own: a radical vision of welfare policies in Europe and beyond?' *Gender and Development.* vol. 9. no.1. pp. 82–9.

Schild, V. 2002. 'Engendering the new social citizenship in Chile, NGO's and social provisioning under Neo-liberalism' in *Gender Justice, Development and Rights.* eds. M. Molyneaux and S. Razavi. Oxford: Oxford University Press.

Schuler, S.R., S.E. Hashemi and S.H. Badal. 1998. 'Men's violence against women in rural Bangladesh: Undermined or exacerbated by micro credit programme'. *Development in Practice.* vol. 8 (2). pp. 148–57

Sen, A. 1990. 'Gender and Cooperative Conflicts' in *Persistent Inequalities: Women and World Development.* ed. I. Tinker. Oxford: Oxford University Press. pp. 123–45.

——. 1999. *Development as Freedom.* Oxford: Oxford University Press.

Sen, A. et al. 2003. 'Continuing the Conversation: Amartya Sen talks to Bina Agarwal, Jane Humphries and Ingrid Robeyns'. *Feminist Economics.* vol. 9. nos. 2–3. pp. 319–32.

Sen, S. 2003. 'Politics of Gender and Class: Women in Indian Industries' in *Family and Gender: Changing Values in Germany and India.* eds. M. Pernau, I. Ahmad and H. Reifield. New Delhi: Sage Publications. pp. 296–321.

Silberschmidt, M. 2001. 'Disempowerment of Men in Rural and Urban East Africa: Implications for Male Identity and Sexual Behaviour'. *World Development.* vol. 29. no.4. pp. 657–71.

Singh, A. and A. Zammit. 2000. *The Global Labour Standards Controversy: Critical Issues for Developing Countries.* Geneva: South Centre.

Soni-Sinha, U. 2001. 'Income Control and Household Work-Sharing' in *Gender, Globalisation and Democratisation.* eds. R.M. Kelly, J.H. Bayes, M.E. Hawkesworth and B. Young. Oxford: Rowman and Littlefield Publishers. pp. 121–36.

Standing, G. 1999. *Global Labour Flexibility: Seeking Distributive Justice.* London: Macmillan Press.

—— 2003 'Human Security and Social Protection' in *Work and Well-being in the Age of Finance.* eds. J. Ghosh and C.P. Chandrasekhar. New Delhi. Tulika Books. pp. 579–602.

Staveren, I. van. 2002. 'Comments on Noreena Hertz' in FENN, 'Gender Tools for Development: A Feminist Economics Perspective on Globalisation'. Seminar Report. The Hague: Institute of Social Studies.

Van Parijs, Philippe. 2004. 'Basic Income: A Simple and Powerful Idea for the

Twenty-first Century'. *Politics and Society*. vol. 32. no.1. March. pp. 7–39.

Vij, D. 1999. Advertisement. 'Superwoman—is she for real?' *The Tribune*. 25 September.

Wolf, D. 1992. *Factory Daughters: Gender, Household Dynamics and Rural Industrialisation in Java*. Berkeley, CA: University of California Press.

Young, B. 2003. 'Financial Crisis and Social Reproduction: Asia, Argentina and Brazil' in *Power, Production and Social Reproduction*. eds. I. Barker and S. Gill. New York: Palgrave Macmillan. pp. 103–123.

Yuval-Davis, N. 1999. 'The Multi-Layered Citizen: Citizenship in the Age of "Glocalization."' *International Feminist Journal of Politics*. 1(1): 119–136.

12

The Plasticity of Gender in Social Policy Formation

PATRICIA MOHAMMED

Introduction.

Once we embrace 'gender' as embodying more than the condition of woman in relation to man, and we begin to interpret gender equity and equality as being fundamental to the transformation of a society, then the concept and its applications become very plastic. This plasticity is evident in the theoretical conceptualisation of women, gender and human security used by both Amartya Sen and Martha Nussbaum in the 'capabilities approach', terminology which they have introduced to and extended the philosophical base of development economics. While the collective economic and social good is the goal of all development, the ultimate aim is that of human security of each individual. Human security is not restricted primarily to issues of poverty or violence, or threats to the body politic, but to the freedoms required by each individual to feel secure as a human being. Sen and Nussbaum have privileged individual human capacity and dignity as the main goal of development. Both implicit and explicit in their work is the embrace of seminal ideas in feminist theory and feminist ethics, that human security issues must acknowledge and work with the fact that there are deeply rooted gender differentials in access to power and resources. In most societies, whether this differential is created through cultural belief systems of gender roles or ethnic and racial stratification in the division of labour, the possibilities for female freedoms to develop their potential and capacities are generally more limited than those of the male.[1] In general, women's access to resources have been mitigated by their capacity to struggle for their human rights, particularly in areas such as domestic violence, sexual and reproductive health and national political decision-making.

Martha Nussbaum affirms a 'liberal' view that is compatible with the feminist conception of the value of women as persons. At the heart of this tradition of liberal political thought is a two-fold intuition about all human beings: that by virtue of being defined as human, we are all equal in dignity and worth, no matter where we are situated in society. She notes that the primary source of this worth is the power of moral choice in the ability to plan a life in accordance with one's own evaluation of ends. At the heart of Nussbaum's liberal theory of justice and human rights is her version of Amartya Sen's concept of substantial freedoms or capabilities.[2] Sen developed this notion as a way of addressing questions of justice and human development. Nor does the capability approach concern itself with the distribution of resources alone, because resources have no value in themselves disconnected from their promotion of what women and men actually do and are. The capability approach asks social planners to enquire into the needs individuals have for resources and their diverse abilities to convert resources into functioning.[3] Des Gasper comments that it is this conversation which Sen has profoundly stimulated between economists and philosophers, and 'his ability to link cases, concepts, explanatory and normative theory, and policy proposals' which is at the heart of his approach. This approach has appealed to the inter-disciplinarity of our present time and to the increasing ethical requirements of policy-makers and practitioners on the field, not only of delivery but also for accountability of their ideas and practices.

This chapter takes its point of departure and inspiration from the work of Sen and Nussbaum, interpreting its sentiments and messages as they appeal to feminist scholarship and to policy-making in the sphere of gender and development. First, the section on 'the personal and the individual' recognises a parallel in the ideas emerging in second wave feminism that the 'personal is political'. The narrative form is used here to look at the lived experience of one woman in Trinidad who within and despite the constraints of historically bound ideas of gender and ethnicity, achieves what we might define as an expression of human security and economic freedom. Second, the section, 'the conceptual is political', draws in the experience of assisting with two national gender policies in the Caribbean, those of the Cayman Islands and Trinidad and Tobago to see how the plasticity inherent in the concept of gender makes it both valuable and highly relevant in the work of 20th century philosophers like Sen and Nussbaum for recasting how and why we need to think about human security.

The personal and the individual

The popular idea of the Indian female entrepreneur in the Caribbean, and in Trinidad in particular, is that of the single-minded, overly thrifty, yet resourceful woman, the careful and trustworthy manager of her husband's business, guardian of both domesticity and ethnicity. What is often left unspoken and submerged in this representation is the extent to which thrift and economy were a necessary part of the migrant's make-up in order to return as a success to the homeland. Such popular ideas obfuscate the larger demographic picture, that success stories may be far fewer than we think. In the case of women's role in entrepreneurship, this common image of the successful and thrifty Indian female assumes the ubiquitous presence of supportive and respectful male partnership. My maternal grandmother, was hardworking and humourless, the reasons for the latter I could not have appreciated when I was young but can only do so in retrospect. She ran a dry goods shop which she operated from the front room of their private home, and simultaneously sold cloth by the yard from bales of material she transported to market sites in Princes Town and Debe, two small towns in Trinidad. The oldest children were left to look after the shop while she sold cloth at the market during the weekdays. On weekends she would resume work in the shop and deal with the domestic affairs of the household. I cannot recall her resting or doing something leisurely. By this means, she reared and educated twelve children, to my knowledge, single-handedly providing the income for the entire household. My grandfather seemed, in the contemporary gender jargon of the region in relation to masculinity, to be 'marginal' to any of these income-earning activities or authority in their familial home.

Among other assumptions is that women entrepreneurs will invariably benefit from the businesses they have built up. This is not always the case. We need research to acquaint us equally with those whose labour was and continues to be exploited by their own families and spouses. There is furthermore, the unchallenged view that women who accrue wealth are motivated primarily by an irrational desire for accumulation, for themselves and their families. Little thought is given to the psychological and personal reasons why they may choose, or are forced by circumstances, to become entrepreneurs, or for that matter what kinds of skills they possess which make them successful at building businesses.

Early travel writers to the Caribbean had been instrumental in popularising such notions of Asian women's thriftiness and have established some of these stereotypes for posterity. In 1887, William Agnew Paton describes this scenario in his visit to San Fernando.

> 'Across the way from the shop of the Hindu silver-smith, we noticed a coolly woman squatting in the door-way of a shanty of more respectable and attractive appearance. ... The coolly woman was loaded down— adorned would faintly express her preposterous state of ornamentation— with all the different varieties of precious metal-work known to the members of the trade ... at first I was inclined to believe that she had on her person the entire stock and capital of the largest wholesale jewellery establishment on the island, and had been placed in the door-way to make exhibition of the great and varied assortment offered for sale by the wealthiest house in its line of business. Such, however, was not the case—she was a Hindu doctor's wife; not only the companion of his

joys, the partner of his sorrows, his better half, and evidently, all his treasures—she was also his business partner, the drummer for the concern, and the signboard to attract custom to his dispensary.[4]

Not content with depicting her as the pimp for her husband's suspect doctoring skills, Paton etches out further popular beliefs pertaining to accumulation among the Indian population. He continues:

A coolly man, no matter what may be his vocation or his money winning-power, no sooner is able to put by some thing for a rainy day than he ties himself on to an artificer, cunning to work in silver and gold, and causes to be beaten into bangles, gewgaws, chains, bracelets, or other forms of female ornaments, any spare change he may have in his belt or in the folds of his turban—to the end that he may encircle the toes or neck, adorn the ankles or thumbs, or other parts of his wife's or daughter's, or if he be a bachelor, sister's or sweetheart's body, thus endowing her practically with all and sundry his worldly goods and earthly possessions. She thus becomes his savings bank and trust company and he regards her in the light of an investment—non interest bearing it is true, nevertheless subject to draft at sight, doubtless very precious to him and handy to have about the house.[5]

Roaming through the West Indies in a whirlwind tour of ten islands in period of just over six months, Harry Franck makes another sweeping observation in 1920.

Both the Chinese and the Hindu residents of Trinidad are thrifty, many of them are well to do, for the former have indefatigable diligence in their favour; and the latter, who neither gamble nor steal, have no serious faults, except for the tendency to carve up their unfaithful wives.[6]

The times have changed. Common wisdom is that all these faults have accrued and accelerated disproportionately. Be that as it may, we do not want to create false myth heroines of Indian female entrepreneurs nor of continuing to essentialise notions of the shopkeeping woman or man, for this has tended to be the dominant theme of the past.

What is lacking in the stories told by travellers and outsiders are the imperatives which drive such women like my grandmother to become entrepreneurs; the necessity of making a living not only for survival but to better the lives of their children. In this regard they are not unlike any other group or similar class of women in the societies of Trinidad and elsewhere in the world. The difference perhaps is in the cultural traditions on which the individuals in one ethnic group draw compared to another to make a living, and the extent to which they are willing to subsume their own needs for that of their children and families. The latter is something of a cliché attached to women in relation to their families, and particularly to the Indian female, certainly within the confines of the culture. At the risk of further entrenching such stereotypes, but also to establish a truism of how such a life is lived, I wanted to mine the details of how successful mothering and entrepreneurship are achieved by letting one woman tell her own story. The academic community often derives its material from the lives of others, retelling this in its clinical language. The voice of the real entrepreneur is absent while the authorial voice controls truth. I relate the story of this woman as she herself tells it,[7] keeping as far as possible, her voice, rhythm of speech and language. We shall call her, 'Mrs Singh'.[8]

Tara was born in the small village of Edinburgh[9] in Chaguanas, central Trinidad, in 1944, one of seven children, of whom she was the oldest.

> Meh father had a bull cart so meh mother used to work in the canefield, cutting cane and loading, she used to go to help him load the cane to sell it.... When I stop school, I was 13 years, I cook, wash, mind children, full water in the pipe, daub, I used to *lepay, lepay* means to wipe the place clean like how we have mop and thing now.... The boy whey like me, he was a mechanic, he used to pass in the main road and I used to full water. He passing and watching, when I bringing in the water to swing in the yard, he used to ride through and see which yard I swinging in. He came and ask, he ask meh uncle, and meh uncle bring him to ask meh father and grandmother. He was a mechanic, doing he own mechanic work.

Marriage was a welcome escape from the responsibility prematurely entrusted on the young girl. At the age of 15 she was married according to Hindu rites to a husband who was five years her senior.

We had a Hindu wedding, kept right in Edinburgh on the main road. Then I married and came here to live. When I came here to live, well was me and meh husband and meh mother-in-law, she were old, I used to have to see about she, she was still moving about but she used to make· little garden and ting but she never work no where. I married 1959. We just had a little shed, a little galvanise shed, where he used to fix cars from. From there now we start to work together, I used to make garden, plant rice, sell in the market, I used to had a plucking depot, meh parents had a little land in the main road where I from, and we used to go and buy chicken and pluck and sell chicken, me and meh son. The two children had 17 years, the big girl de done married I think. Mr. Singh had decide to set up tyre retreads, he had a friend working IDC (Industrial Development Cooperation), across the road where the vagrant them does dey in town, they giving a loan, he have a Chinese person working there, he used to come to fix he car here, so he tell Shridath, meh husban, like better he take a loan and extend the garage and fix the galvanise, right, so Shridath telling the Chinee boy, he say boy I go take a loan but I eh want to build no garage yet, I go have same garage, but I better open a tyre place.

It wasn't expensive then, that time the US was two dollars, so he borrowed about a hundred and something thousand, that was about six per cent or five per cent, not plenty about three per cent, not plenty, right. He start with that and he work together with all the children, well nobody never work eh, to say that to go in any other place to work, while they growing up they work together with the father with me and with the five children.... He never do hub recap, he never do cold recap, then after he start to build up and ting, then he start to pay off the loan, then he take a next loan. I was 25 years when he start, easy easy we build eh, we eh build to say we have plenty money one time and we build, when he go in the bank, he buy a sweepstake and he win a 15,000 dollars and he build this kitchen.

We never pay nobody to work you know, meh son recap, meh daughter one ah dem used to build the tyres, and send it to meh son, meh son used to load it in the thing to recap, he used to put it and take it down and after he take it down he roll it out from the mould, and then when it cool out, the next set ah girls, is more girls, the next two girls they used to clean it, sit down and clean it, one ah them clean it, one ah them when it cold it fix, she painting it, and the one whey used to build the tyre we used to load it and she used to drive the van and go and visit the tyre shop, the people who give us to recap, they only paying you to recap it, when we start we didn't have the money to buy all the material to make it and sell it for a big amount of money, them bring in the facing and everything, we only getting the rubber and recapping it.

It was difficult in the beginning but we used to make out because I used to plant meh own garden, I plant eddoes, cassava, pepper, dasheen, ah ha me own dasheen bush, ah had meh own seasoning, ah ha meh own home fowl, ah ha meh own duck, you know, like all that, we only had to buy like salt and oil and sugar and flour and thing. We ha we own rice, we ha we own dry coconut, you know, all these things we have we plant. When I come I plant all these things here, and meh mother-in-law used to make garden too, we have vegetables, so we work together all of us to make what we have, and we never say that we never, to say like partying, and we dress well up to mark and we going out and we spening money, because that time ah didn't have money to spend. I minding the little kids and carrying on the little business and we seeing that everything going in order. We never go out a lot anyway, anytime we have a little chance we doing something, planting something, seeing about fowl. I had animals, I had five cows and I used to sell cow milk, the time my kids get ready in the morning to go to school, I done milk, five o'clock I done get up, cook for them, go in the pen, milk the cow, wash 12 bottle and full the milk, so time them take this thing and go to get the car, a mister, the father friend used to carry them Chaguanas to school, they selling 12 bottle a milk until they reach the car, they had to walk down, the father dey home working and doing something, if he eh in the tyre shop, he straightening and painting some lil car and ting na, we used to still have the garage working because up here wasn't busy to get plenty work, is now it busy, but it wasn't busy that time.

Long time the loan payments wasn't so much, five thousand, six thousand an ting, it wasn't so much, tings wasn't so much because what we build at that time, we can't say we go build it now you know, because the amount of money you have to pay in loans now. But little by little we build and build and now we have a tyre business, a lil grocery and lil shop there and all the children have they business. I develop, work and make it for them and when the fadder dead well I give it up to them because I can no more afford to hustle again, because I am 61 years, and then I had a triple bypass so I can't do nothing now, so them have their children now to maintain.

In my life, when I married like how them married, them life change, because they father and mother was there to see that everything go all right with them and to provide for them, but in my way now, my husband didn't have no father and he had an old mother and my father and mother had plenty children, so they couldn't help me in no ways, they couldn't help me, them had to help the small ones, I was the biggest and I get out of the house and I had to fend for myself, and I had to see that how I could scrape a penny, because I want to say what I would take and buy, I doh need it because I is never a party girl, a wedding girl and ting. Now I could go where I want and come when I want and when I see anything I could say if I eh want to buy it, when I dey with my children and they see I watching it they go buy it and bring it for me.

The second one she married, the oldest, 27 years, but all the balance married, 15, 16, 19. Hear na, in my days I had to cook, no Kentucky Fried Chicken motor bike eh comin to deliver food, and I had to cook in *chulha*,[10] no stove, I had to go down the hill dey in the garden and pick up some dry wood and bring it come and cook. It easier now, all ah them trying to get something to do to make a lil shilling more, in my days, I alone had to go and make a shilling and to mind five children, but now, the children have their daughters going to school, it different now.

This is an almost verbatim transcript of an interview with Mrs Singh who lives quite happily in Edinburgh village in Chaguanas, Trinidad, today. By the time her husband died, Mrs Singh and her family had moved from owning one to many shops.

She is proud that her family has never had to depend on a pay cheque from anyone at the end of the month.

A compulsion to create a better life for their children, as well as notions of self-sacrifice, pervades the stories of many women's lives. The sociobiologists would have us believe that women's natural altruism is at the root of reproduction and nurturing. No ethnic group has a purchase on this. Nor do people in their individual lives behave as a composite of ethnic or gender stereotypes. Indian women are today to be found in all professions and though they may figure high among the merchant classes, they can by no means be limited to this class or occupational group. Mrs Singh's life is like no other, and is like many others. Identities are formed through the crucible of representation. I would add in the construction of gender identities it is also a product of a persistent re-representation of stereotypes.

The conceptual is political

How do we as gender theorists, gender policy makers, gender and development specialists and social philosophers make sense of the multitudes of stories such as that of my grandmother's and Mrs Singh's, each with their own uniqueness, each biography offering another set of variables and wrestling away at the theories we construct and the convenient equations and theoretical explanations we propose? Not all women are entrepreneurs or good mothers; not all men are violent patriarchs or good providers. Nor can we summarily place people in camps of good or evil, violent or passive. Feminist epistemology has been most responsive to the personal within the political, becoming more so with each passing decade. Feminist activism and scholarship, since its formal inception in the Caribbean from the late 1970s, began to take on the question of masculinity[11] and derived from the history of gender relations in these societies, to unwittingly employ a concept of gender in defining and ameliorating the position of women in society. My own approach in feminist theory has been unapologetically, to work with a relational concept of gender, situating the female experience as central, in relation to constructs and ideologies of masculinity.[12] How each individual theorises and imagines feminism, conceptualises gender and creates a philosophic base from which to define practice and policy is again influenced by personal and collective ethnic and societal histories and experiences. If human security means protecting vital freedoms, connecting different types of freedoms, then it also means allowing for the best means by which each society can work through its notions of gender empowerment and freedoms.

In this section I play with this concept of gender plasticity.

Plast: Combining form indicating a living cell or particle of living matter (Oxford English Dictionary).

Marking an undergraduate student essay in a semester's end examination paper in the course on Sex, Gender and Society, at the University of the West Indies, St Augustine, Trinidad, I came across the phrase 'the plasticity of gender'. Coined by a younger and fresher scholar, this perception of gender was interesting. Plasticity was not a term that we had generally employed while trying to explain the malleability of gender identity or the non-static nature of the gender discourse. Nor had this interpretation been applied to describe the ways in which gender was so melded into other social categories that it was difficult to isolate it as a variable. Neither had I come across this sense of the concept in feminist literature which, over the last two decades, has become more nuanced, interdisciplinary and multifaceted. As with all good theoretical ideas, like that of Amartya Sen's 'entitlements and capabilities' the concept is simple, obvious and allowing for creative applications. It can be potentially useful as another way to think of gender and its continuously expanding and changing application, at times under different names in different spheres and with different meanings. This chameleon like quality of gender is perhaps even more appropriate as we continue to pull and stretch gender to fit the agenda of development and social policy.

My treatment in this section allows for an elastic etymology emerging from idiosyncratic word association and perception, cobbled together with stricter scientific definition—in other words playing with similes and metaphors, with semantics, to visualise how gender works or may not work in society. Traditionally, academic knowledge has privileged the natural sciences and social sciences positivist modes over the humanities. Gender thinking has forced us to reconsider these artificial knowledge divides. This experiment synthesises different modes of thinking and draws some of its data from the experience of formulating two national gender policies, that of the Cayman Islands and of Trinidad and Tobago, over the last four years.

Plasticine

The first word image which comes to mind in relation to plasticity is plasticine, a substance made from clay and other inorganic materials provided for children's play. Children model their reality out of this substance and use their imagination to take green and red abstract lumps and pummel these together into shapes which represent, for them, a mother, a father, a cow, a house or a basket of fruit. Colour and texture are incidental to the sculptured whole. One is reminded of the ways in which we have continued to use gender, constantly moulding it to fashion an imagined reality. We have no defined equilibrium or blueprint to draw on for creating gender identities or systems of gender justice, or gender freedoms—other than perhaps fictional works with happy endings. We cull ideas from bits of experience, tried and tested models which have flaws but offer possibilities, to create ideals which we hope are achievable.

At the same time, we locate such ideals in the specific circumstances in which gender policies are being framed. An illustration is useful here. While both gender policies in the Cayman Islands and Trinidad and Tobago in the Caribbean are underpinned by development goals for these societies, the departure point for gender differs in each.

Cayman Islands

Cayman Islands is a smaller, younger society in some ways; its history, founded upon the seas, has evolved with a notion of a distinctive sexual division of labour comprised of seafaring men and land-bound women. The women who laboured simultaneously in farming and domestic life made for a femininity adept in matters domestic and in public life, when men were at sea.

In 2000 the Permanent Secretaries in several of the Ministries in Cayman were women and they were also well represented in key sectors of the economy including education and publishing. There was a popular perception in the society, therefore, by the end of the 20th century, that Caymanian women did not need empowerment and that there was no need for a national gender policy. Still a dependency of the United Kingdom, with a strong currency, and an economy fuelled by offshore banking and financial services, the Cayman Islands are reliant on migrant labour at every level. Questions which concern gender practitioners are central to the ways in which it must continue to map its future. For example Cayman Islanders depend on the migration of Jamaican female domestics who are employed to care and nurture the children of their employers, but who are at the same time actively discouraged from bringing their own family. Housing shortages on a small high-cost-of-living island exacerbate this problem and justify the rules established by immigration authorities to limit the lifestyle and opportunities available to migrant workers. In this small Christian society, concerned with the respectability and reputation and control of its 'native' women folk, other migrant women from neighbouring Central and South America who are brought in to work in bars and clubs, are perceived as temptation to Caymanian men, and reports are often made by fearful women to have them deported.

Apart from the contemporary problems now under heavy scrutiny such as the under-performance of boys in education, and the ubiquitous challenges associated with domestic violence, issues of gender here are also closely tied up with issues of defining and preserving an identity which is perceived to be Caymanian as defined by its first peoples and for safeguarding its national boundaries and wealth for those who are Caymanian-born or those who have been accepted by Caymanians either through marriage or longevity of service on the islands.

Trinidad and Tobago

Trinidad and Tobago has a different history, of large migration waves beginning from the 18th century, of a nation identity still being formulated through divided ethnic lines, and of uniquely different cultures—European, African, Asian, and Middle Eastern—mixing and blending gender belief systems and religions over the last 200 years. There are persistent differences in gender belief systems, due to varied religious and cultural practices. But, as in Jamaica, gender awareness has been heightened in this society as a result of decades of activism. Women of all ethnic groups have had access to primary, secondary and tertiary level education from the 1960s onwards and female participation in areas such as teaching and in the public and private sector has been continuously expanding. By 1977–78 females already comprised 43.9 per cent of total graduates in all faculties at the University of the West Indies, St Augustine, Trinidad.[13] Legislation such as the Sexual Offences Act (1987), the Domestic Violence Act (1991) in Trinidad and Tobago became highly contested and politicised documents as a result of gender and feminist consciousness and activism by the decades of the 1980s and 90s. With the turn of the century, progressive initiatives such as the recent official collection of statistics for unpaid housework and other activities establishing time spent by both sexes in unremunerated work signal a greater sophistication of ideas in relation to gender equality and social policy. Nonetheless, other salient issues remain unaddressed. With increasing wage or salaried work for both men and women outside of the home, childrearing has become more incompatible with employment. Public and private sectors must respond to the problems of after-school childcare which beset the majority of working people, whether in white collar or blue collar occupations. While culture and religion provide a backdrop against which gender norms navigate, the society must view gender roles as constantly shifting and changing, requiring new mechanisms for dealing with the challenges to gender relations in the home and workplace, including gendered-sensitive rights of disabled women and men.

Gender policies must be tailored to fit the concerns and specific needs of each society in terms of its own history, economic and social status and means of production. This observation may indubitably be made of all social policy. In the engineering of gender relations, however, which aims to make the public aware of the private and intimate components of life, there is a need for a heightened sensibility and a reconfiguration of the gender problem to suit the moment.

Pleistocene

The similar sounding scientific and archaeological term Pleistocene provides an equally insightful concept for excavating the understanding of gender. A number of scholars believe that the onset of the Pleistocene ice age, that caused the deterioration of the earth's climate during the last two million years, was responsible for the evolution of human anatomy and cognition. This argument contrasts with the common idea that the human specie represents a revolutionary breakthrough rather than a conventional adaptation to a particular ecological niche. What the Pleistocene adherents argue is that human culture is nothing more than a straightforward adaptation to climatic deterioration and that our survival depends on our capacity to adapt to environments via cultural traditions.

Gender cannot be disassociated from scientific discourses of human evolution and cultural adaptation. We need to read the data from our fossilised imprints to admit possibilities of drastic shifts in how we envisage gender, a shift that has already taken place from the classic anthropological 'man the hunter and woman the gatherer' paradigm. In social policy formation, the mutual exchange between biological and social gender must underpin our arguments and policy choices. In gender policy terms how must we conceive the open field of transgendered and transsexual identities, or the rights of individuals who do not adhere to an heterosexual norm established by church and society in the West,[14] of the not yet explored potential which each sex has for contribution to social betterment and to the mental and physical well-being of human society.

What possibilities are there for an expanding female labour force within the public sphere and simultaneous expanding of nurturing roles for men in households and other sectors such as nursing i.e. the incorporation of 'care' as as economic and ethical principle in social policy? These are questions being asked of our frail human mental capacities for accepting biological and cultural adaptation. What tracks can a gender policy now lay down for reconfiguring futures. The core role of governments and other development actors is to endow citizens with the required conditions for actualising human functioning, to provide them with necessary capacities and opportunities, what Martha Nussbaum, building on Amartya Sen's work, refers to as 'central human capabilities'.[15] Economic, political, legal, and other social arrangements should be evaluated according to their capacity to expand people's capabilities or valuable freedoms—those freedoms which are interpreted as being outside of a normative goal which society has thus far prescribed for reproduction and survival. The evaluations should also envision overlapping consensus among people with different conceptions of what is good for a society.

Plastic

Let us look at plasticity through its direct stem, plastic. Artists use plastic in reference to those arts in which something was made, three dimensionally formed, such as sculpture, artifacts and carnival costumes, rather than the two dimensional graphic or fine arts. The plastic arts for a fine artist is always lower down the evolutionary scale of art, not real, but contrived, verisimilitude rather than truth, such as plastic knives and forks and plastic flowers—not the real thing. Plastic things are made with synthetic materials that have a polymeric structure which can be moulded when soft and then set. In much the same way perhaps gender roles themselves were moulded, then became set. But, plastic has its uses. Plastic goods and products are lighter, more adaptive to fit many occasions, offer a constant array of new possible uses, including interestingly the universal way in which it has now been adapted to the currency market so that the word 'plastic' is interchangeable for 'money' as in, 'Can I pay with plastic?'

Analogous plastic processes occur in the growth of the gender industry. Add women and stir and create another synthesis, another vantage point from which we have begun to intervene in many social problems. A quote by Amina Mama[16] is useful here:

> Gender studies has grown, not so much because of the feminist challenges that the term implies, but because over 20 years of feminist intervention into the international development industry have created a space for particular kinds of gender discourse. ... Women in Development, Gender and Development, Gender Mainstreaming—these have become such buzzwords that it is accommodated ... not the least because it sounds as if it might attract some funds.

Drawing on the contemporary idiom again, gender has become more plastic, good for credit. Plastic has other connotations and qualities which can be applied. A popular notion of plastic gave rise to the idiom 'scandal' bag in Jamaica to refer to the see-through synthetic bags in which items are packed at the store, transparent, for all the world to see. Gender, derived from a fierce feminist activism, aims like some plastic, to achieve this transparency and accountability in its transformational politics.

Plasticity

This brings a stream of conscious logic to plasticity, this time drawing again on its definition from the natural sciences. In physics, plasticity is a property of a material that undergoes plastic deformation in response to an applied force. Plastic deformation is a non-reversible change. This is unlike *elasticity*, a term which is used by economists to mean something that is highly responsive to changes in something else. For example, elastic demand means that the quantity demanded changes when the price changes. Elasticity is therefore a measure of responsiveness. It tells how much one thing changes when you change something else that affects it. But it means that it can revert to a previous size, or length, or value.

Is gender in fact elastic or does it have the qualities which render it as plasticity? I am reminded again of thematic recurrences in gender policy formulation processes. In public consultations, gender issues stretch to embrace every ill or concern people have, whether it is lack of potable water supply, or lack of jobs for men and women. At the same time, there is an undercurrent threaded through this public debate, that the mass of problems in society are caused because of women's 'abdication from their natural roles', a gem which was articulated by one gentleman in the Cayman Islands.[17] Gender is by no means elastic in this regard. While responsive to numerous conditions and issues, there is no automatic revert mechanism to some former situation where women are safely tucked away in their homes and men are engaged in running things. Nor is there a fixed paradigm of a normative sexual division of labour and equilibrium in gender relations to which the pendulum must swing. In this sense gender is defined by a plasticity, by a constant synthesis dependent on new materials and new cultural adaptations, such that eventually what appears to be a synthetic product reconfigures itself as conventional and traditional again.

In conclusion, I think the term plasticity is a useful one, necessarily limited by some of the less complimentary connotations inherent in its stem—plastic. Nonetheless, the *plasticity of gender* speaks to its many meanings as developed above. One of these clearly is its linguistic nuances and shifts, such that sex and gender, although not interchangeable for the gender theorist, are both words which have undergone shifts in meanings and use in the 20th century. Second, it inherently allows us to conceive of expanding the boundaries of what it is to be masculine or feminine. Third, its malleability in relation to larger development issues, ensures that gender issues are not outside of all development issues and remain central to empirical investigations, to analysis and to policy intervention and to philosophy. Gender as a conceptual tool of analysis, has already proven itself in the classroom, in activism and in its continuously transformative activist arm—the feminist movement. Were it not thus proven, with other crucial social concepts and categories such as ethnicity and class, to have value in organising our knowledge of the complexity of human social relations, then the concept of gender would become in time another meaningless buzzword for the development industry. That it has allowed thinkers like Amartya Sen and Martha Nussbaum to expand the concept of human capabilities and freedoms in the 20th century is already a response to its plasticity and wide application by a range of disciplines and scholars. However, more needs to be done to incorporate difference, cultural specificity and multiple identities. The ideas from the mid-20th century onwards which have expanded our ways of seeing and thinking about human security rely on the fundamental characteristic inherent in the concept of gender, not the least of which is its plasticity: its adaptability, convenience, responsiveness, capacity for moulding and remodelling, respectful of different histories and climates and taking on as many colours, nuances and shapes as there are peoples and societies.

Notes

[1] This statement does not assume a heterosexual and normative sense of society, but accepts that society both rejects and embraces the idea of non-normativity in sexuality and gender relations.

[2] Martha C. Nussbaum, *Sex and Social Justice,* Oxford University Press, 1999.

[3] Des Gasper, 'The Work of Amartya Sen An Appreciation', *Ideas,* A Newsletter, May 1999. Institute of Social Studies, The Hague.

[4] William Agnew Paton, *Down the Islands: A Voyage to the Caribbean.* New York, 1887. pp. 200–201.

[5] ibid.

[6] Harry A Franck, *Roaming through the West Indies,* D. Appleton-Century Company, London and New York, 1920. p. 384.

[7] I am most grateful to Nazma Muller who carried out this interview and several others for me in preparation for this paper. The narrative sequences contained here were extracted from a paper first delivered at a conference on Indians and Entrepreneurship at the University of the West Indies, St Augustine in 2003.

[8] Mrs Singh is a pseudonym applied for the purposes of anonymity. I thank 'Mrs Singh' for allowing this interview and the use of her life story.

[9] A village in Chaguanas, Central Trinidad and Tobago, West Indies.

[10] Traditional stove made out of earth and using firewood.

[11] The debates on masculinity have long been part of the gender discourse in the region, fuelled to some extent by a male scholar Errol Miller whose

books, *The Marginalization of the Black Male* and *Men at Risk* provided the polemic against which many other publications and essays are now emerging, among them, Rhoda Reddock, *Interrogating Caribbean Masculinities: Theoretical and Empirical Analyses*, UWI Press, Kingston, 2004.

12 Patricia Mohammed, *Gender Negotiations among Indians in Trinidad 1917–1947*. ISS/Palgrave, The Hague and UK, 2001, based on a PhD thesis at the ISS. Geertje Lycklama was one of my supervisors at the Institute of Social Studies, the others being Renee Pittin, ISS and Bridget Brereton at UWI.

13 Central Statistical Office statistics cited in Patricia Mohammed, 'Educational Attainment of Women in Trinidad and Tobago, 1946–1980', vol. 5, *Women and Education, Women in the Caribbean Project*, Research Papers, ISER, Cave Hill, 1982.

14 This is by no means a far-fetched idea. Culture and society in the past and present have admitted variations in gender and sexuality. Relationships we would call homosexual, especially between men and youths, played an important role in ancient Greek society. All distinctions of transgenderism: transsexuals, transvestites, hermaphrodites, and intersexuals are drawn to a special role in India called *hijras*.

15 Maxine Molyneux and Shahra Razavi, 'Gender Justice, Development and Rights, Democracy, Governance and Human Rights', Programme Paper No 10, United Nations Research Institute for Social Development, January 2003.

16 Amina Mama, 'Critical Capacities: Facing the Challenges of Intellectual Development in Africa'. Inaugural Address Prince Claus Chair in Development and Equity, delivered on 28 April 2004 at the Institute of Social Studies, The Hague, Public Lecture Series 2003, No. 4, p. 13.

17 See Critical Stakeholders Workshop Report, Ministry of Community Development, Women Affairs, Youth and Sports, George Town, Cayman Islands, October 2001.

13

Engendering Science and Interdisciplinary Environmental Research for Environmental Security

The Case of the Nariva Swamp

RHODA REDDOCK[1]

Introduction

A quite well developed literature has emerged in relation to women, gender and the environment internationally. Since much of this has been linked to the field of Women/Gender in Development most studies have been carried out in countries of the Economic South. Reviews of this literature have identified a number of sometimes conflicting and contrasting approaches. What is common to all of them is that 'gender' continues to be marginal to the mainstream literature and teaching on environmental studies. Scholars in this growing field, with its many branches such as environmental engineering, environmental science and environmental studies, continue to research, write and teach as if this scholarship did not exist.

In the discourse on human security (Sen and Nussbaum 1992), the issue of environmental security has received limited attention. Yet recent developments in relation to climate change, and the resulting biophysical disasters bring home the need to include such an analysis and the gendered aspects into our understanding of human security. This relates to our understanding of both the contributing factors and the social, economic and environmental results of environmental disasters, both in the North and the South.

297

Cecile Jackson (1993), identifies two main schools of thought in relation to this subject—the ecofeminist school of which Vandana Shiva is its most well-known exponent and the 'women and environment' approach, based on the traditional 'Women in Development' emphasis on 'integration of women into development and recognition of the multiple but differing roles of women. This is summarised in the following quotation:

> There is a large literature, in part scholarly, in part polemical, on the relation between women and the environment. The debate has tended to polarise between two approaches: a 'women and environment' and an ecofeminist school. The first grew out of the WID (Women in Development) approach to project and planning interventions. It emphasised the importance of women in their role as environmental resource managers, their vulnerability to declines in resource availabilities, and the need to develop environmental programmes directed at assisting women, essentially in parallel to, and separately from, men's programmes.... The ecofeminist school has a different ideologically driven flavour. It derives from a philosophy of feminism grounded in women's affinity with the forces of nature, as opposed to men's urge to control and manipulate the natural world through application of the scientific method. It similarly advocates respect and support for women's efforts to conserve the environment. It puts greater stress however, on the active initiatives displayed by women in defence of environmental resources in various Third World settings (Joekes, Heyzer, Oniang'o and Salles 1994: 137–8).

Joekes et al. propose an alternative approach which they term the developmentalist approach as one which acknowledges the many situations where women have primary responsibility for use of natural resources, but suggest that these tasks are not as universally ascribed to women as the literature suggests. Men they argue, often contribute to fuel wood collection and other tasks, even if the modalities by which they do so may differ and reflect other social patterns of disadvantage to women. The question is, they stress, how and under what circumstances, variations occur and how women's interests are affected. They also seek to examine the broader question of patterns of resource and land use as bases for total livelihoods in rural areas (Joekes et al. 1994: 138–9).

Jackson also identifies two trends in the mainstream literature and approach to the environment. These she terms— *Technocentrism* and *Ecocentrism*. The former she argues has been the dominant approach to the environment for centuries and is currently reflected in the management and technical approach to resource use and planning. These approaches she notes, have by definition excluded any concern with women or gender except for the latter, which has seen women as part of the problem. Jackson identifies the ideological role of the scientific method in shaping approaches to science, knowledge and technological progress. She notes:

> The ideology of scientific and technological progress may not be responsible for initiating the exploitation of women and nature, but it appears to have contributed to these processes. The mythology of the scientific method as objective, neutral and value free has veiled the degree to which technocratic environmentalists and environmentalism expressed particular class and gender perspectives in what were perceived as problems, in the diagnosis of causes, and in the remedial actions taken. Technocratic environmentalism has no space for the politics of gender interests (Jackson 1993: 652).

Ecocentrism on the other hand is also seen as having origins in past centuries, in its challenge of rationalism and science and its emphasis on alternative knowledges based on feelings, emotions, instincts and morals. These two trends can be easily linked with the two key gender-based approaches cited above. Ecocentrism however, which has been associated with neo-Malthusianism in its emphasis on the negative impact of population growth on the environment, has particular implications for women (Jackson 1993: 658).

Ecofeminism has been highly criticised as being essentialist and ascribing certain natural and essential characteristics to women and by extension men. On the one hand it is noted, scholars have critiqued the dichotomous division between nature and culture and the automatic definition of women into nature as a result of their capacity for childbearing and lactation.[2] But on the other, the natural association between women and the environment is challenged as being linear and ignoring the diversity of historical experiences which women may have experienced in different social and historical contexts.

In contrast to the above Jackson argues for a materialist and feminist approach, which takes into consideration the historical and cultural variability that exists internationally. She notes, that although Marxist approaches towards the environment have not always been credible, yet Marxist/materialist thought does provide some insights, which are useful in the analysis of gender and environmental contexts. These she identifies as:

> the unity of nature and culture; the social construction of nature; the manner in which material conditions and history inform environmental ideas and perceptions and the internal differentiation of society which leads groups to have different environmental relations.
>
> A key problem of the ecofeminist approaches is that they fail to recognise either the diversity of lived environmental relations which different women experience, or the power structures in societies which mediate environmental relations and the ebb and flow of competing environmental ideologies. Accounts of how class relations impinge upon resource access reveal considerable variations...
>
> Gender differentiations means that men and women of the same household relate to resources in different ways and these variations are inserted into class relations. The outcomes, however, are not predictable— poor women may be more or less environment friendly in their behaviour than poor men or rich men/women, depending on their rights, responsibilities, knowledges and bargaining positions within their households and communities (Jackson 1993: 663–4).

This approach presented by Jackson above, presents a useful framework within which to understand the study of the Nariva Swamp, a protected wetland in Trinidad and Tobago, which is presented below. At the same time however, as explored in this study, natural landscapes are also 'symbolic terrains of contestation between different social actors for access to and control of natural resources' (Sletto 2002: 389).

A wetland of international importance

The Nariva Swamp, which is located in the central part of the East Coast of Trinidad,[3] is the country's largest freshwater wetland, occupying approximately 90 square kilometres. The wetland basin supports an extensive range of species, including wildfowl, manatee and anaconda. Indeed, 614 species of animals and 319 species of plants are dependent upon the Swamp (Bacon et al. 1979). A number of rivers, including the Guatecare, Bois Neuf, Navet, Charuma, Biche and Nariva feed into the wetland. The Nariva Swamp was declared a forest reserve in 1989.

The Kernahan/Cascadoux communities are to be found on the south-eastern tip of the Swamp on the periphery of the Swamp Basin, or flooding regime. Consequently, these communities are subject to varying degrees of flooding according to the annual rainfall distribution. Although there are other communities in the area covered by the Swamp, these two are the most dependent on the natural resources available in the Swamp for day-to-day survival. Starting out as illegal squatter communities on state lands, these communities through a combination of resistance and accommodation negotiated for their formal recognition by local and state authorities.

Kernahan consists largely of freshwater marshland, with some elevated areas. The local ecosystem supports palm swamps, mangrove swamps, freshwater marsh and freshwater swamp wood. However, indigenous vegetation is gradually being cleared to make way for agricultural and 'cash' crops especially watermelon. Conversely, Cascadoux is slightly elevated and situated on a mud volcano, spanning an area of approximately 50 hectares. This volcano dominates the local topography and vegetation. Whereas Kernahan is predominantly a lagoon area, Cascadoux maintains a large degree of forest. The entire area experiences tropical conditions, characteristic of the rest of Trinidad and Tobago, with a dry season from January to May and a wet season from June to December. Natural resources available within these communities range from various endemic floral and faunal species and those used for agricultural purposes.

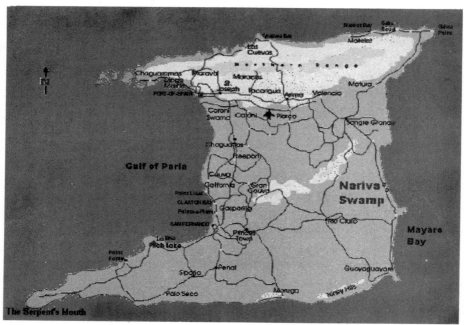

Location of the Nariva Swamp in Trinidad

The first migrants to the area were predominantly men who settled temporarily in Cascadoux in the early 1940s as rice cultivators or employees in the surrounding coconut estates. Cascadoux settlers, ethnically mixed (Indo- and Afro-Trinidadian),[4] came from towns such as Sangre Grande and Arima in the north-east of Trinidad and initially constructed temporary camps within the forests. In the 1970s the Ragbir family, of Indo-Trinidadian descent, moved to Cascadoux and raised 14 children. Descendants of this family constitute the majority of the Indo-Trinidadian population in Cascadoux.

The history of Kernahan is quite different, possibly because it is less accessible than Cascadoux. In contrast, its settlers, largely of Indo-Trinidadian descent, originated from the southern part of Trinidad, such as Debe and Penal areas with swamp-like conditions and a tradition of rice cultivation. By 1962 there were two permanent camps in isolated Kernahan, which increased dramatically over the next 10 years.

Initially, the men would spend several weeks in the wetland cultivating the land and then return home to sell the produce and visit their families. Hence, the arrangement was never intended to be permanent. A range of factors, including the availability of large areas of land, and its fertility, and the lack of income-generation options elsewhere culminated in the permanent settlement of the Kernahan and Cascadoux communities.

Gradually, women and children began to migrate in, and communities with various activities began to be established. Hurricane Alma of 1974 inadvertently assisted in the clearing of forested areas, and hence agricultural production could be increased to support the growing population. By the 1980s, it was accepted that Cascadoux was a village in its own right and the Cascadoux Village Council was conceived as a body to represent its inhabitants. According to researcher Gabrielle Hosein, the village council reflects its origins in the village *panchayat* structure,[5] which she describes as one where 'men are expected to know more but where outrageously outspoken women can have some influence.'[6] The formalised Village Council system brought it in line with state recognised forms of community organisation in the rest of the country, which may have specific characteristics due to local cultural and historical factors.

The lands were used for the cultivation of short-term cash crops to support an expanding population, caused by further in-migration which escalated in the mid-1980s, when the government, in an effort to improve local food security, proposed to initiate a 1500-acre rice production scheme in the Kernahan area. Cultivators were provided with subsidies as an incentive for large-scale rice farming. This was controversial as such schemes have had a seriously detrimental effect on the flora and fauna of the area, as well as on the small-scale rice farmers. It became the focus of widespread environmental agitation, led by women environmentalists, described by the media as 'The Battle for Nariva', culminating in the declaration of the Swamp as a protected wetland and the eventual end to the rice project and to small-scale rice farming.

Environmental awareness, both locally and internationally led the state to prohibit the catching of conch and cascadura[7] in the Bush Bush Sanctuary, established within the Swamp in 1968, as part of a national programme for the protection of swamp resources. Additionally the environmental struggles of the women in the Ministry of Forestry's Wildlife Section and the Pointe a Pierre Wildfowl Trust,[8] led to its declaration as a site of international ecological importance according to the Ramsar Convention in 1992.[9] In 1993, it was placed on the Montreux Record, which lists wetlands whose ecological character is threatened. As a result of these actions and direct interventions of environmentalists and researchers, a sense of environmental consciousness began to grow among the villagers.[10]

The villagers of Kernahan were for the most part, Hindu. However, the majority has converted to Pentecostal Christianity through the work of American missionaries. Small pockets of Hindu and Sai Baba adherents still coexist with the Pentecostal majority. The early Cascadoux community comprised Muslims, Hindus and Presbyterians and has remained similar, although many Hindus here have also converted to Pentecostalism.

The quality of life and living conditions have changed significantly, particularly for women. Over the 50 years since migrants began to settle in the area, girls have the opportunity to attend school and to choose their marriage partners, although many do not or leave at an early age.[11] Some of them even anticipate the possibility of earning an independent income. However, in these communities, changes in gendered norms and sanctions occur slowly and women must still obey many rules of propriety and honour in their dress, their behaviour and social interactions and they live with the threat of domestic violence. Girls would benefit from more information about their bodies, health and sexuality, their rights and options. Generally, women who have some education have more control over the quality of their lives. When examining how to achieve socio-economic and ecological sustainability, such information can assist in understanding the underlying factors that should inform policy and planning.[12]

The Nariva Swamp: a gendered case study[13]

The Nariva Swamp, was selected over other areas due to the national conflicts and contestations taking place at that time regarding the use of the area and its resources. The wetland has a history of hosting activities that have deleterious effects on the environment, such as logging, large-scale rice cultivation, over-fishing and now seismic oil exploration. The scale of human pressures and dependency on the land has made it an area of acute interest at a local, national and international level and an example of the conflicts between the state and farmers' concerns with food security and the imperatives of ecological security which may appear less immediate.

This research was considered particularly groundbreaking in that it aimed to incorporate gender analysis into an interdisciplinary study of a contested ecosystem. This innovative and experimental project, sought to examine the socio-economic, cultural, political and ecological factors impacting upon the sustainable use of the Nariva Swamp. Further, it was anticipated that this research could provide a gender sensitive database of material, which would ensure that policy initiatives emanating would empower women and the communities in general. This could be achieved by sensitising them to the biophysical environment and the impact of their use of its resources; to produce research material that integrated a gender analysis into an interdisciplinary framework; and finally, to thoroughly evaluate 'the scientific method' as understood and practised by natural and physical scientists as a tool for researching environmental situations.

The research study comprised four principal components.

The first was designed to develop a gender analysis of this ecosystem, examining how its natural resources were utilised differently by men, women, children and youth of both sexes and subsequently to use this information to develop proposals for sustainable use.

The second component involved the exploration of power relations and governance within the households, the community and at national levels, with a particular focus on the historical perspective. This component focused on the history of state policy in the Swamp over the last century, tracing the changing policy approaches of colonial and post-colonial governments and the process contributing to its current status.

The third component focused on household and community level governance issues and the economic, gender, socio-economic and other differentials. This enabled researchers to grasp the manner in which the local administrative and control structures functioned in order to develop a community, despite the precarious natural, political, economic and social environment.

The fourth component integrated material on gendered social relations within households and the wider community, economic configurations and cultural practices of the women and men living in the Swamp and their location within and relationship to the biophysical environment.[14]

Research methodology

This study went beyond many of the development-oriented women/gender and environment studies carried out in other parts of the world. For one it was conceived as an interdisciplinary study, which would bring together a number of academic disciplines that do not normally work together. In particular it raised issues about 'the scientific method' and the debates around it. One question raised was whether we were trying to introduce a new variant/approach to the scientific method or whether there was only one scientific method in which case this research could be perceived as non-scientific. As noted by Lélé and Norgaard (2005):

> What starts out in the pure sciences as only a problem of subjective choice of taxonomies or models burgeons into the issue of the value-laden nature of natural science when working on phenomena of social relevance. But most natural scientists have been brought up on the notion that science is value neutral. This belief proves to be a barrier both to working across disciplines and to doing good science.

One final concern driving the research exercise was a commitment to empowerment of the women of these communities and the exploration of possibilities for facilitating gender consciousness and heightened sensitivity to the biophysical environment within the community and in policy prescriptions.

The overall research was conducted in each of the 78 households of Kernahan and the 33 households of Cascadoux and spanned almost one year. A team of four young researchers—economist, ecologist, agricultural scientist and political scientist/gender studies scholar (three female and one male) carried out the field research. Two project coordinators, a sociologist and gender studies scholar and a plant biochemist, coordinated the overall study. Interestingly, an animal scientist carried out the historical study of state policy in the Swamp over the 20th century.

The methodological philosophy adopted was one aimed at establishing strong interpersonal connections with the members of the communities and hence avoiding the patterns of the rapid rural appraisals, which have more commonly been used in the region. Methods of gathering and validating data were drawn from both the natural and social sciences (and were influenced by feminist methodological concerns). Hence they involved the application of both qualitative and quantitative methods and participatory approaches. Qualitative techniques employed included participant observation, transect walks, historical and social mapping, direct observation, semi-structured interviews, focus groups, oral narratives, genealogies, and archival research on secondary data. The quantitative methods comprised the use of questionnaires, water and soil testing and the collection and analysis of demographic data.

Central to the epistemological framework of this project was a critique of traditional scientific methods of accumulating data. Approaches characteristic of Participatory Rural Appraisal (PRA) methods were used as they provided an alternative to traditional methods used in environmental research. In addition to integrating and empowering the communities, this approach permitted members of a community to create their own representations of their realities and their relationships to the environment. PRA is a structured methodology that perceives community participation in the research process as essential. Moreover, it seeks to gain multiple perspectives, recognising that local knowledge is as equally important as academic knowledge. It provides a forum for interactive learning and the sharing of knowledge as well as giving voice to members of the community. This was combined with ethnographic observation techniques and sustained interaction with community members.

The expansion of traditional PRA methods to include feminist epistemological concerns and ethnographic techniques emerged from the recognition of the limitations of this approach. As noted by Ilan Kapoor (2002: 104), although starting from a premise of participation and theorising from the bottom up, by privileging the existing structures, this approach may be less successful in addressing issues of power, hierarchy and even participation by its very point of departure.

To accumulate material the researchers lived within close proximity to the communities for a period of approximately nine months. They were able to develop strong connections with the villagers, through various means, such as sharing daily tasks, having informal discussions and 'liming'.[15] It was envisaged that such activities would build a sense of trust between the researchers and the villagers and result in a more comprehensive understanding of their existence and links with the environment.

More challenging however were the efforts to integrate gender into the research exercise. Trained in mainstream scholarship, which did not include gender analysis and also one which was antagonistic to interdisciplinarity, researchers at times felt ambivalent or even resentful of the challenges to their existing worldview. Researcher Sharda Durbal, trained in agricultural science and environmental science describes this below:

> Permeating the entire research process was my difficulty in grappling with the concepts of gender, ethnography, PRA and the methods to be utilised in such a study. The need to collect data and incorporate it into a framework for analysis ... posed a particular problem for me, particularly as I came from a science background. Cook and Fonow (1986) appropriately describes (sic) this problem as follows: 'we have been trained to think in terms of a positivist schema which equates the term methodology with specific techniques for gathering and analysing information.'... I had no prior understanding or knowledge of the ethnographic process or the use of reflexive accounts in the documentation of the research process. Methodology was a key issue for me as I worked in fear of my results being considered superficial by a life science body. My readings and discussions with various people however allowed me the freedom to better understand why and how to use and work with the methods that were being introduced to me (Durbal 2000: 19).

The mapping techniques used, drew heavily on information from villagers as well as observations in the field. They aided in the generation of data on the history and development of the communities with respect to changes over time, the use of the natural resources and decision-making processes between men and women. Some of these maps included gendered resource maps, seasonal charts and historical maps. These were useful tools for fieldworkers, as local people often have a deeper knowledge of their surroundings and awareness of the subtle changes over time and these maps were local conceptualisations and representations of space based on peoples' lived experiences reinforcing Sletto's argument that maps are now being reread as ideological representations of the social contexts and interests of their creators (Sletto 2002: 390). These maps encouraged the villagers to think reflexively about their position and role within the environment. In the words of researcher Sharda Durbal:

Mapping exercises were done with individuals and groups of different ages, sex and number of years lived in the communities. Villagers were asked to describe the development of the communities, the plant and animal life, the people, the use of resources and the changes in the area over different periods of time. These methods also assisted in creating greater awareness within the community of the importance and benefits of wetlands, as they were able to see from their own descriptions and drawings the change in the use and availability of resources over time and how this has affected livelihoods and the environment in which they live. ... Maps drawn by women served as a reminder of the first families to settle in the area, whereas men's maps showed the vastness and dense nature of the forest at that time (Durbal 2000: 12).

The use of questionnaires was seen as complementary to ethnographic and other qualitative techniques. Indeed, many of the observations and informal discussions with villagers supported the questionnaire responses. Yet a major contradiction of the use of PRA methods proved to be the gendered limitations placed on women in these communities. It was easier to access male participation in the collective research activity with community members than female participation. This was due mainly to the sanctions on mobility for women as well their heavy responsibilities for housework, childcare and subsistence agriculture (gardening). This experience supports the contention of Kapoor who pointed to the coercion and intimidation that prevented free and equal deliberations in PRA exercises (Kapoor 2002).

The use of Geographical Information Systems (GIS) was also integrated into this approach, particularly in the research on Gender and Natural Resource Use. This technique generated land-use maps including gender-differentiated spatial-use maps of the area and their changes over time. Nature and transect walks through the community and adjacent areas, accompanied by biologists, provided an opportunity for the villagers to identify the species around as well as determine which of these resources were used by the community, how they were used and by whom. Data on the history of the area, medicinal plants, cultural practices and use of resources were recorded. It gave the researchers and younger villagers an opportunity to learn from the older members about the natural and social history of the area and the behaviours of plants and animals in the natural environment.

Many findings were further substantiated through direct and participant observation by the researchers. The constant presence of the researchers in the villages aided this process of verification or refutation. Although no claims of empowerment can be made for this exercise, the approach used also involved the sensitising of villagers on a range of ecologically related issues. Educational workshops were organised for example on the importance of wetlands, and on bush fire prevention and women of the community were taken on field trips.

In relation to the empowerment component of the research, there were many issues which emerged. On the one hand as noted in the Composite Report:

> We were faced with the task of facilitating, mobilising and organising in a community divided by religion, class and physical location. Family networks, age and gender also contributed to the difficulty of these tasks. Existing community groups provided an opportunity to more easily organise youth for ecotourism activities. However, these groups were not really active.

It was acknowledged that even such methods as PRA are not without their limitations. Ultimately, the data belong to the researcher, and very rarely are truly collaborative efforts achieved. *Give Back Sessions* can be instrumental in reversing this sense of exploitation and lack of ownership by the people being researched. Additionally, the researchers realised that collecting data about the villagers' personal lives was problematic as their time was precious and few were keen to have such information published and potentially made public knowledge. Hence, issues of ethics arose during and after the research period as villagers objected to some of the information presented in one of the reports as community members could be easily identified. The team had to undertake to withdraw the documents and have them rewritten;

not in a way that sacrificed substance but one which protected their identities.

The researchers were reflexive about their experiences in the field, recognising that their own gendered identity and social class and cultural assumptions heavily influenced the research data collected. For example, it was noted that the male researcher was considered more accessible to the men, especially when discussing illegal activities, such as cultivating marijuana and trading arms. Conversely, female villagers were reluctant to speak openly with the male researcher unless their spouses were present which in turn altered the content of the conversations.

Interdisciplinarity, feminist scholarship and environmental studies

This research was envisaged to be interdisciplinary and multidisciplinary. The researchers and research coordinators came from various disciplinary backgrounds. It is entirely feasible that they brought to the field their own perception of what should be important fields of study. This project envisaged that environmental studies generally could benefit from such an interdisciplinary approach taking into consideration all inhabitants of the ecosystem—human, plant and animal—and sought to rectify the neglect of the local communities by actively incorporating them in the research process. There is now a stronger focus on the socio-economic and socio-political issues affecting the area. It must be noted however, that residents respond much more favourably to projects in which short-term benefits are evident.

Equally important is that the feminist epistemological concern with integrated knowledge has not always been achieved. Feminist interdisciplinary work seeks not simply to integrate the content of different disciplines but also to synthesise knowledge in a way that creates something more than the sum of their parts (Finger and Rosner 2001: 1). It also aims to challenge structured barriers among scholars and to generate horizontal learning which could enrich disciplinary work as well as contribute to new integrative paradigms and 'has the potential to transform not only *what* we know, but also *how* we know ...' (Finger and Rosner 2001: 500).

The reality is however that very little feminist scholarship is truly interdisciplinary and less still that combines work from the social, natural and applied sciences. This is not surprising as interdisciplinary work is not easy. Scholars need to be open to unfamiliar language, epistemological frameworks, publication requirements and different conceptualisations of acceptable knowledge, science and research.

There is still much resistance to interdisciplinary studies within the academic community. The view was expressed during the course of this study that the social scientists should do their own studies and leave the natural scientists to do theirs and that interdisciplinarity diluted or weakened the depth of the research.

Gender, power and the Nariva ecosystem: knowledge systems and sites of struggle

The integration of gender analysis in environmental studies allowed us to examine the differential interactions of women and men, boys and girls with the biophysical environment and the differences in their use of the environment. The examination of women and men's experiences in production, reproduction, interpersonal relationships and management of community and other activities revealed areas of knowledge not normally considered, for example the gendered use of spaces and of nature—both plant and animal, for household and family use, economic exchange, ritual and religious purposes, and leisure. The inclusion of gender also highlighted differential access to resources such as land, water etc., as well as negotiation and conflict at the community and household level.

Indeed environmental issues can become multiple and interconnected sites of struggle, as has been the case in Trinidad and Tobago and elsewhere. For instance, Jackson noted that in Zimbabwe, greater emphasis is placed on reforestation and the planting of species suited to construction, which was generally a male responsibility (and big business concern) as opposed to firewood, which was a female responsibility (and household need) (Jackson 1993: 656).

Recent attempts have been made to increase the involvement of communities in management and decision-making related to the natural resources. One approach has been the thrust for income generation through ecotourism initiatives prompted by state agencies and NGOs. It focuses on forest and wildlife conservation with the provision of hospitality and tour guide services as a means of income generation. Such an approach seeks to integrate the villagers and acknowledges their dependence upon the environment whilst also answering to pressures for conservation of resources.

For example, the practice of introducing 'buffer zones' to protect reserves such as the Bush Bush Sanctuary, is now seen as a move away from top-down approaches and towards greater community participation and awareness. In the 1980s, the Trinidad and Tobago Wildlife Division of the Ministry of Agriculture sought to actively involve the community in developing policies to manage the area as a mechanism to promote conservation whilst also benefiting the community.

Unfortunately, conflicts between groups at the community level may hinder or prevent entirely such a programme. Additionally, it has been noted that in fact few buffer zone strategies have succeeded in merging conservation with land use systems of local people. Indeed there has been a very low level of participation of the community in recent projects. A number of reasons have been suggested for this. Green, Joekes and Leach note that:

> 'Conservation with development' programmes generally advocate protection of a core reserve area, with management plans for surrounding buffer zones focused on a varied mix of state/commercial and local livelihood interests. Local level support for reserve protection is sought by giving forest dwellers a stake in revenues generated within the reserve, perhaps through ecotourism, or by ensuring their access to locally valued forest products, for instance, in 'extractive reserves'... Gender issues are rarely mentioned in this literature; it is safe to assume that they lie outside the main concerns of the approach, which thus strongly risks

compromising women's resource interests (Green, Joekes and Leach 1998: 261).

It may be that external parties have developed most projects based on the perceived needs of the villagers and thus have focused on knowledge transfer rather than community empowerment. Additionally, participation is usually sought from the most visible of community members (most often men), to the exclusion of others. Thus, external stakeholders must realise that community politics and perceived favouritism can stymie effective community participation. Furthermore, villagers may be disinterested because their expectations of immediate short-term results are not fulfilled.

Cheryl Lans in her analysis of 'State Policy and Governance on The Nariva Swamp', shows in her historical overview of forestry policy in Trinidad and Tobago how in relation to the state forestry sector, the sexual division of labour was reflected in different allocations of prestige and power, where mainstream 'forestry' was seen as a more prestigious male bastion and 'wildlife and national parks' a female, hence 'softer' area suited to women with biology degrees (Lans 2000: 43).

In interviews with staff of the Ministry of Agriculture,[16] it was reported that during the 1980s, conflict emerged between the male leadership in the Forestry Division, and the predominantly female 'troublemakers' of the Wildlife Section. This is reflected in this extract from an interview on the response to the World Bank National Parks Plan. According to the interviewee:

> They didn't think that National Parks and Wildlife was as important as Forestry. Forestry was concerned about cutting trees, taming the environment … the Forestry Officers were not conservation minded. The Wildlife Section's budget was small, the chain of command was too long, there were no substantive posts, they were managing large acreages and they needed more manpower (Interview, Environmentalist, September 1999, cited in Lans 2000: 44).

With the increasing emphasis on environmental issues over forestry production in the global context, however, increased opportunities and resources emerged for the implementation of the co-management and community-based initiatives preferred by the women employed in the Wildlife Section. This raised concerns and some conflict with the predominantly male staff in the Forestry sections, many of whom perceived this as an erosion of their former power and recognition (Lans 2000: 44–5). Hence the reason, Lans notes, advocacy in relation to the protection of the Nariva Swamp was undertaken mainly by women employed in the Wildlife Section of the Ministry as well as women environmentalists in non-governmental organisations.

Lans notes further that many of the criticisms of the women environmentalists used references to their emotions and their bodies. While she is aware of Jackson's admonitions against equating women with concern for the environment, persons interviewed for her research shared the view that in Trinidad, women were more involved in advocacy on environmental issues than men and that the actions of woman environmentalist Molly Gaskin, had been central to the visibility of the Nariva Swamp in the national consciousness (Lans 2000: 47). These women succeeded in shifting the policy on the Swamp from one related to economic production and land settlement to one associated with conservation and protection.

The approach to Ramsar was a key mechanism in this plan. Not surprisingly, the 1993 Kushira Conference at which the Nariva Swamp was added to the Montreux Record of Ramsar Sites 'where changes in ecological character have occurred, are occurring or are likely to occur as a result of technological developments, pollution or other human interference', was attended by Carol James, then head of the Wildlife Section, Nadra Nathai-Gyan also of the Wildlife Section, and Molly Gaskin and Karlyn Shepherd of the Pointe a Pierre Wildfowl Trust as NGO representatives (Lans 2000: 48). In the ensuing struggle against large rice farmers who had begun rice production in the Swamp, a woman Theresa Akaloo, President of the Rice Growers Association and member of one of the large rice-growing families, emerged as the main spokesperson, supporting Jackson's view that women can be found at different locations on the environmental continuum.

Delving further into the gendered use of spaces, of nature and differential access to resources the study shows how in the communities of Kernahan and Cascadoux, activities and spaces are perceived in gendered terms. The mechanised cultivation of rice is largely a male activity whereas women are involved in root crop production. Just prior to our intervention, rice cultivation was significant and given a great deal more attention than root crop cultivation. In the 1980s the government introduced a subsidised scheme for rice farmers and yet women's production was given no attention. Due to public activism by environmental groups, large rice farming was eventually disallowed in the Swamp. Generally speaking higher value crops such as watermelon are under the control of men whereas the crops considered of lesser value, bodi,[17] and ochro, are the responsibility of women. Women are more involved in harvesting and crop maintenance and men are usually involved in land preparation. Additionally, while both women and men fish for cascadura in the channels, women use nets and not traps as men do. According to Sharda Durbal:

> The fact that women do not use traps may be attributed to the fact that the material used for making the traps (Roseau branches) is found in forested or lagoon areas. Roseau is also covered with large thorns, which may also deter women from collecting them (Durbal 2000: 45).

Fishing activities reflect differences in gendered space and access to resources. Fishing is primarily a male activity and is carried out in the deep forests of Bush Bush and Anho. Generally, women do not enter the forest, as it is not considered safe for them. Both men and women maintain the opinion that if they venture into the forest unaccompanied and fall into danger, then they deserve it as they had no right to be there in the first place. In general, women's activities take place closer to the villages, whereas the men's activities, hunting and fishing, take them some distance away from the villages. Women's mobility was in many ways proscribed in the villages and women had far less freedom of movement than men. This would not be obvious from casual observation but recognised after closer and deeper observation and interaction.

Ecofeminism emphasises women's intrinsic link to the environment, sometimes to the extent of downplaying men's knowledge. Women are thought to suffer more than men from the results of environmental degradation due to their relationship with it. It must be acknowledged however, that understanding of the use of the environment as gendered helps to identify differences in use of space and hence differing relationships of men and women to the environment.

Critiques of ecofeminism have been at pains to caution any tendency to link an affinity with 'nature' to women and indeed, it was found that women in the Kernahan and Cascadoux communities were much less knowledgeable about their flora and fauna than men. A main reason for this however, was the controls on mobility, patriarchal dominance and domestic violence, which characterised women's lives in that community. Women had fewer opportunities to interact with nature, and in spite of its proximity, the forest was out of bounds for them. In addition, as a community of recent migration, the tradition of ancestral knowledge was less well developed in this space. Yet women were quite central to environmentalist initiatives at other levels, especially when educated and able to operate with greater social and physical mobility.

Gender dynamics at the community and household level

Although Kernahan and Cascadoux are often treated as one village, there are differences between them as well as in each community's perception of the other. (Those from Kernahan perceive the two villages as one whereas those from Cascadoux see the communities as distinct from each other). Firstly, there are differences in the degree of gendered sanctions. In Cascadoux there was a greater proportion of women who were equal or primary decision-makers in their household, unlike women in Kernahan, and some of them wear short pants, drive vehicles and earn their own income.

Evidently women in Cascadoux experience fewer constraints. This was no doubt related to the differences in gendered power relations between the two ethnic groups.

In both communities household decisions are made through a process of negotiation between men and women. In less equitable households, issues may be discussed jointly but the decision will finally lie with the senior male. Religious doctrines, traditions and gendered sanctions reinforce the notion that the man is the head of the household, especially in the Indo-Trinidadian community of Kernahan. The mixed and Afro-Trinidadian women in Cascadoux have greater involvement in production and many earn their own income and have greater autonomy than those in predominantly Indo-Trinidadian Kernahan. In general they have a greater tendency to be single, sole supporters of their households.

Of the ten households where women were found to have greater decision-making power and autonomy, in three in Kernahan and one in Cascadoux the senior male was unable to work, in one in each community the woman was widowed, while two in Cascadoux were single and one divorced. One woman in Kernahan exercised authority with the support of her spouse (Basdeo 2000: 12). Gendered sanctions therefore appear to be less salient in Cascadoux. This implies that there is a greater level of equity between men and women in this settlement.

Gendered sanctions refer to the rules and norms that govern men's and women's behaviours and which penalise individuals for transgressing gender-appropriate lifestyles through institutional and community-based forms of social censure. It is possible to identify a pattern among such sanctions; women's behaviour and mobility are subject to greater constriction than that of men's. This is the case within *both* communities. Women's transgressive behaviour is subject to greater criticism, largely through the medium of gossip, than that of men's.

Kernahan inhabitants put more strain on the environment as they rely on it more as a source of income. In contrast, Cascadoux villagers hold a variety of different occupations. It must be said that the younger males of both communities aspire to hold jobs outside the agricultural sphere and many seek to leave these areas. Educated young women seek to find jobs such as teaching, with less emphasis on full-time family responsibility.

In both villages the relevance of indigenous knowledge about plants and animals was given greater value and recognition by the older members of the communities. There was a distinct absence of the transferral of knowledge to the younger generations. A greater emphasis was placed on religion, over the environment, as a collective cause. It is even possible that widespread conversion to Pentecostalism may be a factor to explain the virtual exclusion of indigenous knowledge. Further studies could reveal the intricate relationship between religious beliefs and environmentally sustainable practices. For the majority of the villagers, evangelical Christianity had entirely replaced other religions, such as Hinduism, and perhaps has even obscured all other forms of knowledge and worldviews. This has extensive implications for how people view land, spirituality, intimate relationships and the resolution of material problems. Hence, religion, spirituality and perhaps alternative forms of knowledge must be taken into consideration in developing strategies for socio-economic and ecological sustainability, as such knowledge greatly influences how people perceive and inhabit their surroundings.

Within the two communities, there are marked differences in how men, women, boys and girls use the village space. In general, the household is a domain largely used by women and one to which they are confined due to the sexual division of labour. Conversely, men's work is outside the home. When not working men and boys may often be found 'liming' outside. Hence, in organising meetings to address community issues, it is essential to understand this differential usage. An extensive array of notes on which groups or individuals would not go to certain places and the times that residents were available to attend meetings had to be formulated and used to get the relevant people together to promote environmental awareness and cohesion within the community.

Conclusions

This study was in many ways an exploratory one, which challenged many mainstream approaches to environmental research. First it sought to integrate gender analysis into environmental studies and to locate people as gendered beings, as a key component of the ecosystem. Second it sought to experiment with interdisciplinary and multidisciplinary methodologies, using a multidisciplinary research team. The expansion of, or challenge to, the scientific method was also another issue, which may not have been resolved, possibly because of different understandings of what is the scientific method. While some efforts at action research were incorporated through the involvement of the community in the research process as well as in education and sensitisation activities;[18] and while efforts to empower community members especially women were attempted through community interactions, informal discussions, formal workshops and field trips, it is difficult to evaluate the extent to which this was achieved.

The study also aimed to document and critique state policy toward agricultural resource use and settlement in the Nariva Swamp. In the case of Trinidad and Tobago, there is a perceived crisis in the state's leadership and governance on environmental issues that local organisations are striving to alleviate with the collaboration of international organisations and donor agencies. This has intensified with the plans to start oil exploration after the completion of this study and current plans for extraction. The environmental struggles of the women in the government's Wildlife Section, the Pointe a Pierre Wildfowl Trust and other environmental activist groups, have brought about significant changes. Such decisions and negotiations have gendered implications.

'Indigenous knowledge' within these communities is also gendered, with men having a greater understanding of the natural environment, which they may have gained from ancestors. These results challenge the popular notion that women are somehow intrinsically linked to the environment in a way that men are not. Programmes seeking to empower women by increasing their participation in environmental projects often overlook the reality of their continual re-negotiation of resource use and management and intra- and inter-household bargaining strategies. These result from patterns of gender inequity, which may differ according to ethnicity, socio-economic standing and age.

It seems that, gradually, environmental consciousness is becoming established among the villagers.[19] Young people especially are grasping this notion and working towards projects of sustainable use of the swamp. For young women, however, marriage and childbearing often put an end to their activity in this regard. Effective ecological sustainability of the area is contingent upon gender sensitive interventions by the various organisations, including the state and NGOs, and their programmes geared towards community education.

The members of both communities have had a long history of reliance upon the land as a means of income, even to the detriment of the local environment. The villagers accept the priority of income over environment. The lack of consensus and the prevalence of inter- and intra-house conflict have resulted in the absence of collective enthusiasm towards environmental issues. Consequently, this has hampered the community in addressing such issues as well as voicing personal concerns. The extent of the community's ability to influence external interventions, such as state policies, is dependent upon its ability to have consensus and collective mobilisation.

These findings are relevant to projects of political decentralisation which seek to transfer aspects of political power and authority to localised governance structures. These efforts are usually proposed as ways of enhancing and democratising decision-making, allocation of resources, and revenue generation to independent and autonomous local level public agencies and are seen as crucial for attaining improved human security (Mani 2005: 1). This study suggests that such efforts are doomed to failure if not grounded in critical understandings of the gender, class, ecological and community dynamics. The approach used addressed community members as people with their own needs, social and cultural imperatives and contradictions, and not only as the accidental inhabitants of the ecosystem. What this study brings out clearly is the interrelationship between human security and environmental security.

Many issues were raised in this study that require future examination. It is hoped that this study and the issues and debates resulting from it, can contribute to a growing body of interdisciplinary, participatory and gendered international knowledge on endangered ecosystems; knowledge which is becoming increasingly important to issues of human security and well-being.

Notes

[1] This paper is based on a research study coordinated by Grace Sirju-Charran and Rhoda Reddock and carried out by researchers Rishi Basdeo, Nicola Cross, Sharda Durbal, Gabrielle Hosein and Cheryl Lans between 1999 and 2000. Major funding was received from the Canadian International Development Agency (CIDA)-CARICOM Gender Equality Programme and CIDA-Canada through the Island Sustainability, Livelihoods and Equity (ISLE) Project.

[2] Although one of the earliest discussions of this (Mies 1981) argues that this relation is not natural but cultural and derived from women's historical experience of their bodies as means of production.

[3] Trinidad is the larger of a two-island nation-state of Trinidad and Tobago in the southern Caribbean, very close to Venezuela on the South American mainland.

[4] Ethnic identities have been important in defining political, social and economic life in Trinidad and Tobago since the mid-19th century. For more on this see B. Brereton 1979.

[5] The *panchayat* developed in India and is one of the oldest systems of democratic local organisation. It refers to both a community organising system as well as to a council of leaders, originally mainly male, who would resolve conflict and adjudicate in matters of local governance. Versions of this system were taken to Trinidad by immigrant indentured labourers in the late 19th and early 20th centuries.

[6] Personal reflection, 14 March 2004.

[7] Cascadura/cascadoo/cascadu—armoured catfish (*Hoplosternum littorale*) cited in Sletto 2002: 404.

[8] A non-governmental environmental organisation.

[9] The Convention on Wetlands is an inter-governmental treaty signed by

governments in Ramsar, Iran in 1971. It provides the framework for national action and international cooperation in the conservation and wise use of wetlands and their resources. The Montreux Record, is a register of wetland sites on the List of Wetlands of International Importance where changes in ecological character have occurred, are occurring, or are likely to occur as a result of technological developments, pollution or other human interference. It is maintained as part of the Ramsar Database.

[10] Additionally, the Caribbean Network for Integrated Rural Development (CNIRD) expanded such awareness by initiating the construction of an ecotourism visitors' centre in Kernahan. But attitudes towards this centre vary tremendously. Some villagers made disparaging remarks, asking what good had it done for them.

[11] This is not the norm for Trinidad and Tobago, there tends to be higher school enrolment and attendance of girls than boys. See CARICOM Secretariat, Gender-Based Differentials in Education Database Project.

[12] Since the completion of this research exercise, the Canadian oil exploration company, Talisman Ltd. approached the Environment Management Authority (EMA) of the Government of Trinidad and Tobago for permission to carry out seismic exploration in the Nariva Swamp. An initial refusal by the EMA was responded to with a legal challenge which was eventually resolved in favour of the company.

[13] The Centre for Gender and Development Studies (CGDS) at the University of the West Indies, St Augustine envisaged the idea of the *Nariva Swamp: A Gendered Case Study* project in 1995 through its participation in the Island Sustainability, Livelihood and Equity Programme (ISLE). The project was subsequently coordinated by the CGDS and funding for the research project was obtained through the Canadian International Development Agency (CIDA)-CARICOM Gender Equality Programme.

[14] The project encompassed four areas of research study, from which the following reports were produced: 'Gender and Natural Resource Use in Kernahan and Cascadoux'; 'State Policy and Governance in the Nariva Swamp: A Historical and Gender Analysis'; 'Community Level Governance in Kernahan and Cascadoux'; and finally 'Socio-Economic, Cultural and Gender Analysis of Kernahan and Cascadoux'. In addition to these a Composite Report was prepared in January 2001.

[15] Liming—passing the time, hanging out with others, socialising.

[16] Full title at the time—Ministry of Agriculture, Land and Marine Resources.

[17] A long green bean, in common use locally.

[18] The research methods and findings have also been the basis for the production of two educational documentary videos. *Living with the Wetlands: Women, Men and the Nariva Swamp* and the other which was scheduled for completion in 2005.

19 According to the villagers, the action-research components of this study as well as the involvement of unmarried, educated young women (and one young man) in this independent scholarly activity did contribute in some ways to this.

References

Bacon, Peter, J.S. Kenny, M.E. Alkins, S.N. Mootoosingh, S.N. Ramcharan and G.B.S. Seebaran. 1979. 'Studies on the Biological Resources of Nariva Swamp, Trinidad'. Occasional Paper no. 4. Zoology Department. St Augustine: University of the West Indies.

Bailey, Barbara and Myrna Bernard. 2003. 'Gender Differentials in Educational Performance at Secondary and Tertiary Levels of Caribbean Education Systems'. CARICOM Gender and Education Database Analysis. Research Project. mimeo. CARICOM Secretariat.

Basdeo, Rishi. 2000. 'Community Level Governance in Kernahan and Cascadoux: A Gender Analysis'. Research Report. Centre for Gender and Development Studies. St Augustine: University of the West Indies.

Brereton, Bridget. 1979. *Race Relations in Colonial Trinidad, 1870–1900.* Cambridge: Cambridge University Press.

Centre for Gender and Development Studies. 2001. 'The Nariva Swamp: A Gendered Case Study, with Special Reference to Kernahan and Cascadoux'. Composite Report. Centre for Gender and Development Studies. St Augustine: University of the West Indies.

Cook, Judith and Nancy Fonow. 1986. 'Knowledge and Women's Interests: Issues of Epistemology and Methodology in Feminist Sociological Knowledge'. *Sociological Enquiry* 56. no. 1. pp. 2–29.

Cross, Nicola and Gabrielle Hosein. 2000. 'Socio-Economic, Cultural and Gender Analysis of Kernahan and Cascadoux'. Research Report. Centre for Gender and Development Studies. St Augustine: University of the West Indies.

Durbal, Sharda. 2000. 'Gender and Natural Resource Use in Kernahan and Cascadoux'. Research Report. Centre for Gender and Development Studies. St Augustine: University of the West Indies.

Finger, Anke and Victoria Rosner. 2001. 'Doing Feminism in Interdisciplinary Contexts'. *Feminist Studies* 27. no. 2. summer. pp. 499–503.

Green, Cathy, Susan Joekes and Melissa Leach. 1998. 'Questionable Links: Approaches to Gender and Environmental Research and Policy' in *Feminist Visions of Development: Gender Analysis and Policy.* London: Routledge.

Jackson Cecile. 1993. 'Environmentalisms and Gender Interests in the Third World'. *Development and Change.* vol. 24. pp. 649–677.

Joekes Susan, Noeleen Heyzer, Ruth Oniang'o and Vania Salles. 1994. 'Gender, Environment and Population'. *Development and Change.* vol. 25.

Kapoor, Ilan. 2002. 'The Devil's in the Theory: A Critical Assessment of Robert Chambers' Work on Participatory Development'. *Third World Quarterly.* vol. 23. no. 1. pp. 101–117.

Lans, Cheryl. 2000. 'State Policy and Governance in the Nariva Swamp: A Historical and Gender Analysis'. Research Report. Centre for Gender and Development Studies. St Augustine: University of the West Indies.

Lélé, Sharachchandra and Richard B. Norgaard. 2005. 'Practising Interdisciplinarity'. *Bioscience.* vol. 55. issue 11. November. pp. 967–975.

Mani, Devyani. 2005. 'Strengthening Decentralised Governance for Human Security'. Nagoya, Japan: United Nations Centre for Regional Development (UNCRD). (First Draft).

Mies, Maria. 1981. 'The Social Origins of the Sexual Division of Labour'. ISS Occasional Paper. no. 85. The Hague: Institute of Social Studies.

Nussbaum, Martha and Amartya Sen. eds. 1992. *The Quality of Life.* Oxford: Oxford University Press.

Sletto, Bjørn. 2002. 'Producing Space(s), Representing Landscapes: Maps and Resource Conflicts in Trinidad'. *Cultural Geographies.* 9. pp. 389–420.

Contributors

SUNILA ABEYSEKERA is Executive Director of INFORM, Human Rights Development Centre, Sri Lanka. She is a key feminist and human rights activist in South Asia and was awarded the United Nations Human Rights Prize, Asia region, in 1998 on the 50th Anniversary of the Universal Declaration of Human Rights. She has participated in a number of teaching and training programmes in human rights, women's rights, and conflict, development and gender. She works in collaboration with UNIFEM; Asia Forum on Human Rights and Development; International Women's Rights Action Watch (IWRAW); Asia Pacific Forum on Women; and Global Alliance against Trafficking in Women (GAATW). She has published widely on women, conflict and human rights.

AMRITA CHHACHHI is Senior Lecturer in the Women, Gender and Development Programme at the Institute of Social Studies, The Hague, Netherlands. Her research and teaching interests address two areas: globalisation, gender, labour, poverty and social protection; and gender, culture, identity politics and conflict. She has published widely on these themes, including 'Women, Gender, Identity Politics: South Asia' in *Encyclopaedia of Women and Islamic Cultures* (general editor, Suad Joseph, Brill Academic Publishers, Leiden, 2004); *Confronting State, Capital and Patriarchy: Women Organising in the Process of Industrialisation* (co-editor R. Pittin,

Macmillan, 1996); and *Eroding Citizenship: Gender and Labour in Contemporary India* (forthcoming). She is on the editorial board of the journal *Development and Change*. She has been involved in establishing women's studies in the West Indies, Namibia, Yemen and Bangladesh and with feminist, peace and anti-nuclear coalitions in the South Asian region.

NOELEEN HEYZER is Executive Director of UNIFEM, New York. She was also the Chair, UN Interagency Task Force on Women's Empowerment to implement the Cairo Plan of Action, UNFPA (1995–1996); Chair, UN Operational Working Group on the implementation of the Platform for Action of the Fourth World Conference on Women (1996–1997); Co-chair of the UN Council of the Micro-credit Summit to reach 100 million poorest families with Juan Somavia, Director General of the ILO (1997-ongoing); Head of the international delegation to engender the peace process in the Middle East (2000); Co-convenor of the Round Table on Human Rights and HIV/AIDS with Mary Robinson, UN High Commissioner for Human Rights, and Carol Bellamy, Executive Director, UNICEF, during the General Assembly Special Session on HIV/AIDS (2001); Chair, UN Interagency Task Force on Gender Equality and HIV/AIDS (1999-ongoing); Alternate Chair of the United Nations Development Programme Staff Rebuttal Panel (2001-ongoing).

RACHEL KURIAN is Senior Lecturer in the Politics of Alternative Development Programme at the Institute of Social Studies, The Hague, Netherlands. Her publications include 'India: To Act and Learn' in *The Next Steps: Experiences and Analysis of How to Eradicate Child Labour* (editor B. Grimsrud, Oslo, Fafo, 2002); *World Employment: A Gender Perspective Thematic Report of Industrialised Countries* (Stockholm, SIDA, 2000); with L. Hanmer, N. de Jong, and J. Mooij, 'Are the DAC Targets Achievable? Poverty and Human Development in the Year 2015' in *Journal of International Development* (1999); 'Women's Work in Changing Labour Markets: The Case of Thailand in the 1980s' in *Women,*

Globalization and Fragmentation in the Developing Countries, (editors, H. Afshar and S. Barrientos, London, Macmillan, St Martin's Press).

PATRICIA MOHAMMED is Professor of Gender Studies, Centre for Gender and Development Studies, St Augustine, Trinidad and Tobago. From 1994–2002 she was Head/Lecturer at the Mona Unit of the Centre for Gender and Development Studies, Jamaica. Her publications include: *Gendered Realities: Essays in Caribbean Feminist Thought; Gender Negotiations among Indians in Trinidad: 1917–1947; Caribbean Women at the Crossroads,* (co-author), and *The Construction of Gender Indicators for Jamaica* (editor). She was Editor of *Rethinking Caribbean Difference,* a Special Issue of *Feminist Review* 59 (June 1998) in which she wrote 'Towards Indigenous Feminist Theorising in the Caribbean'. She is on the Advisory Board of *Global Networks: A Journal of International Affairs* (published by Blackwell). She is also a member of the Editorial Collective of *Small Axe: A Journal of Caribbean Criticism* (published by Indiana University Press), and is a Contributing Editor to *Feminist Review Collective* (published by Palgrave Journals).

JOYCE OUTSHOORN is Professor of Political Sciences at the Joke Smit Institute of the University of Leiden, Netherlands. Until 1987 she was Senior Lecturer in Political Science at the University of Amsterdam. From 1993–2000 she was Chair of the Netherlands School of Research in Women's Studies (Nederlandse Onderzoeksschool Vrouwenstudies). She has published widely on issues of the women's movement, emancipation policies, abortion and prostitution. Recent publications include *The Politics of Prostitution: Women's Movements, Democratic States and the Globalisation of Sex Commerce* (editor, Cambridge, Cambridge University Press, 2004); 'Gendering the "Greying" of Society: A Discourse Analysis of the Care Gap' in *Public Administration Review* 62 (March/April 2002); 'Regulating Prostitution as Sex Work: The Pioneer Case of the Netherlands', *Acta Politica* 39 (Summer 2001); 'Policy-Making on Abortion: Arenas, Actors and Arguments in the Netherlands' in *Abortion Politics, Women's Movements, and the State* (editor, D. McBride, Stetson, New York/Oxford, Oxford University Press, 2000).

RHODA REDDOCK is Professor in Women's Studies and Head of the Centre for Gender and Development Studies, University of West Indies, Trinidad. She was awarded the Vice-Chancellor's Award for Excellence in Teaching, Research, Outreach and Administration for the 2001–2002 academic year and the 7th Triennial Caricom Award for Women in 2002. She is a member of the Council of Women Working for Social Progress and a founder member of Caribbean Association for Feminist Research and Action (CAFRA). She has written and edited numerous books, papers and articles which include *Women, Labour and Politics in Trinidad and Tobago: A History* (named Choice Outstanding Academic Book in 1996); *Elma Francoise, the NECSA and the Worker's Struggle for Change in the Caribbean*; *Ethnic Minorities in Caribbean Society*; *Women Plantation Workers: International Experiences*; *National Liberation and Women's Liberation*; *Women and Slavery in the Caribbean: A Feminist Perspective*; *Indian Women and Indentureship in Trinidad and Tobago 1845–1917: Freedom Denied*; *Interrogating Caribbean Masculinities: A Reader.*

CARLA RISSEEUW is Professor of Cross Cultural Gender Studies, Department of Anthropology and Development Sociology, University of Leiden, Netherlands. She is also a filmmaker and has worked on issues of land rights (Kenya, Sri Lanka) and gender and the organisation of home-based women workers (Sri Lanka). While maintaining her 30-year long links with the Sri Lankan organisation of women workers, she has also turned to the study of family, care, welfare and gender in the Netherlands with a comparative exploration of the issue of ageing in the Netherlands and Sri Lanka. Recently she published with three Indian colleagues on the retracting Dutch welfare state; its public and private care arrangements, as well as the specific sociocultural and historical issues of family and friendship.

GITA SEN holds the Sir Ratan Tata Chair at the Indian Institute of Management, Bangalore, India, and is Adjunct Professor at the Harvard School of Public Health, USA. A leading international researcher on the links between gender justice and globalisation, she works with non-governmental and international organisations in an advisory capacity, including UN Research Institute for Social Development, WHO Advisory Committee on Health Research and the International Women's Health Coalition. She is the research coordinator on globalisation for the DAWN network of researchers, activists and policy-makers. She serves on the boards of numerous other organisations.

THANH-DAM TRUONG is Associate Professor in Women, Gender and Development Studies at the Institute of Social Studies, The Hague, Netherlands. Her research addresses the relations between gender, culture and economy with a focus on East and South-east Asia and specially on international migration and trafficking. She has also published on Buddhism in the context of the debate on 'Asian Values and Social Change', and on gender, human development and human security.

IMANI TAFARI-AMA currently lectures in Jamaica. Her PhD thesis is entitled 'Blood, Bullets and Bodies: Sexuality and Inter City Violence in Jamaica' (2002).

VIRGINIA VARGAS is one of the most well-known feminist leaders of Latin America. She is co-founder of the Peruvian feminist centre, Flora Tristan in Peru. She has published many articles on women's citizenship and the women's movement and is actively engaged in the World Social Forum.

SASKIA WIERINGA is Director of the International Information Centre and Archives for the Women's Movement in Amsterdam. She is also an affiliated senior researcher at the University of Amsterdam. She has written and edited 14 books, including two books of fiction, and numerous scholarly articles, mainly on the women's movement, sexuality and gender planning. *Female Desires: Women's Same Sex Practice in Cross-cultural Perspective* (co-edited with Evelyn Blackwood, Columbia University Press, 1999) has won the Ruth Benedict prize. Other recent books are *Sexual Politics in Indonesia* (Palgrave Macmillan 2002); and the novel *Lubang Buaya* (Metafor Jakarta, 2003). She is the President of the International Association for the Study of Sexuality, Culture and Society. Her main research interests are women's empowerment, gender indicators, sexuality and HIV/AIDS. She has been involved in setting up women's studies in Yemen, Sudan, the Caribbean, Namibia and Bangladesh.